LEGACIES OF CRIME

Legacies of Crime explores the lives of seriously delinquent girls and boys who were followed over a twenty-year period as they navigated the transition to adulthood. In-depth interviews with these women and men and their children – a majority of whom are now adolescents themselves – depict the adults' economic and social disadvantages and continued criminal involvement, and in turn the unique vulnerabilities of their children. Peggy C. Giordano identifies family dynamics that foster the intergenerational transmission of crime, violence, and drug abuse, rejecting the notion that such continuities are based solely on genetic similarities or even lax, inconsistent parenting. The author breaks new ground in directly exploring – and in the process revising – the basic tenets of classic social learning theories and in confronting the complications associated with the parent's gender. *Legacies of Crime* also identifies factors associated with resilience in the face of what is often a formidable package of risks favoring intergenerational continuity.

Peggy C. Giordano is Distinguished Research Professor at Bowling Green State University. Her research – published in leading journals such as *Criminology, American Sociological Review,* and the *American Journal of Sociology* – has long focused on the causes of juvenile delinquency and particularly on similarities and differences in male and female pathways to criminal involvement. A Fellow of the American Society of Criminology, Giordano's analyses of the adult lives of a sample of delinquent youth have twice won the American Sociological Association's James F. Short, Jr. award for best article. This book extends this research in a unique exploration of the lives of the children of the original study subjects.

CAMBRIDGE STUDIES IN CRIMINOLOGY

Editors

Alfred Blumstein *H. John Heinz School of Public Policy and Management, Carnegie Mellon University*
David Farrington *Institute of Criminology, University of Cambridge*

Recent books in the series

Rethinking Homicide: Exploring the Structure and Process Underlying Deadly Situations, by Terance D. Miethe and Wendy C. Regoeczi

Situational Prison Control: Crime Prevention in Correctional Institutions, by Richard Wortley

Prisoner Reentry and Crime in America, edited by Jeremy Travis and Christy Visher

Choosing White-Collar Crime, by Neal Shover and Andrew Hochstetler

Marking Time in the Golden State: Women's Imprisonment in California, by Candace Kruttschnitt and Rosemary Gartner

The Crime Drop in America (revised edition), edited by Alfred Blumstein and Joel Wallman

Policing Gangs in America, by Charles M. Katz and Vincent J. Webb

Street Justice: Retaliation in the Criminal Underworld, by Bruce Jacobs and Richard Wright

Race and Policing in America: Conflict and Reform, by Ronald Weitzer and Steven Tuch

What Works in Corrections: Reducing Recidivism, by Doris Layton MacKenzie

Police Innovation: Contrasting Perspectives, edited by David Weisburd and Anthony A. Braga

The Prison and the Gallows: The Politics of Mass Incarceration in America, by Marie Gottschalk

Understanding Crime Statistics: Revisiting the Divergence of the NCVS and UCR, edited by James P. Lynch and Lynn A. Addington

Key Issues in Criminal Career Research: New Analyses of the Cambridge Study of Delinquent Development, by Alex R. Piquero, David P. Farrington, and Alfred Blumstein

Drug-Crime Connections, by Trevor Bennett and Katy Holloway

Lengthening the Arm of the Law: Enhancing Police Resources in the Twenty-First Century, by Julie Ayling, Peter Grabosky, and Clifford Shearing

Legacies of Crime

A Follow-Up of the Children of Highly Delinquent Girls and Boys

Peggy C. Giordano
Bowling Green State University

CAMBRIDGE UNIVERSITY PRESS
Cambridge, New York, Melbourne, Madrid, Cape Town, Singapore,
São Paulo, Delhi, Dubai, Tokyo

Cambridge University Press
32 Avenue of the Americas, New York, NY 10013-2473, USA

www.cambridge.org
Information on this title: www.cambridge.org/9780521705516

First published 2010

Printed in the United States of America

A catalog record for this publication is available from the British Library.

Library of Congress Cataloging in Publication data
Giordano, Peggy C.
   Legacies of crime : a follow-up of the children of highly delinquent
   girls and boys / Peggy C. Giordano.
      p.   cm. – (Cambridge studies in criminology)
   Includes bibliographical references and index.
   ISBN 978-0-521-87971-2 (hardback)
   1. Juvenile delinquents – United States – Longitudinal studies.   2. Juvenile
   delinquents – Family relationships – United States.   3. Juvenile
   delinquency – United States – Longitudinal studies.   4. Criminal behavior –
   United States – Longitudinal studies.   I. Title.   II. Series.
   HV9104.G549 2010
   364.36–dc22   2010000463

ISBN 978-0-521-87971-2 Hardback
ISBN 978-0-521-70551-6 Paperback

To my parents,
Doris and Jim Cochran

Contents

Acknowledgments

Interviews conducted in connection with the Ohio Life-Course Study (OLS) took place over a twenty-five-year period and involved the active collaboration and hard work of many colleagues and students. Special thanks must go to Stephen Cernkovich, a co-investigator on the adolescent phase of the OLS, the Toledo Youth Survey, as well as the related adult follow-up studies. Steve played a central role in the collection and analyses of these data, and our collaborative work on the respondents' lives and criminal careers is key to an understanding of the family environments their children must navigate. Ted Groat also played an important role as co-investigator on the adult follow-ups, particularly in analyses of the qualitative data, formulating ideas about desistance processes, and, most important, offering encouragement over the long haul. These early interviews were funded by grants from the National Institute of Mental Health (grants MH29095, MH46410, and MH52268), while a grant from the W. T. Grant Foundation enabled us to complete the most recent third wave of interviews focused on issues of parenting and the well-being of the next generation of children. Monica Longmore and Wendy Manning, co-investigators on the parenting project, brought useful social psychological and demographic perspectives to the investigation and offered immeasurable quantities of intellectual, practical, and moral support. The Toledo Adolescent Relationships Study (used for some comparisons to OLS children) was funded by The Eunice Kennedy Shriver National Institute for Child Health and Human Development (grant HD36223), and was also completed in collaboration with Manning and Longmore.

Many outstanding interviewers have participated in each wave of data collection, but Claudia Vercellotti deserves special mention, as she not only completed a large number of the structured interviews, but almost all of the open-ended life-history interviews quoted at length in these pages. Claudia possesses a unique sensitivity and openness, nonjudgmental attitude, and gentle humor that have been central to the respondents' willingness to share many aspects of their lives with us. She also worked tirelessly to track difficult-to-find respondents and offered valuable insights on matters ranging from the dynamics within specific families to more general theorizing about religion, romantic partners, and the long-term effects of drug abuse. I would also like to express my gratitude to the adult and adolescent respondents themselves, for their willingness to participate in interviews that required introspection and candor, and recall of experiences that may have been difficult or painful to discuss.

The OLS study and related projects involved a sometimes dizzying array of concrete activities, troubleshooting, and human relations work that Jennifer Rudolph, Abbey Eng, Meredith Porter, and Colleen Scott, as research coordinators, managed with calm and creativity. Colleen Scott has been most directly involved in the production work required to complete this book, and she has made the entire process both possible and a very rewarding experience. We also appreciate the editorial and production assistance of Ed Parsons, Jason Przybylski, Charanya Ramanathan, Virginia Anna Faber, Anna Staudt, and others at Cambridge University Press.

Others who contributed directly or indirectly to the ideas or analyses described in the book include: Wendi Goodlin, Ryan Schroeder, Jill Deines, Jen Brown, Donna Holland, Eric Jorrey, Pat Seffrin, Rob Lonardo, Wendi Johnson, Deanna Trella, Erin Crane, Kenyatta Phelps, Meredith Pugh, Charles McCaghy, John Laub, Ross Matsueda, and Emma Engdahl.

Finally, I would like to express my love and gratitude to understanding family members who have taught me much about the meaning and impact of intergenerational ties: Doris, Jim, and Bob Cochran; Caroline Giordano; Ted, Jon, Andrew, and Liz Groat; and Brian Woodcock.

CHAPTER ONE

Introduction

Every time she comes she always gets mad at my grandma... like she choked my grandma before she went to jail. I'm always like, I don't want to hit her and stuff, but like I have a hammer and I sit it right next to my bed. 'Cause I know if my mom comes in messed up on drugs, she gets real violent... and she always comes up and rips the phone jack out of the wall and stuff. I just have to be ready...

[Jason][1]

We first met Jason's mother Stacy in 1982, when she was a teenager herself, in connection with a study of incarcerated juvenile offenders. We were interested in why and how girls become involved in delinquent behaviors and had been interviewing the total population of Ohio's state institution for girls and a comparable sample of delinquent boys. Over the years, we thought often about these teens, wondering what had become of that very delinquent "class of '82" (Giordano, Cernkovich, & Pugh, 1985). In 1995, we began the lengthy process of trying to locate the original study participants, who were then an average of 29 years of age and living in various locations throughout Ohio and, in some instances, the surrounding states. We were eventually able to locate and re-interview over 85 percent of the original respondents.[2] Those interviews revealed that many of these women and men had, like Stacy, experienced continued difficulties and problems with the law (Giordano, Cernkovich, & Rudolph, 2002).

---

[1] We have changed the names of all respondents quoted or described and any other individuals referenced in their life history accounts. We also typically changed place names, such as high schools or locations of employment, in order to assure the anonymity of the respondents.

[2] Waves 1 and 2 were funded by the National Institute of Mental Health grants.

Although the Ohio Life-Course Study (OLS) follow-up had focused on these young women and men as they made the transition to adulthood, it was impossible to ignore their children – as they crawled on the living room furniture, traipsed in and out of apartments, or appeared as important subjects within the respondents' own life histories ("After they took Kristen away...").

In 2003, recognizing that the majority of the children born to our sample members were entering the adolescent period themselves, we once again set out to find these families, but this time, the interviews we conducted focused primarily on issues of parenting and child well-being.[3] In addition to the original members of the sample, we were also able to interview at least one, and sometimes all, of their adolescent children. The book focuses on the lives of 125 families and includes analyses based on interviews with 349 parents, children, and other caregivers. The in-depth life-history narratives of these adults and children are central to the story we will tell; yet, analyses based on structured data collected over a 20-year period add to our understanding of effects on children of the parents' experiences and the nature of continuities observed across the two generations.

What is growing up like for a young boy like Jason, whose mother has been arrested over seventy times? How does it feel to see your father only on infrequent visits when he is out of prison? How does a parent's life of crime and drug abuse affect your own chances of surviving adolescence relatively unscathed and the likelihood that you will avoid getting into serious trouble yourself? And are children of female and male offenders similarly affected by their parents' problem lifestyles? This book addresses these questions, providing an up-close examination of family life as experienced by a cohort of young people, all of whom have at least one and sometimes both parents with a significant early history of delinquent involvement. In the following chapters we (i) make tangible the realities of growing up in these families; (ii) document how this cohort of children has fared – academically, socially, behaviorally, and emotionally; and (iii) identify specific social mechanisms connected to intergenerational continuities in substance abuse, crime, and violent behavior.

[3] The follow-up of the OLS parents and their children (wave 3) was funded by the W.T. Grant Foundation.

We also examine success stories, focusing on young people who have managed, against considerable odds, to avoid a replay of their parents' problem childhoods.

The scholarly literature contains surprisingly few studies of the so-called intergenerational transmission process. Numerous studies have documented that delinquent youth are more likely than other adolescents to report having a parent with a criminal history, and some longitudinal studies have demonstrated significant associations between parental behaviors, such as aggression, and similar behaviors in their children. However, most studies have theorized about parenting practices or genetic similarities as underpinnings of these rates of "concordance." Fewer studies have focused on the social-learning processes that may foster such behavioral continuities. While we recognize that both biological predisposition and parenting style play a significant role, the focus of this investigation is on the social dimensions of the phenomenon. Our objective is to explore in more detail direct and subtle learning influences within the family context. However, we add to the classic treatments of learning mechanisms by more fully embracing a social psychology of social learning processes. Our view is that a comprehensive understanding of intergenerational influences requires attention to the child's emotional reactions to parents' actions, as well as to the ways in which parents may transmit "definitions favorable to the violation of law" (Sutherland, 1947). Consistent with our social-psychological approach, we argue that it is critical to consider identity-formation processes, since the child's emerging identity gives added coherence to developing attitudes and emotions, eventually fostering either similarities with one's parents or a break with family traditions.

We hope this book will be useful to students and researchers who focus on the causes of crime, as well as to family scholars and readers who are interested in gender. The findings from this in-depth portrait also have policy implications. For example, a number of practitioners are understandably concerned about the significant challenges faced by the children of incarcerated parents. Yet we gain substantially from a broader life-course treatment and from giving additional attention to the child's own point of view. Thus, while prior work has focused heavily on negative effects of separation while the parent is incarcerated, the children we interviewed frequently did not narrate this as the most traumatic of their experiences. Jason's narrative, quoted at the outset, provides an initial illustration of a more complicated perspective on incarceration's effects.

ORGANIZATION OF THE BOOK

Chapter Two situates the study within several research traditions. We focus first on what is known about the intergenerational transmission of crime and related problem outcomes. Because offenders' own adult circumstances undoubtedly influence the character of their children's experiences, we also consider research that has offered a life-course perspective on criminal involvement. One of the unique features of this sample is that over 50 percent of the respondents we followed in this longitudinal investigation are women; thus it is also important to consider prior research on women and crime that explores the uniquely gendered aspects of these life-course processes. Finally, our review encompasses studies and programmatic efforts that have focused specifically on the children of incarcerated parents. We conclude the chapter with a short overview of our social-psychological theoretical perspective, developing a symbolic interactionist approach to intergenerational transmission in more detail in Chapter Six.

Chapter Three, on methods, describes our research odyssey as we attempted to locate these highly disadvantaged respondents and introduces the reader to these adults and their children. Our goal is not only to describe their general characteristics (i.e., gender, age, race/ethnicity) but also to depict the marginal living circumstances in which we found many of them. This general background is useful for understanding the adult and child outcomes we elaborate on in subsequent chapters. In addition, we outline our interview procedures at each of the three interview waves and describe related study samples we relied upon for purposes of comparison.

Chapter Four develops a more complete portrait of the OLS respondents as adults, based on both quantitative and qualitative data. It is impossible to gain an adequate appreciation of the character of the children's lives (and, in turn, the mechanisms linking the two generations) without considering the realities of the parents' own backgrounds and current circumstances. The chapter presents aggregate data about the parents' crime, violence, and drug-abuse patterns, but it also highlights significant variations within this sample. For example, the sample contains women and men whose lives are characterized by a pattern of what appears to be complete "desistance" from crime, those whose difficulties are more intermittent, and others who have evidenced a pattern of sustained involvement in criminal behavior. This portrait of the parents also includes attention to their lives beyond the levels of criminal activity. Thus, we also investigate marriage and childbearing experiences, levels of educational and occupational attainment, and the emotional well-being of these original respondents. Finally, we focus on the parenting experiences of these women and men. We compare our results to those obtained in connection with a related adult follow-up study and another survey of over 1,000 randomly selected parents of adolescents.

Chapter Five explores the key question: on average, how have these children turned out? Providing an adequate answer requires multiple comparisons and considering effects, or "legacies," that go beyond the child's own involvement in delinquency or lack thereof. We present basic data on the instabilities and victimization experiences that characterize many OLS children's lives, and we subsequently document how these children compare to a random sample of youths on a range of outcomes, including delinquency, substance use, violence, contacts with the law, academic achievement, difficulties in school, involvement with delinquent peers, sexual risk-taking, and psychological distress.[4] As in Chapter Four, we develop a portrait that depicts the realities of the children's circumstances, but from the child's vantage point. Our study design also permits a unique set of comparisons between these children's reports and those provided by the parents when they were teens. The final section of Chapter Five examines variations in delinquency within the sample of OLS youth and the parent and child factors that are associated

---

[4] The study of Toledo teens that we use for comparison purposes, the Toledo Adolescent Relationships Study (TARS), was funded by The Eunice Kennedy Schriver National Institute of Child Health and Human Development.

with these variations in victimization experiences and self-reports of delinquency involvement.

While Chapter Five is largely concerned with the extent of intergenerational transmission, Chapter Six explores how and why it occurs. In this chapter, we rely primarily on the qualitative data. We move beyond prior work on specific parenting practices by developing a revised social learning perspective on the transmission process. This symbolic interactionist perspective highlights not only what is learned, and how this learning occurs, but also incorporates the child's reactions to what is taking place within the confines of these families. In short, our overarching goal is to illuminate unique aspects of navigating childhood with antisocial, violent, and/or drug-involved parents, as contrasted with a more generic focus on parenting styles or levels of attachment to parents.

Chapter Seven follows from the previous discussion of mechanisms, but focuses specific attention on the more successful youths within this sample. We discuss prosocial influences found in prior research on resilient youth (individual and social factors that are generally recognized as protective), but again our primary interest is in adaptations that are relatively specific to success in navigating this type of risk environment. As in our discussion of cross-generational continuities, we highlight the role of identity formation processes in shaping these more favorable outcomes. As will be evident from Chapters Five and Six, it is important to measure success in relative terms, as very few of these children have excelled using traditional markers such as high levels of academic performance. Thus, we also view success as simply managing to avoid major legal contacts, in addition to the specific adaptations unique to this type of sample, such as taking on the parent/caregiver role within the family.

Chapter Eight discusses the importance of our major findings for theories of intergenerational transmission, and then concludes by exploring policy implications for future work with offenders and for programs aimed at positively influencing the well-being of their children.

CHAPTER TWO

Literature Review and Conceptual Framework

While it is intuitive to expect that parental criminality will have an influence on children's behavior (the apple doesn't fall far from the tree), surprisingly little research has focused directly on the intergenerational transmission *process* itself. Most of what we know about patterns of crime over two generations is based on retrospective studies: researchers have shown that delinquents are more likely than conforming youth to have a parent with a criminal history. Parental criminality is thus a well-accepted *risk factor* for juvenile delinquency. Follow-up studies pose a related but less often researched question: when we track juvenile delinquents through their transition to adulthood, what happens to their children? *Prospective studies* of this type are not as plentiful, if only for practical reasons, that is, it takes a long time for the young people originally studied to mature, find romantic partners, have children, and then for their children to reach an age when their own delinquent acts begin to occur.

Several recent longitudinal studies have been underway long enough to incorporate assessments of the behaviors of the children of the original respondents, and both the classic risk-factor studies and these more contemporary prospective investigations provide a useful background for the current study. While both kinds of studies have documented links between the behavior of one generation and of the next, we conclude from our review of the literature that our understanding of the mechanisms underlying intergenerational transmission is nevertheless markedly less than complete. It is also important to consider the theory and research from the *life-course* tradition, as our intergenerational study also fits under this broader conceptual umbrella. Although life-course investigations usually focus on the patterning of crime and other experiences for a given set of focal respondents rather than their children, what we know about juvenile delinquents' lives as adults is clearly key to an understanding of the family environments their children must navigate. The basic emphases of the life-course approach have also influenced our theoretical emphasis, particularly since, in addition to continuity, this perspective underscores the importance of attending to the dynamic processes associated with change.

Many criminologists working in the intergenerational and life-course traditions have focused their research on male respondents. This stems from the reality that many of the classic longitudinal investigations started with samples of boys, which was consistent with boys' generally higher rates of delinquency. Yet every jurisdiction includes a small number of girls whose behavior is deemed sufficiently serious to warrant official intervention, and even studies based on general population samples document variations in the delinquency levels of girls and boys. Thus, while long-term follow-ups of "problem" girls are uncommon, an expanding literature on issues of *gender and crime* adds further background to the current study.

Finally, we review the expanding literature on *children of incarcerated parents*. This literature overlaps considerably with our interests here and forges the link to policies and programs designed to assist children with backgrounds similar to those of the OLS children. We conclude this review and critique of prior work by introducing the key dimensions of our own theoretical perspective.

PARENTAL CRIMINALITY AS A RISK FACTOR

An influential British study, the Cambridge Study in Delinquent Development, has contributed to the literature as both a "risk-factor" study and as a prospective longitudinal investigation (for an excellent review of major results of this 40-year study, see Farrington, 2003). The Cambridge study, which focused on 411 young boys from south London, is distinguished by interviews with and other data on these respondents that spans the ages of 8 to 46. For our purposes, a singular asset of the study was the ability to track the conviction histories of parents, siblings, and other relatives through a centralized registry of official arrests and incarcerations. Early in the study, Farrington and colleagues found that the delinquent youths in their sample were significantly more likely to have a convicted parent. While convictions of the father especially, appeared to raise the odds of the child's delinquent involvement, having delinquent older siblings, mothers, and even younger siblings was also associated with a greater likelihood of delinquency. The authors have concluded that "having a convicted parent (mother or father) was consistently among the best childhood predictors of juvenile offending and antisocial behavior in the study males" (Smith & Farrington, 2004: 230–231). Since the investigators tracked the young men over a considerable period of time, they were also able to document that having a convicted parent was significantly associated with antisocial behavior at ages 18 and 32, as well as a pattern of chronic offending. Related to this basic finding, they observed that "the concentration of offending in a small number of families was remarkable in the Cambridge Study. Less than 6% of the families were responsible for half of all convictions of all family members (fathers, mothers, sons, and daughters) of all 400 families" (2003: 150).

While the Cambridge study thus highlighted parental criminality as a strong risk factor in child delinquency, the authors did not emphasize social-learning processes, arguing instead that parenting processes were key to an understanding of such cross-generational links. As evidence, Farrington (2003) pointed out that it was actually quite rare for fathers and sons to co-offend with one another and, in addition, that they had uncovered "no evidence convicted fathers directly encouraged their sons to commit crimes or taught them criminal techniques. On the contrary, convicted fathers condemned their sons' offending" (p. 150). Farrington also noted that the risk of parental criminality was not influenced by *when* the fathers offended (i.e., the conviction could have occurred prior to the birth of the child or while the child was very young). In short, the authors concluded that there was "no direct behavioral influence of criminal fathers on delinquent sons" (p. 150). Instead, their data uncovered much evidence of "maladaptive parenting" including "poor supervision, inconsistent discipline, parental conflict, and lack of affection and support" (Smith & Farrington, 2004: 232).

Studies conducted in the United States accord with the results of the Cambridge study. Evidence of parental criminality typically emerges in these studies as a strong correlate of the child's delinquency involvement. This appears to be the case whether the research designs focus on general youth samples or include incarcerated or other high-risk youth, often viewed in comparison to a control sample (Glueck & Glueck, 1950; McCord, 1977). It is also important to note that unlike the Cambridge study, some of the U.S. samples reflect greater diversity. For example, Loeber and Stouthamer-Loeber (1986), relying on data from the Pittsburgh Youth Study, showed that the association is similarly strong for African American and for white males in their sample group. In addition, the association appears to be robust across different historical eras (see, e.g., Burt, 1925; Healy & Bronner, 1926).

PROSPECTIVE STUDIES

If one were to walk into a juvenile institution and query the young people incarcerated there about their family backgrounds, it is likely that many reports of parental criminality would be recorded (along with evidence of broken homes, lax supervision, and child abuse). However, it is a different matter to follow up these youths as they have made the transition to adulthood and to observe the extent of cross-generational continuity reflected in the delinquent behavior of their children. While the number of truly prospective studies of parental criminality is not large, such studies, in general, document significant but less dramatic effects than have been revealed through the risk-factor or retrospective approach. A number of studies have focused broadly on aggression rather than on delinquency/criminality, but these studies are nevertheless generally relevant and consistent in their findings. For example, in a study of 600 respondents who were drawn from Columbia County, New York, and followed prospectively, Huesmann et al. (1984) found that the respondents' aggression at age eight predicted later reports of aggression on the part of their children. Farrington also found continuity in bullying behaviors over two generations. However, Farrington's (1993) results indicated that approximately 30 percent of the respondents who had been bullies had children who bullied, and many of the children of the aggressive youth in the Huesmann et al. sample were not similarly aggressive. Such findings, then, provide evidence of continuity and heightened risk, but they also document that an intergenerational cycle is far from inevitable.

Because a considerable length of time is required for children to reach the ages when delinquency is at its traditional peak, a number of contemporary longitudinal studies have examined the behavioral tendencies of the young children born to members of original samples. Cairns et al.'s (1998) Carolina Longitudinal Study followed up girls as well as boys, and, focusing on those who had given birth at relatively young ages (average age 19), found continuity in the behaviors of the toddler-age children of the aggressive boys but not of the girls.

More recently, a special issue of the *Journal of Abnormal Child Psychology* on intergenerational transmission included results from several different longitudinal studies, and importantly, investigators attempted to coordinate their measurement strategies and reporting of intergenerational effects (Capaldi et al., 2003; Shaw, 2003). Although the character and the ages of the samples in the studies varied, most of the research efforts centered on very young children, and the results generally accord with the conclusion of Thornberry et al. (2003): "intergenerational continuity in antisocial behavior is evident, albeit somewhat modest" (p. 171). In addition, the researchers were interested in investigating some of the key mechanisms responsible for observed continuities, and similar to Farrington's observations, many investigators concluded that parenting practices were a critical part of the process. Thornberry and colleagues, for example, found that factors such as parental warmth and consistency of discipline were associated with delinquency as an adolescent and, in turn, with the problem behaviors of the children (hostility, aggression, disobeying rules). Thornberry's investigation, based on data from the Rochester Youth Development Study, is also noteworthy for its inclusion of both girls and boys, thus permitting the authors to explore the possibility of gendered cross-generational effects. The researchers concluded that, while parenting "mattered" for both the boys and girls, the findings also indicate a more direct link between fathers' delinquency and their children's early behavior problems. In contrast, only parenting behaviors and financial stress were related to variations in reports of early antisocial behavior in the children born to the girls in the original study. Since women are more often the close-in caregivers for children, and women's delinquency careers are more limited, Thornberry et al. (2003) argued that these factors, particularly parenting practices, would likely influence (mediate) any early antisocial tendencies on the part of girls.

Although we agree with the conclusions of these researchers that such factors as parental warmth and consistency of discipline are key to understanding delinquency in general and cross-genera-tional effects in particular, in our view insufficient attention has been given to the role of social learning processes as a dynamic associated with intergenerational transmission. Correspondingly, we have little knowledge about the specific mechanisms involved in such learning processes.[1] As noted at the outset, this is a gap in the existing literature that we are most interested in addressing. For example, while Thornberry et al. (2003) find that there is a direct link between the father's delinquency and the child's behav-ior problems that seems unrelated to parenting practices, they do not explore the possibility that this association may reflect a learn-ing component. Instead, the authors theorize that it could stem from genetic influences, and they highlight the need to explore the role of "other social and psychological factors," including: (i) edu-cational attainment, (ii) social capital, (iii) family structure, (iv) the nature of the relationship with the partner, and (v) the influence of the other parent. We agree that it is critically important to assess these factors in connection with intergenerational patterns; yet in our view the lack of attention to social learning mechanisms is limit-ing to the development of a comprehensive understanding of cross-generational mechanisms.

[1]   A number of studies highlighting the role of parenting practices do theorize that similarities observed across generations in parenting involve modeling, thus they generally emphasize the learning of parenting practices. In this study, we wish to focus on domains other than parenting (as traditionally defined) that increase risks for cross-generational continuities.

Findings from the Cambridge study did reveal that antisocial males in the study were more likely than their nondelinquent counterparts to maintain a "deviant lifestyle" in adulthood (Farrington, 1995). In a recent examination of intergenerational effects, Smith and Farrington theorized that since parenting variables did not fully mediate the relation between antisocial parents and children, "an important mechanism of intergenerational continuity is the maintenance of an antisocial lifestyle, including deviant peer and partner relationships" (2004: 243). The lack of attention in many studies to social-learning processes does not necessarily reflect a lack of interest in these dynamics; rather, it may stem from basic difficulties in capturing and modeling such mechanisms, particularly when using traditional quantitative approaches. For example, while questions have been devised that reliably index different types of parenting practices, it is a challenge to develop items that tap the more subtle processes through which parents may transmit values, attitudes, and behavior patterns to their children. Indeed, it could be argued that to the degree that there remains concordance across generations once parenting and other factors such as SES have been taken into account, this in itself can be taken as evidence of a social learning process.

Another complication is methodological but has substantive and theoretical implications. While the studies cited earlier include many important design features (multiple assessments over a large number of years, information gleaned from multiple reporters, including parents, children, and sometimes, school personnel), the sample groups that are often relied upon do not typically include large numbers of delinquent youth. Importantly, such surveys have allowed us to generalize about the range of variation observed in general populations of adolescents, and their results are not influenced by possible criminal-justice system biases. Nevertheless, such designs are often limited in their capacity to fully explore the life-course experiences of serious/chronic offenders (e.g., periods of incarceration, drug abuse, and the like) because few such individuals are typically captured through random survey methods. This is often the case even when investigators oversample in high-risk areas, such as inner-city or high-crime neighborhoods. In short, most youths in a given cohort or population-based sample are not very delinquent, and they become even less so as they mature into adulthood. This makes it difficult to examine the generational transfer of behavior patterns when the criminal careers of the majority of focal respondents have often never really "taken off" to begin with.

THE LIFE-COURSE PERSPECTIVE

Sampson and Laub (2001), major proponents of the life-course perspective within criminology, focused much of their research on a group of boys who had reached what they describe as a "reasonable threshold of frequent and serious offending" (p. 12). Their analyses of data collected by Sheldon and Eleanor Glueck beginning in the 1940s was consistent with the authors' theoretical interests in understanding more about juvenile delinquents' later adult patterns of persistence or desistance from crime. The Gluecks' follow-up of two groups of boys is distinctive because it included 500 delinquent youth from the greater Boston area, who had been incarcerated at one time in a state institution, and a comparable sample of nondelinquent youth. The Gluecks amassed interview and arrest data when the men averaged 14, 25, and 30 years of age, and Sampson and Laub later reinterviewed a subset of these respondents as much older men (n = 50) who at that time averaged 70 years of age. Laub and Sampson also eventually collected arrest data for the total sample covering the intervening years up to age 70. The Gluecks' study and Laub and Sampsons' analyses, then, provided an excellent long-term vantage point for examining the lives and criminal careers of youths who are familiar to juvenile justice personnel, but who may not be found in large numbers in neighborhood-based surveys. Our study was conducted decades later but is similar in this basic respect – the girls and boys in our sample were also targeted based on their incarceration in state-level juvenile institutions. Thus, the Gluecks' study has been useful as an anchor for and, at times, a counterpoint for our own analyses, as well as the child follow-up.

Although neither the Gluecks nor Sampson and Laub followed up with the children of the original sample, the study is nevertheless often cited as one of the risk-factor studies documenting intergenerational linkages.[2] Early on, the Gluecks observed that parental criminality was much more common in the backgrounds of the delinquent sampler than in control group sample (1950). Sampson and Laub's analyses helped to develop the life-course perspective on crime by focusing attention on variations in the criminal behavior of the Glueck men as they became adults and on the life-course experiences that appeared to be related to those variations. Sampson and Laub documented that members of the original sample of delinquent youth were more likely than the control group to continue to offend as they made the transition to adulthood; yet, even when they concentrated on this delinquent sample, they observed considerable variability in the degree to which and the pace at which the men desisted from their earlier criminal involvement. An important finding was that major transition events such as marriage and stable employment were sources of redirection; conversely, they did not find strong support for the idea that early risk factors (including negative family circumstances) foreclosed the potential to make positive adjustments later on (Laub, Nagin, & Sampson, 1998; Laub & Sampson, 2003). A key contribution of this study, then, is that evidence of both continuity and change emerges, given the perspective afforded by the longer life-course vantage point. Past behavior is generally a solid predictor of future behavior, but change (whether termed maturational reform, desistance, or redemption) is possible and frequently found in long-term follow-ups.

Sampson and Laub's focus on themes of continuity and change accords well with the emphasis here on intergenerational transmission. Parental criminality and aggression make it more likely that children will evidence the same behaviors, but as the developing research tradition described earlier attests, virtually all studies also document discontinuities across the generations. Even without assessing the specifics of parenting, it is intuitive to expect that the children born to men who in adulthood had achieved social and economic stability and had clearly desisted from crime, might be better off than the children of less stable, more criminal men. Sampson and Laub described a range of adult adaptations made by the Glueck men – from solid

---

[2] See Snarey (1993) for an analysis of parenting on the part of the control-group sample members.

family types who stayed married to the same person all their adult lives to those who drifted in and out of crime to those whose violence, alcohol abuse, and other criminal actions persisted over many years.

Sampson and Laub's research is also useful because it illustrates the play of historical era as an influence on the course of the men's lives. The men studied by Sampson and Laub came of age in the 1940s and thus were influenced by numerous possibilities and constraints that are specific to this cohort. For example, a number of men served in the military in World War II, a set of experiences that appeared to have generally beneficial effects on criminal involvement (Sampson & Laub, 1996). Social pressure to move ahead with "shotgun marriages" and cultural norms against divorce also likely influenced marriage's stabilizing potential. In addition, even though the men all had juvenile arrest histories, and some had also acquired adult arrest histories, and on average had low levels of education, the availability of manufacturing jobs in the relatively prosperous postwar period was also a generally positive societal-level influence on the character of the men's lives. Sampson and Laub's findings and other researches have generally shown that stable jobs benefit the desistance process (see, e.g., Horney, Osgood, & Marshall, 1995; Mischkowitz, 1994; Uggen, 2000). In addition, economic resources increase one's attractiveness as a marriage partner and are inversely associated with marital conflict and dissolution (Conger et al., 1990; Edin & Kefalas, 2005; Oppenheimer, 2003).

As we discuss in more detail in Chapter Four, the aggregate portrait that emerges from Sampson and Laub's study of the Glueck men resonates in many respects with our more contemporary follow-up. However, along with shifts in the social and economic processes described earlier (declines in the likelihood and stability of marriages, reduced opportunities for those with little education to secure stable employment), several other time-sensitive factors also place the study historically and contrast with our emphases in this investigation. Consistent with the basic tenets of life-course theorizing, then, these shifts have implications for understanding the unique character of the life-course experiences of our focal respondents, as well as the distinctive family circumstances ("legacies") their children have inherited.

In Sampson and Laub's analyses, women only make an appearance as wives or girlfriends of the focal respondents. Yet, the generally low base rates of women's criminal involvement at the time the Glueck men matured into adulthood may have influenced the authors' view that the partner's level of criminality has little impact on what they labeled the "good marriage effect." As the authors stated, even without knowing a specific wife's criminal history, it is likely that such an individual represented a favorable network influence, since gender differences in crime were so lopsided. However, this basic reality, along with more general theoretical predilections, may have been pivotal in the development of their focus on social control rather than social learning processes. Thus, the authors essentially bracketed the spouse's role in fostering definitions favorable or unfavorable to violations of law (Sutherland, 1947), concentrating instead on the extent to which marriage/job stability provided an element of "social control" over the men's conduct. In their early work, Sampson and Laub conceived of marriage as an investment process – over time, the men's commitment to marriage increased to the point that they did not wish to jeopardize it by engaging in criminal activities. In the more recent book, which includes new interviews with a subset of the Glueck men, the authors argued further that marriage provided structure and new routines that are also important to an understanding of the "good marriage" effect (Laub & Sampson, 2003). All of these dynamics are consistent with a social control theoretical lens.

This emphasis on informal social controls over the individual thus extends the logic of control theory, a perspective originally developed in connection with the causes of juvenile delinquency, to an understanding of variations in the later adult lives of these same individuals. Thus, young people become antisocial in large measure because they are not effectively controlled by parents, and, if they are lucky enough to turn their lives around later on, it is because of the new controls associated with significant life changes (i.e., marriage). And we can see the continuing impact of the control point of view in the heavy focus on supervision and other parenting practices as critical mediators of intergenerational continuities, as described in the literature review earlier. Hirschi, a key architect of the control perspective, argued strongly against the idea that families teach their children about crime – he said, for example, that criminals do not typically commit deviant acts in front of the children; instead, an individual, "even if he is himself committing criminal acts, does not publicize this fact to his children" (1969: 108). This is consistent with Sampson and Laub's contention that the spouse's level of criminality is not an important consideration, and with Farrington's assertion that parents do not offend with nor wish to see their children offend. Thus, viewed from several different life-course vantage points, we must conclude that the idea of learning about crime or, alternatively, about a more prosocial way of life is seen as less pivotal to crime causation than are the dynamics that are typically linked with theories of social control.

An alternative viewpoint, and one we wish to develop further in this book, is that most control notions are fully compatible with social-learning principles (see, e.g., Conger, 1976); thus, we do not wish to discard but instead to add to the considerable insights that have emerged from research relying on the former perspective. Hirschi's disdain for theoretical integration and his view of the incompatibility of these perspectives notwithstanding (Hirschi, 1987), the parent may be lax in monitoring the child and also teach attitudes and behaviors that make crime more likely. One spouse can not only provide structure and routine for the other, but also has many chances to be an exemplar of an antisocial or prosocial way of life.

As we discuss in more detail in subsequent chapters, most criminologists readily accept (and our own research has also demonstrated) that delinquent girls such as those we have followed up may be negatively influenced by their romantic partners (Giordano, Cernkovich, & Holland, 2003; Leverentz, 2006). This focus on women's experiences undoubtedly has sensitized us to the role of romantic partners in both the social learning and the social control sense (i.e., a woman's marriage to a violent drug-dealing ex-convict is unlikely to facilitate the desistance process, even in the presence of strong bonds of affection). However, we hope that our discussion and analyses make a contribution to more general theorizing about life-course/crime connections as well.

As we suggested earlier, marriage has historically represented a settling down for men because women were very unlikely to be involved in crime and other antisocial behavior. This mismatch in rates is still present, but is arguably less pronounced than in earlier eras. Increases in drug use and the markets that support them and in women's arrest and incarceration rates (often for drug related offenses) are thus important to an understanding of the contemporary world of crime, and to the character of social networks and their influence. Thus, a female partner, like a male partner, can either be a good or a bad influence, depending on the criminal/prosocial orientation of these significant others (Capaldi Kim, & Owen, 2008). Similarly, both parents have a chance to be positive or problematic influences on their children's lives. Again, temporal shifts in the character of the criminal landscape (e.g., the debilitating effects on families of crack cocaine use) undoubtedly has fostered our emphasis on learning mechanisms that may coalesce with other more heavily researched dynamics such as lack of supervision and neglect.[3]

PRIOR RESEARCH/THEORIZING ABOUT GENDER AND CRIME

While we hope that our research adds to the literature on intergenerational and life-course processes, one of the unique features of the study is that young women make up over 50 percent of the original sample group, and an even larger percentage of the "parents" for purposes of the current investigation. Thus, it is important to situate our analyses not only within the above research, but also within the context of the literature on gender and crime. If an essential theme within the mostly male tradition of life-course research is that of continuity and change, core concerns within the gender and crime literature are questions of similarity and difference. Thus, researchers continue to grapple with the issue of whether and to what degree theoretical perspectives, and even basic facts about crime that developed largely

---

[3] Even if we were to focus exclusively on crime committed by men/boys in earlier eras, in our view it is likely that social learning/social influence processes would be implicated in the individual's patterns of criminal involvement. For example, even very early accounts of cross-generational transmission, while oriented toward genetic influences, recognized the important role of "criminogenic family values" (Dugdale, 1877).

around male-focused studies, "fit" with the life experiences of women and girls.

It is typical to associate the interest in divergent perspectives with the development of feminist scholarship, but even prior to this period (the 1970s saw an increase in feminist treatments of various crime topics, including issues of causation), a number of researchers posited gendered pathways to crime. For example, Riege (1972) and Rittenhouse (1963) argued that, while boys were often motivated by "status strivings," "relational strivings" were critical to an understanding of the behaviors of the smaller subset of girls who became involved in delinquent behavior. Thus, early on, the notion developed that girls' involvement in delinquency could be conceptualized as an attempt to "fill a relationship void" (see also Konopka, 1966). This idea actually fits well with a much broader, more recent literature on gender that highlights girls' strong relational orientation (Gilligan, 1982; Simon, Eder, & Evans, 1992).

Our early research took issue with some of the earliest discussions of unique-pathways because we thought that young women, like their male counterparts, might also be influenced by "status strivings" (particularly those stemming from economic disadvantages) and other social dynamics that had been emphasized in research on male delinquency. We found that the perceptions of blocked opportunities for educational and occupational achievement were related to girls' as well as boys' self-reported delinquency, and that the delinquent attitudes/behaviors of friends were strongly related to girls' own levels of involvement (for a review see Giordano & Cernkovich, 1997). As it became much more common to include significant numbers of girls in study samples, an array of findings on school, family, and neighborhood influences on girls' delinquency accumulated, generally supporting the idea of some common etiological influences (Zahn, 2009).

Feminist theorists have nevertheless provided a much needed alternative lens by highlighting the unique concerns of girls and women and the ways in which gender inequalities influence girls' behaviors as well as those of agents of social control (whether the family or the police). In the initial development of this line of theorizing, however, scholars such as Leonard (1982) suggested the need to discard traditional "male-based" theories, arguing that they are "biased to the core, riddled with assumptions that relate to a male – not a female – reality" (p. 181). Given our focus here on social learning theory, it is useful to revisit Leonard's position on this perspective.

> Generally speaking, women are shielded from criminal learning experiences. Even within the same groups as males (like the family), their social position is unequal, and they are frequently taught dissimilar attitudes. More isolated from criminal norms and techniques, they are also more consistently taught law-abiding behavior and are expected to act in accordance with the law ... Boys and girls are taught quite different standards and, with this, subtly different attitudes toward law breaking. (1982: 108)

Although it has been extremely important to highlight that boys and girls are often socialized quite differently, the distinction Leonard makes does a better job of explaining the continuing gender gap in rates of delinquency and crime than the actions of young women who do become involved in various forms of antisocial behavior. In addition, there is, in our view, nothing distinctively "male" about living in a disadvantaged neighborhood, failing in school, or wanting to fit in with one's friends (all traditional predictors of male delinquency that have also proven to be robust predictors of variations in adolescent girls' involvement). At the family level, such bread-and-butter predictors as parental supervision and warmth/caring have also repeatedly been shown to be strong influences on delinquency in girls as well as boys (Kruttschnitt & Giordano, 2009). While the limited body of research on intergenerational transmission has often focused on male parents and male children, we do not believe (and our data will show) that girls who grow up within close range of parental criminality are impervious to these family circumstances.

Thus, while we do not agree that traditional theories such as social control and social learning should be abandoned, we do agree that attention to gendered processes is also critical if we are to develop a comprehensive portrait of girls' choices, constraints, and indeed their criminal involvement. A key point raised by feminist scholars is that continually relying on a generic conceptual tool kit is ultimately limiting to the theory development process. For example, feminist perspectives on crime have heightened awareness of the role of victimization experiences, in particular the role of sexual abuse, as an important and highly gendered background factor that helps to explain girls' involvement in delinquency (Katz, 2000).

In addition to elucidating connections between victimization and offending, this perspective sheds light on the impact of inequitable gender relationships and more concretely negative male influences. For example, Chesney-Lind and Shelden's (1998) research on runaways finds that over time, young women living on the streets often face heightened risk for abusive relationships and further victimization and exploitation by male companions. Bottcher (2001) stressed that "studies of adolescent gender show that patterns of male domination and female subordination are increasingly apparent during the teenage years," noting that "the portrayal of female subjugation and sexual exploitation is unremitting in qualitative and journalistic accounts of delinquent youths and gangs" (p. 899). This emphasis is also found in the literature on adult criminal behavior, often based on studies of incarcerated women. Richie (1996), for example, argued that many women are essentially "compelled to crime" by the coercive actions of male partners (as, e.g., when women's criminal involvement amounts to carrying out the wishes of their male partner) or that many law violations are actually better understood as attempts at self-preservation (i.e., fighting off an abusive husband). This focus on relationships that are characterized by constraint and coercion contrasts with the more egalitarian emphasis of the research on peer relationships and delinquency as it has developed in the more generic or male-based research literature.

A third and related point that is highlighted within the gender and crime literature is that offenses that are more prevalent among girls and women, such as prostitution, also reflect patriarchal gender relationships and adaptations that are uniquely marginalizing. As Miller (1986) observed in her ethnographic account of women involved in prostitution in Milwaukee, this "life" represents a nexus of illegal activities and contacts and "street" orientation that often becomes very difficult to escape (see also Barnard, 1993). An important consideration is the high level of stigma attached to behaviors that violate double standards of sexual conduct. In addition, even less obviously gendered behaviors such as drug abuse are often viewed as more alarming when women engage in them. The combination (e.g., as epitomized in the label "crack whore") is especially stigmatizing both from society's point of view and, often, from the standpoint of women's own perceptions (Sterk, 1999).

Although theorizing in the gender and crime area thus developed in opposition to traditional criminological perspectives, there has been increased recent interest in moving toward a more integrated perspective, that is, one that takes into account both gendered and generic processes (Heimer & Kruttschnitt, 2006). For example, sexual abuse is frequently documented in the histories of delinquent girls, but the majority of girls who experience sexual abuse do not go on to become delinquent or criminal adults (Widom, 1989). This suggests that a focus on a gendered dynamic such as sexual abuse does not in itself offer a comprehensive account of the causes of girls' delinquency. Attention to such experiences in combination with other more traditional risk factors may be required to round out our understanding of the mechanisms involved in the etiology of girls' delinquency.

Gaarder and Belknap (2002) found support for this more complex view in their analyses of the life histories of a sample of girls who were transferred to adult court because of their involvement in relatively serious offenses such as aggravated robbery and felonious assault. These researchers found evidence of both gendered processes, such as victimization, and negative romantic-partner influences, and also of disadvantaged backgrounds, lack of success in school, involvement with delinquent peers, and parental criminality/drug abuse. Similarly, in an analysis of the OLS women's descriptions of their growing-up years (the parents for purposes of the current study), we found that the majority (over 70%) of the women's narratives contained references to both gendered and generic themes. No narrative produced by these young women contained only references to gendered processes, and just 29 percent consisted of references only to mechanisms stressed by traditional delinquency theorists (Giordano, Deines, & Cernkovich, 2006). Miller and Mullins (2006) called for a more integrated approach to theory development as well, based on their study of girls' motivations for violent and aggressive actions. In an analysis of data from in-depth interviews with at-risk and delinquent girls, the

researchers found that the young women they interviewed frequently
described their violent/aggressive actions in ways that often paral-
leled the motivations expressed by male delinquents (i.e., wanting to
gain respect/status or needing to show toughness). Yet the authors
also found evidence of gendered meanings, such as the tendency of
girls to fight over a romantic interest or because of insults to one's
appearance. This study thus describes the attitudes and behaviors
of girls in a way that overcomes some of the theoretical excesses of
earlier research (e.g., Dobash et al.'s declaration that when women
use violence it is almost always "in defense of self and children in
response to cues of imminent assault" [1992: 80]).

Why do these depictions of the causes of female delinquency and
crime "matter" for purposes of the present study, focused as it is on
the dynamics of intergenerational transmission? In our view, a thorough understanding of what got the women where they are is necessary in order to adequately depict their lives as adults and, in turn, to
capture the generic as well as unique vulnerabilities of their children.
If we were to emphasize only generic considerations, this would effectively foreshadow a portrait of the adult women as poorly educated, living in poverty, and perhaps associating with delinquent peers. While
the women's lives do vary considerably, as we show in more detail
in Chapter Four, this picture is generally quite accurate. Focusing
only on those features of the women's lives, however, ignores many of
the realities that have been effectively depicted by feminist researchers, including romantic ties to abusive, antisocial partners who may
reside within the household. We also might bypass any attention to
the women's psychological well-being and drug use as strongly influenced by earlier sexual abuse experiences as well as their current circumstances. These realities are all a part of what makes up the child's
family environment, thus influencing parenting practices and other
mechanisms involved in the intergenerational transmission process.

THE CHILDREN OF INCARCERATED PARENTS

Recent estimates indicate that approximately 17 million children in
the United States have a parent who is incarcerated in one of the
nation's prisons (Glaze & Maruschak, 2008). Thus, the burgeoning

literature on societal effects of parental incarceration is another research tradition that provides a useful background for the current investigation. It is consistent with statistics on gender disparities that more studies have examined effects of male incarceration, but there has been increased attention to female prisoners and their children, often with a view toward improving services to families affected by the parent's incarceration (Bloom, 1995; Gabel & Johnston, 1995; Travis, McBride, & Solomon, 2005). Research and theorizing in this area ranges from broad-based societal or neighborhood-level analyses of effects of "mass incarceration" to more focused investigations examining the extent to which children of prisoners are at risk for school and behavior problems and other adjustment difficulties (Hagan & Dinovitzer, 1999; Western & McLanahan, 2000; Western & Wildeman, 2009). This research is potentially useful as it provides a different window on intergenerational effects.

Murray and Farrington (2005) examined the background characteristics of boys who participated in the Cambridge study and found that parental imprisonment was associated with a variety of delinquent outcomes, controlling for traditional risk factors and even the parents' prior convictions. More recently Murray and Farrington (2008) conducted a comprehensive review of the research on effects of parental imprisonment, focusing on studies that included a control group or relied on general population samples and provided information on the strength of the association with child antisocial outcomes. Their analyses document significant effects of parental incarceration.

Because mothers are typically the primary caregivers for children, researchers and practitioners alike have noted multiple problems that occur when a mother must serve out a sentence, often at a considerable distance from the family's residence. Thus, researchers have documented that the children of such mothers face difficulties finding suitable alternative caregivers and have also highlighted the stigma and loss associated with the incarceration event. Researchers have shown that children of incarcerated mothers in particular may experience psychological distress, school failure, and behavior problems (Arditti, 2005). Some of the studies in this tradition have relied on parental reports about the child, which may not provide the most accurate assessments of the child's level of functioning (since the parent is unable to observe problems directly and may, for example, have only limited knowledge of how the child is faring in school).

A more fundamental issue is that researchers in this tradition have typically located the sources of the child's difficulties primarily in the stress that accompanies the parent's incarceration (Hairston, 2007). This differs from the life-course treatment that we develop in this analysis, which recognizes that the parent may have experienced several periods of jail time and/or incarceration during the child's growing-up years. Further, the parents' criminal activity may be experienced as a direct source of family discord and personal stress. Indeed, while at any given time a significant number of U.S. children have a parent who is incarcerated, a much larger number have a parent who has been incarcerated as some point during the child's lifetime (Raphael & Stoll, 2009). This is an important point because during periods when the parent is not incarcerated, the child may, for example, worry that the parent will be arrested again and may also be directly and negatively influenced by the parent's actions. These ongoing anxieties accumulate alongside and may even surpass more immediately visible stressors associated with the parents' incarceration period(s).

Some researchers have attempted to disentangle the impact of these various effects, what Murray and Farrington (2008) refer to as "pre-existing adversities," as contrasted with the influence of parental incarceration itself. For example, Stanton (1980) compared the children of jailed mothers and the children of mothers on probation, reasoning that both sets of parents might be similar in levels of adversity, including criminal involvement. Stanton did find that reports of problem behavior were significantly higher for children of the jailed mothers. Nevertheless, as Murray and Farrington note, the jailed mothers tended to have more prior convictions and less favorable educational and occupational circumstances, which may have influenced this result. Murray and Farrington argue that an experimental design would provide the ideal test of the true effects of incarceration. Since this is impractical, they focused on five quasi-experimental studies, finding independent effects on child outcomes in three of them and no effects of incarceration in two (once parental criminality and other "adversities" had been taken into account). While recognizing the need for more research in this area, the authors go on to describe factors that may explain the observed associations (i.e., serve as mediators) between parental incarceration and negative child outcomes. Their review stressed "trauma of parent-child separation," stigma associated with the incarceration, and social and economic strains that result from the parent's absence, rather than social learning mechanisms.

MECHANISMS UNDERLYING INTERGENERATIONAL TRANSMISSION: A FOCUS ON SOCIAL LEARNING PROCESSES

While the dynamics emphasized by Murray and Farrington and other scholars are critical to an understanding of effects of parental crime and incarceration, our primary objective is to shed further light on the social learning mechanisms associated with the intergenerational transmission of crime. Our interest in the dynamics of social learning undoubtedly stems from a general affinity for this theoretical viewpoint, as well as from our conclusion that the dynamics underlying social learning have not been adequately explored. However, the neo-Meadian perspective on intergenerational transmission discussed in more detail in Chapter Six can also be considered a grounded theory, since specific emphases emerged from analyses of the data, particularly from the in-depth qualitative interviews that were conducted with parents, children, and other caregivers.[4] We have also been influenced by recent developments in symbolic interactionist theorizing, which have provided inspiration and a more formal conceptual anchor for emerging ideas.[5]

[4] Grounded theory emphasizes that concepts and understandings should emerge from, that is, be grounded in a thorough analysis of the data rather than being developed "a priori" and subsequently tested empirically. In addition, this perspective has more often been associated with the collection and analysis of qualitative rather than structured or quantitative data (Glaser & Strauss, 1967).

[5] The neo-Meadian theory we describe was initially developed through our analyses of interviews with the OLS parents (see, e.g., Giordano, Schroeder, & Cernkovich, 2007); subsequent analyses of the child interviews and sections of the parent interview that related to parenting behaviors led to our view that the neo-Meadian approach could be extended as a useful framework for illuminating the dynamics associated with intergenerational transmission.

It could be argued that social learning mechanisms are so intuitive that they require little more in the way of explanation or elaboration. Some concepts identified within the scholarly literature are similarly straightforward: notions of *modeling* or *imitation* clearly evoke social learning processes but do not in themselves provide a clear window on the specific ways in which social learning occurs. Indeed, evidence favoring modeling/imitation often consists of the observed concordance between parent and child behavior itself or is considered residual, leftover after such factors as parenting practices have been taken into account.

Early on in the development of criminological theory, Gabriel Tarde ([1890] 1912) focused attention on the idea of social imitation as a counterpoint to Lombroso's (1876) biologically oriented treatments of the origins of criminality (i.e., the notion of the "born criminal"). Tarde's ideas about imitation thus suggested the general utility of attending to social influence/learning processes, rather than focusing exclusively on innate individual differences. Both Tarde's "law of close contact" and his emphasis on the primacy of "superior to subordinate influence" provide a basic rationale for our focus on learning as an important dynamic that is associated with intergenerational transmission. The family context qualifies as a close-in context within which social influence is likely to take place, and the parent's position is considered to be superior to that of the child. Tarde did not, however, provide many specifics about mechanisms involved, particularly where the focus is upon small groups, such as family settings. While recognizing the importance of close contact, he often analyzed broader social processes such as collective behavior and the influence of one social class upon the other (e.g., the idea that those in the lower social echelons often imitate the behavior of those placed higher in a system of stratification).

Edwin Sutherland's (1947) theory of differential association drew on Tarde's insights but further developed the dynamics of social learning and influence processes. Sutherland believed that "the principal part of the learning of criminal behavior occurs within intimate primary groups" (p. 6) and encompasses the same mechanisms involved in learning any other pattern of behavior. Yet Sutherland's emphasis on the centrality of *communication processes* adds a level of specificity about mechanisms; it also positions social learning theory squarely within the broader sociological tradition of symbolic interactionist theories. One's intimate associations do not simply provide behavioral models to imitate but, through recurrent interaction and communication, continually impart "definitions" that are either favorable or unfavorable to the violation of law. This focus on the range of attitudes, motives, and rationalizations others provide is consistent with the symbolic interactionist emphasis on meanings, and foregrounds the cognitive underpinnings of behavior, including criminal activity. Sutherland also highlighted that some associations are likely to be more influential than others ("differential associations may vary in frequency, duration, priority, and intensity" [p. 7]). These conditions describe the parent-child bond well: interactions with the parent are important to the child and occur early, often, and in most instances, throughout the life course.

In our view, Sutherland's basic insights and subsequent elaborations of the theory of differential association (notably Akers' (2002) social learning theory) are a needed addition to the conceptual emphases of social control and related perspectives. In attempting to explain variations in delinquency involvement, control theorists do focus heavily on the parent-child bond, but they also concentrate almost exclusively on what is attenuated or missing (lack of attachment, lack of supervision). Certainly, a lack of proper supervision is one of the most robust correlates/predictors of delinquency, but we do not believe that a focus on informal social controls provides a complete picture of daily life within families. Accordingly, neither does it provide a comprehensive perspective on the dynamics underlying intergenerational transmission.

Classic social learning approaches thus provide a useful general background for thinking about parents as a major source of learning and influence. It is somewhat ironic, then, that so much of the research on social learning processes has concentrated on same-aged-friends and peers rather than family influences. Indeed, Warr (2002: 73) observed that "to many students of crime, the very notion of peer influence is synonymous with Edwin Sutherland's theory of differential association …" Research in this tradition has provided general support for basic postulates of the learning perspective, in that the delinquency of one's peers has proved to be a consistent predictor of a youth's own delinquency (Haynie, 2001; Simons, Wu et al., 1994). Researchers have shown links between parental attitudes and the child's behavior, but this entire area is not as well-developed as the area that is focused on parenting styles/practices. This may stem from the belief that the parent's antisocial days are in large part behind them, lessening their role as a source of direct transmission, as well as from the difficulty of studying a family's content, as contrasted with its formal characteristics (e.g., family-structure types, authoritative vs. authoritarian parenting style).

Our study of the OLS respondents and their children provides an excellent opportunity to address this gap in the literature because we have focused on a group of parents whose deviant actions have often extended into their children's growing-up years (Giordano, Schroeder, & Cernkovich, 2007; see also Chapter Four of this book). In addition, the in-depth life-history narratives we elicited provide insights about life within such families and the mechanisms involved that are more difficult to glean from quantitative approaches. In the process of analyzing these qualitative data, we have found it necessary to revise the classic social learning paradigm in order to incorporate several potentially important concepts with implications for intergenerational transmission – *self and identity*, *agency*, and *emotion*.

SELF AND IDENTITY

In its focus on the social origins of meanings (definitions favorable or unfavorable …), Sutherland's (1947) theory of differential association fits well within the symbolic interactionist tradition. Yet Mead (1934) and other symbolic interactionist theorists stressed that the same processes of interaction and communication that produce these meanings/definitions are implicated in the development of more general views about the "self." Mead highlighted that the ability to develop a consciousness of self (i.e., to reflect on one's self as an object) is a distinctively human attribute, one that engages cognitive processes – the origins of which are also social. Interactions within the family, then, not only expose children to specific behaviors (i.e., as they observe aggressive acts) and definitions (e.g., parents' liberal attitudes toward marijuana use), but also provide raw materials for these evolving views of self. The parents' identity portfolio is readily available to draw upon, and the "reflected appraisals" they communicate to the child (*you're just like your mother*) also have weight and significance.

Thus, a symbolic interactionist approach to intergenerational transmission necessarily will include attention to identity formation processes. Theorists in the symbolic interactionist tradition highlight that self and identity are important because they have "motivational" significance, acting as a kind of cognitive filter for decision making. This filtering notion is particularly important as the child moves forward in the life course, inevitably confronting novel situations. In these ever-unfolding situations and contexts, parental definitions will not prove to be comprehensive or entirely adequate guides to action; instead, the new choices will be evaluated in light of children's own developing understandings about their current and possible selves (e.g., *Am I the sort of person who will practice a musical instrument? Am I up for this party, this fight?*).

AGENCY

A related insight associated with symbolic interactionist theorizing is that the individual is both "a social product and a social force" (Rosenberg, 1990: 593). Thus, children are not only influenced by their environments but also, as "active agents," influence them. As Mead noted, selectivity of attention and foresight are distinctively human attributes. This idea that individuals exercise human agency, or act so as to create the social environments that nevertheless (as Emirbayer & Goodwin, 1994 suggest), influence them in turn has not typically been incorporated into traditional social learning theories. Indeed, such theories have frequently been criticized for conceptualizing the individual as a "passive vessel," uncritically receiving and then acting on the basis of the particular mix of definitions to which they have been exposed (Box, 1971). In addition, it is not immediately intuitive to think about children in particular as affecting "agentic" moves, since they are seen as subordinate and somewhat constrained within the family context and beyond. Yet Mead's idea of selective attention suggests in a general way that even very young children have "degrees of freedom" to, for example, attend to some members of the family more than others or to search outside the family for definitions that fit with their emerging identities. Thus, self-views and agency are intimately related. Children draw on parents' definitions and views of self but are not exact replicas of them, instead reflecting upon and then acting on the basis of their own unique biographies and emerging consciousness about what they are like and want to be like. These ideas are important to an understanding of continuities as well as *discontinuities* across generations, the latter having received particularly scant attention within the intergenerational literature.

Our analyses will highlight an important role for human agency; nevertheless, it is important to underscore that choice making takes place against a backdrop of structural contingencies and constraints. Choices are bounded, that is, never completely divorced from the social systems (macro-level, immediate social networks) within which they unfold. Indeed, we have argued that across the spectrum of advantage and disadvantage, "the play of agency is in the middle" (Giordano, Cernkovich, & Rudolph, 2002). If individuals are sufficiently advantaged, a show of agency is not necessary (since things typically do fall into place). Conversely if individuals are sufficiently disadvantaged, a show of agency is not nearly enough. For our purposes here, this general observation serves to highlight that there is likely a limit to the idea of children's agentic or creative capacities. Accordingly, to the degree that they are encapsulated within highly deviant and otherwise disadvantaged family contexts, children may have little in the way of social and cultural capital around which to craft a more prosocial way of life, even if they are inclined to do so. This is an important consideration for understanding the lives of the OLS youths and the strong cultural press toward intergenerational continuity that characterizes many of their family environments. As we will describe in more detail in subsequent chapters, the children we studied often coped with a dizzying array of social/economic disadvantages and experienced life in close daily contact with multiple antisocial family members.

EMOTION

When subjective processes have been incorporated into social learning theories, the emphasis has been upon cognitions (i.e., the idea of learning specific attitudes that make crime more likely). However, researchers across a number of disciplines have increasingly focused on the importance of emotional experience to a comprehensive understanding of human behavior and development (Collins, 2004; Massey, 2002; Pacherie, 2002; Turner, 2000). Symbolic interactionists in particular have stressed the degree to which emotions are: (i) social in origin, (ii) not opposed to but directly aligned with cognitive processes, and (iii) consequential for understanding behavioral choices. This is the case whether we focus upon "situated" (in the moment) actions or longer-term life-course "trajectories." Although Mead himself focused primarily on cognitive processes, contemporary symbolic interactionists have suggested that Mead's basic insights can usefully be extended to cover the emotional ream. Thus we use the term "neo-Meadian" when applied to the version of symbolic interactionism we rely on here and in related work (Engdahl, 2004; Giordano et al., 2007).

Extending the notion that meanings are socially constructed, scholars such as the Swedish sociologist Emma Engdahl (2004) have reasoned that emotions and the way they are expressed are also the product of social interaction. Emotions may be defined as "self-feelings," but our sense of what emotions are, taken-for granted strategies for emotion-management, and the experience of emotion itself arise within particular social contexts. Thus, a central criticism of Sutherland's treatment of social learning and of the literature on intergenerational transmission is the relative neglect of emotional processes.

Agnew (1992) and other criminologists developed the notion that anger and other negative emotions are important to an understanding of criminal behavior (Agnew, 1992; Dehaan & Loader, 2002). We build on this general idea, highlighting the social origins of these and other emotions, and exploring the role of emotional processes in relation to cross-generational continuity as well as change. Emotions are integral to intergenerational transmission in two respects. First, parents directly model behaviors such as aggression (the imitation idea) and communicate definitions (e.g., violence is needed or justified in this situation); yet they also provide the child's initial and on-going exposure to what emotions are and how they come to be expressed or managed. This is a fairly straightforward learning argument, one that is simply extended to cover the emotional realm. However, emotions are implicated in a second, equally important way.

Sutherland conceptualized social learning not only in somewhat passive terms, but also as an affectively neutral process. Indeed, the image comes to mind of two sides of a scale containing criminal and conforming definitions, with the heavier side determining the actor's own behavior. Thus, we must depart somewhat from Sutherland's key premise that the learning of criminal behavior incorporates all of the same mechanisms involved in learning any other behavior. While this is true in the technical sense, practically speaking different parent-child learning opportunities will vary in their emotional valence and impact. For example, one may learn from a parent how to fry chicken or make the bed, but these understandings may be interpreted by the child as routine and nonproblematic, hence occasioning little in the way of an emotional response.

In contrast, the child confronted with criminal parents and their antisocial lifestyles will have many opportunities to learn, but these also frequently engender a range of negative emotional reactions to these family circumstances. Thus, the victimization experiences, losses, household moves, and disappointments we describe in more detail in Chapters Five and Six may prove a direct *source* of negative emotions that amplify the child's level of risk for behavior problems and other negative life outcomes. Importantly, it is within these same families that children have had repeated exposure to the forms of unproductive coping strategies and ways of "acting out" that give shape to their emotional responses, and increase the likelihood of the intergenerational transmission of antisocial patterns of behavior.

CHAPTER THREE

The Ohio Life-Course Study

The following quote was drawn from interviewer comments recorded after the first adult follow-up interview with Gina, who was at the time 29 years old and living in Columbus, Ohio.

> I actually went all over town looking for Gina. I was to one end of town and then back to the other. There's no way I would have ever found her, [but] her friend got me to Grandma, Grandma got me to the right building, and then I met the crack heads, and the neighbor got me to Gina. Gina lives in the basement of this huge crack house apartment. She absolutely lives in the middle of nowhere. In fact, I'm still kind of amazed that I even found her in this downtown building. I mean there's no mailboxes, there's no anything. You go down this pitch black hallway. I totally had to trust this woman I was with – that and trust that my can of mace didn't run out! (Laughs) Um, but no, it was a completely dark hallway. I had a flashlight with me but other than that, I mean, it was completely dark and, um, very difficult to see. And you were completely down in the basement where there were no numbers, no nothing. Just lots of doors. And this woman happened to know where she was staying.
>
> But she [Gina] was glad to see me, obviously, with fifty bucks. So that's the first thing I showed her was the money, to prove that I was legit. [She lived there with] her husband, who's many, many, many, many, many, many, many, years her senior, um, she's been pregnant ten times and they haven't all been with Chuck, her current husband. Some of the things that she talked about: her mom died during child birth, giving birth to her. Her dad died when she was two. She was raised by her stepmom – Didn't like her ... [After running away] she was raised by hookers and that they, you know, made her keep going to school. She's not stupid. She's a

lot more street smart then she is smart. [But] She could not tell me, I mean, she's been pregnant ten times and couldn't tell me, couldn't tell me the years of all her kids' births. She's not working right now. Wants to work but isn't working right now. Very scarred up. You can tell she's been in a lot of fights. I mean very, very, very marked up. I mean EXTREMELY marked-up. And she's been through some things. Lost all her kids ... But she does take care of one of Chuck's kids.

Oh, and she was real concerned about my safety, especially my being on the top floor with the crack heads, which I thought that was kind of interesting. I actually find that a lot, like the more interviews I do, whatever the situation is, wherever I am, people are always very concerned about my safety, which is kind of comforting but, I mean, and anyways she had her husband walk me ALL the way out. Made sure I got all the way out and you know, all the way to my car.

The above quote illustrates difficulties we often encountered in the process of locating these respondents after an interval of thirteen years with virtually no contact. The excerpt from this longer narrative also offers a glimpse of the marginal living circumstances of many of the women and men who participated in the Ohio Life-Course Study (OLS). This short quote conveys, too, that Gina's early problem life history ("raised by hookers") has not segued into a happy and productive adult life. Gina is currently unemployed and living in a crack house. She has been unable to retain custody of her children, and even the interviewer's cursory description (very, very, very, marked up) reveals tangible manifestations of a difficult life, including exposure to violence. And yet the concluding remarks our interviewer Claudia Vercellotti offers about Gina and the interviewing process are also important. For example, she describes the frequent concerns for her safety during the interview process. In notes describing other interviews, Claudia also documents the thoughtfulness, sense of humor, or deep religious faith of many respondents. These aspects of the women's and men's narratives are also a part of their identities and personal biographies, even though our interest in intergenerational patterns of crime inevitably draws our attention to their histories of drug abuse, violence, prison time, and other "problem" outcomes.

A BRIEF OVERVIEW OF THE OHIO LIFE-COURSE STUDY

The OLS comprised a series of three interviews that spanned a period of approximately twenty-two years. We interviewed Gina and the entire population of the state institution for delinquent girls in Ohio (Scioto Village) in 1982, when they averaged 16 years of age (n = 127). The sample is diverse (38% African American) and includes young people from all of Ohio's cities and several smaller towns. We also interviewed a comparable sample of boys who were institutionalized at the state level at that time (n = 127). The first adult follow-up interview, from which the above quote is taken, was completed in 1995, when the respondents averaged 29 years (n = 210). The second follow-up, which focused more heavily on issues of parenting and child well-being, was completed in 2003 (total sample = 153; parent sample = 123). In connection with the 2003 adult follow-up we also were able to interview one child, and sometimes multiple biological children of the original respondents, a majority of whom were, at that time, navigating the period of adolescence themselves (n = 158). We also interviewed a primary caregiver when the child was not living with the focal biological parent (n = 38). We describe in more detail below the strategies for locating the respondents at each of the follow-ups and the content of the interviews. We provide a descriptive profile that sets the stage for the more complete analysis of adult and child outcomes that we describe in the later chapters and introduce the related sample groups that we rely upon to make basic comparisons (Toledo Youth Survey [TYS], Toledo Young Adult Survey [TYAS] and Toledo Adolescent Relationships Study [TARS]). Although these control groups are not precisely matched, the studies were carried out at about the same time as the OLS study, focused on Ohio samples with approximately the same age distributions as OLS study members, and included identical interview questions.

INITIAL INTERVIEW WITH THE OLS RESPONDENTS AS ADOLESCENTS

Early studies of delinquent youth often relied on institutionalized samples, but the advent of self-reported delinquency scales as well as concerns about system biases combined to foster a new emphasis on randomly selected samples or on entire cohorts of adolescents. Yet, as noted in the literature review, the heavy reliance on general youth samples has costs, particularly because serious chronic offenders within these samples are often underrepresented. Even quite sophisticated samples of the general youth population often do not locate large numbers of such problem youth. This makes it difficult to study the long-term consequences of serious antisocial behavior on the behavior and well-being of the next generation of children. As noted previously, this low base rate is even more characteristic of female respondents, where low rates of delinquency and crime are observed at every age. Still, we know that there is a small subset of young women who are involved in serious offenses, sometimes at high rates. While many of these girls find their way into institutions, they are difficult to capture in significant numbers via general youth samples.

To illustrate this, in 1981 we conducted a study of a large sample of female and male adolescents via random selection procedures, oversampling in neighborhoods with high crime rates in Toledo, Ohio (n = 941). Yet, even relying on these oversampling techniques, few girls in the TYS study reported serious acts of delinquency, and only a small handful had accumulated police or juvenile court contacts. Because of our interest in female delinquency, we decided to supplement the TYS study by interviewing girls who had been adjudicated as delinquent and were incarcerated in a facility for juvenile offenders. At the time of the study, a single institution in Ohio housed girls from counties throughout the state who had been committed to the Department of Youth Services. In 1982, after securing permission from state and institutional authorities, we interviewed the total population of girls at Scioto Village and a randomly selected group of boys drawn from three male institutions (OLS).[1]

As is often the case with such institutions, the Ohio state facilities were located some distance from the urban centers – Cleveland, Columbus, Cincinnati, Akron, Dayton, Toledo – and the handful of

---

[1] These initial interviews were conducted by Giordano and Stephen Cernkovich, along with a small group of Bowling Green State University graduate and undergraduate students.

smaller cities where these youths originally lived. Thus, in marked contrast to the adult follow-ups, which necessarily took place in Cleveland, Columbus, Cincinnati, and the like, the interview process at the first wave was relatively efficient. We conducted structured, face-to-face interviews with these young people in quiet areas of the institutions such as the library, and with a few exceptions (one of our interviewers had a passing resemblance to the star of a then popular television program, "The Greatest American Hero," and many of the girls kept jockeying to be interviewed by him), the respondents were engaged and cooperative. We also had conducted research in several Columbus area high schools, and the often unwieldy nature of those experiences contrasted with the comparatively smooth data-collection phase we encountered at Scioto Village and the comparable male institutions. We were a minor nuisance to the high schoolers; at the institutions we were something new and interesting to break up the day's routines.

The interview schedule focused on major domains of the adolescent's life and was designed to elicit information on family dynamics, peer networks, school attachment, and performance, as well as on the respondents' self-reported delinquency, arrest, and incarceration histories. In addition, some questions were included that we hypothesized might be important because of our focus on girls (e.g., the gender composition of the friendship group, whether respondents were with their boyfriends when committing delinquent acts). The interview also included follow-up information about the specific contexts and motivations for violence, drug and alcohol use, and property crimes. While the interviews provided us with systematically collected data on all 254 respondents, we also felt that we learned a great deal from these youths during the less structured talk that occurred before and after the interview proper. This informed our decision to conduct in-depth unstructured interviews in connection with the adult follow-ups that occurred much later on. The original OLS sample averaged 16 years of age. Fifty percent of the sample was female; 65 percent was white. Nonwhite respondents were predominantly African American (32%).

Respondents who participated in the TYS were administered a nearly identical protocol to that completed by OLS respondents.

This sample was selected using census tract information, and as mentioned earlier, the design included oversamples in areas with high crime rates. The average age was similar to that of the OLS youths (16 years). The method of administration was face-to-face interviews conducted in respondents' homes. The TYS sample was also diverse, including 50 percent African American youth.

A brief comparison of self-report information drawn from the TYS and OLS respondents illustrates the differences in the nature and levels of delinquency involvement across the two samples (see Cernkovich, Giordano, & Pugh, 1985 for a more detailed examination of differences across the two groups). Comparisons reveal that the OLS respondents report considerably more delinquent behavior than their TYS counterparts. This is the case whether we focus on females or males, on serious or relatively minor offenses. For example, while only 4 percent of the TYS girls report any involvement in theft of property, 64 percent of the OLS girls report involvement in this offense. Similarly, only 10 percent of the TYS females reported running away during the previous year, compared to 70 percent of the institutional offenders. The differences in *levels* of involvement (frequency of these acts) range from 3 to 51 times greater for the institutional respondents than for the TYS respondents. For example, the institutional females report an average of 24 grand theft incidents compared to 0.57 incidents for the TYS youths. Similarly, the institutional girls committed an average of 15 unarmed robberies during the 12-month reference period, compared to only 1 among the TYS girls. Involvement of OLS males is higher relative to female reports, but again, the OLS respondents self-report significantly more delinquency involvement than their male counterparts who participated in the TYS study.

Further evidence of differences in seriousness is provided by a comparison of responses to specific follow-up questions. Given the apparently similar groups who admitted to a particular serious offense such as assault, differences between the TYS and the institutional respondents were found in the specific characteristics of these incidents. For example, while the victims of the assaultive behaviors of TYS youth were more often brothers/sisters or friends, the victims of the institutionalized samples included these groups but also included "strangers," "teachers," and the like. In an adult interview, Rhonda recalled incidents from her juvenile days: "At Garfield I threw some girl through the display case ... I was gettin' in a lot of fights. I hit a teacher, matter of fact, I hit two teachers. That's why I didn't finish high school."

In addition, the institutional offenders were more likely than their TYS counterparts to have assaulted someone while committing a crime. Whereas TYS youth had often engaged in breaking and entering "to warm up," the institutionalized OLS youth admitted to this rationale as well as to breaking and entering for the purpose of "stealing something." Similarly, TYS girls admitted theft of traditional items such as clothing and jewelry, while institutionalized girls admitted to this but also were more likely to have stolen items such as stereos, televisions, or furniture (28%); money or wallets (45.6%); or even guns (21.6%).

Since the TYS sample encompasses a range of levels of involvement, we also compared those youths in the Toledo study who reported the highest levels of delinquency within this sample (individuals who would be considered "serious offenders" when relying on this sample group alone) with the institutionalized OLS respondents. These comparisons revealed that institutionalized youth are not only more delinquent than the "average youth" in the general youth population, they are also considerably more delinquent than the most delinquent youth identified in the typical self-report survey (Cernkovich et al., 1985). These across-sample differences not only shed light on the delinquency "credentials" of the OLS respondents, but may be directly implicated in the differences in our theoretical perspective and the results obtained in prior studies, and in the current exploration of child effects.

For example, in our prior analyses based on the OLS sample, we found that marital status was not a significant predictor of desistance from crime, in contrast to what has been shown in a number of other studies (Giordano, Cernkovich, & Rudolph, 2002). As mentioned in the literature review, prior studies have also suggested that women often abruptly desist from crime upon the birth of their first child. This was also a far from general pattern among OLS respondents. For most young women whose delinquent careers are relatively minor, it may be that passing through these major transitions is a powerful catalyst for reducing or giving up on crime. In contrast, our data depict the desistance process as less likely, more circuitous and difficult, and less clearly tied to traditional transition events (see also Cernkovich & Giordano, 2001).

Such findings also raise the possibility that basic understandings about intergenerational transmission may also be influenced by sample characteristics. For example, as noted in Chapter Two, prior work on the mechanisms involved in intergenerational similarities has focused on poor/inept parenting as a key mediator. This is based in the logic of control theory, the belief that most parents do not actively "teach" their children to become delinquent (a process that would be more consistent with a social learning framework) and findings that are most often derived from unselected sample groups. Perhaps it is the case that, as Hirschi noted, most parents, even if deviant, typically shield their children from their deviant behaviors. However, our interviews with the OLS adults and their children, which are described in more detail in Chapters Five through Seven, clearly reveal that these youths are privy to a great deal of deviant behavior in the form of drug use, violence, and other criminal acts.

These findings undoubtedly have influenced our perspective on intergenerational transmission, including our view of the importance of attending to direct transmission processes in combination with ineffective/inconsistent parenting practices and other structural disadvantages. Similarly, our focus in Chapter Six on children's emotional reactions to their parents' behaviors and lifestyles may be directly related to the level and scope of difficulties that characterize the lives of many of those in the OLS parent generation. For example, within the context of a neighborhood or cohort sample, a "deviant" parent might be one who drinks too much in the evenings after work and is subsequently unable to act as a vigilant monitor of her/his child's behavior. This differs qualitatively from the circumstances many OLS children have experienced, such as the pain/embarrassment, upon alighting from the school bus, of seeing one's father placed in a squad car, or the trepidations involved in repeated trips to retrieve one's mother from yet another crack house. Thus, in our view, although traditional samples are ideal windows on typical adolescents and their transitions into adulthood, they may not fully capture the realities of the lives of many chronic offenders and the multiple ways in which their childhood and adult circumstances influence their children.

THE FIRST ADULT FOLLOW-UP

Although our research studies had always centered on adolescents, especially problem youth, we eventually became interested in learning more about the transition between adolescence and adulthood and the factors associated with variations in adult well-being. In 1992 and 1993 we attempted to locate the respondents who had participated in the TYS, who now were an average of 29 years of age. We refer to this next phase of the study as the TYAS (Toledo Young Adult Survey). We eventually located and interviewed 77 percent of the original TYS respondents. As is typical for such adult surveys, only a small number of the original respondents continued to have problems with the law as adults, although a greater number experienced other difficulties, such as psychological distress, unwanted childbearing, or poor economic prospects. Giordano interviewed the women who had clearly continued a pattern of criminal involvement (one who was incarcerated at the Ohio Reformatory for Women in Marysville, Ohio; another who was in the Toledo jail; and a third recently paroled respondent whose interview took place in a friend's apartment). However, the small number of arrests reported, particularly among females, led us to speculate about the lives of the much more delinquent "class of '82" whom we had interviewed while they were institutionalized for serious offenses. This led to our decision to attempt to locate these young adults, who also now averaged approximately 29 years of age and presumably resided in cities throughout Ohio.

The OLS follow-ups of the original institutionalized youth were significantly more challenging to complete than the earlier related Toledo study. First, Toledo is convenient (about twenty miles away) to our research base at Bowling Green State University, while the OLS required a state-wide search and beyond (e.g., several respondents from southern Ohio were now living in rural Kentucky). In addition, we were working from teenage recollections of the names and addresses of "two people who are likely to be in close contact with you and will know where you are in several years," which had been provided thirteen years earlier, largely from memory. However, we had also asked about first names of respondents' brothers and sisters, and a further asset was the greater tendency of the OLS respondents to leave what have been called "institutional footprints" (Widom, 1984). Thus, while frayed family connections and residential instability were often formidable obstacles to locating respondents, this was offset by the greater likelihood that these individuals were known to police, parole officers, or other official sources, including the state's Department of Rehabilitation and Corrections. We relied on such traditional locating strategies as contacting family members and neighbors and doing credit and other records checks (e.g., military service, Department of Motor Vehicles registrations), and also benefited greatly from the cooperation of professional sources. Sometimes the police were wary of giving out details, but when they were cooperative, we were privy to a wealth of information about last known addresses, aliases, and other contacts that proved invaluable. The Department of Rehabilitation and Corrections had information on any respondents who had been or were incarcerated at the state level. And, foreshadowing the findings about life-course patterns of criminal involvement described in subsequent chapters, it was necessary to negotiate entry into twenty-two different jails and prisons in Ohio and neighboring states, where we interviewed a total of 43 respondents. In this first adult follow-up, we interviewed 10 of the women and 33 of the men while they were incarcerated. These interviews typically took place in the lawyers' cubicles or other quiet areas of the institution.

The conditions under which the in-home interviews took place varied greatly. While the interviewers endeavored to find a quiet area in the home in which to conduct both the structured and in-depth interviews (typically, these were completed during the same visit), this sometimes meant interviewing on the porch, in the yard, in the interviewer's car, or at a park. Many housing situations were cramped, and relatives/roommates did not always respect our privacy requirements. Claudia Vercellotti was especially sensitive and resourceful in conducting these interviews under less than ideal conditions and over time became the primary interviewer for these and the subsequent 2003 parent/child interviews. For example, Claudia learned to gravitate toward hard rather than deeply cushioned furniture, where bugs were often a problem; nevertheless, when "critters" did appear, she had a way of dismissing them and putting respondents at ease about the conditions of their homes, trailers, or apartments. At the same time, as the quote that begins this chapter shows, she provided detailed descriptive notes after completing the interview that provided additional context for the housing/living circumstances and the overall well-being of each respondent. Given the concentration of respondents from Ohio's large cities, descriptions such as the following were not uncommon; this interviewer noted several times that she heard shots fired, and once even had to buy back her own hubcaps from a neighborhood youth who had removed them during the interview:

> Dope deals going all around me, little dope heads ... bunch of them walked up, walking up on my car, I think trying to figure out if I was the police ... Waving their little dime bags around, you know, showing their rocks. I mean it, I was in the hole. I was definitely, definitely in the midst of the madness ... And when I first got there, I could hear there was a fight going on two doors down; there was a dope deal going, out in this man's front yard.

At the time of the first follow-up interview, another respondent, Jeanette, had recently regained custody of her children and moved to a new apartment. Although Jeanette's comments reflected hope about the possibilities for a fresh start, the neighborhood description the interviewer provides offers a more complete portrait of the starting point from which this respondent was attempting to affect a major turnaround.

> Quite a neighborhood ... right in the heart the downtown ... ah ... right in the heart of abandoned buildings on her street ... there didn't seem to be a single other building with a doorway on it, or any windows. Catholic Mission on the end of her street ... those were the only buildings that seemed to have any even hope for any residents in them ... all of them had smashed windows ... no doors. The neighborhood was full of trash ... broken bottles ... cars broken down ... originally I was a little bit concerned about where to

leave my car. It … there is … just … just no option really of … a good place … so I put it next to other cars on a street … and it was there when I came back. Her apartment was quite nice … it was very quiet inside … was pretty much a complete contrast to the neighbour-hood, which was just deplorable … just, ah … next to unlivable I would say … it seemed just alive with criminal activity … I was glad it was in the morning interview … around ten o'clock.

Although the majority of the respondents resided in urban envi-ronments, several women and men in the sample were originally from smaller cities or rural areas, or had moved to these settings as adults. Although these environments often appeared to be more "promising" than the inner city areas, again the housing circum-stances of these respondents rarely reflected solid economic and social standing within their communities. For example, the inter-viewer traveled to southern Ohio to interview David, noting that "the area is beautiful and has rolling hills and beautiful scenery; [but] the houses in his area and his own were coal shacks that didn't look habitable."

David's house is a shanty shack with a coal furnace; the most struc-turally sound part of the house was a neon beer sign planted on the living room walls, which were painted [a] dark green that appeared black. [There was a] huge T.V. and one decrepit, sinking couch and [a] chair; red painted floor with bugs everywhere and a screen for heat cut out of a drop ceiling.

THE CONTENT OF THE FIRST ADULT INTERVIEW

Both the structured and in-depth interviews were designed to address the fundamental question – how are the OLS respondents doing as adults? Our primary interest was to determine continuity and change in criminal behavior, and accordingly, we administered a *self-reported crime* measure similar to the adolescent version, removing any ques-tions about offenses that had only been criminal because of the individual's status as a juvenile (e.g., running away). Since intimate partner violence and drug/alcohol problems often escalate during the adult years and are frequent sources of continued legal difficul-ties, respondents also completed self-report instruments designed to capture *intimate partner violence perpetration/victimization* (a short version of Gelles' Conflict Tactics Scale [Straus, Gelles, & Steinmetz, 1980]) as well as the extent of *problem use of alcohol and drugs* (Jessor & Jessor, 1977). We also included a short index tapping *psychological distress/depression*.

The adult interview continued the adolescent focus on the *quality and character of the respondents' network ties*: we included questions about the nature of relationships with parents and other relatives, friends, and marital/intimate partners. The respondent also completed instruments that provided information about the *criminality of the romantic partner* and *criminal involvement of the respondent's friends*. Since we had not included items about child abuse in the original interview, a retrospective scale measuring *physical and sexual abuse* was included at the time of this adult follow-up.

The research team for this phase of the study included a demographer. Reflecting this, the interview schedule contained numerous questions about the individual's cohabitation and marital history and fertility experiences. Information about the timing and number of births was especially useful in the subsequent phase of the project, which focused on interviews with the respondents who had become parents and at least one of their children. We also ascertained whether each child resided with the focal biological parent at the time of this interview. Educational attainment and occupational experiences, household income, welfare receipt, and other basic details about the respondent's adult life were also assessed. Finally, the protocol included a number of social psychological items and scales (e.g., a measure of self-esteem, self-efficacy, anger identity, gender role attitudes) that further differentiate these respondents.

The open-ended interviews were designed to give the respondents more freedom to present their own perspectives on the direction their lives had taken. Although the primary focus was on their adult years, the life history narratives we elicited often included much detail about their childhood and adolescent years as well. The protocol consisted of eight broad questions that were similar to the structured items in intent and focus. Our objective was to capture respondents' own assessments of how they were doing since we had last interviewed them, and to increase our understanding of the factors associated with criminal persistence or desistance. The interviewer began by asking the respondent about the individuals they had named as good friends during the 1982 interview. This proved to be a not-too-personal "ice-breaker," and served to remind them that we had indeed interviewed them previously (many had completely forgotten that they had participated in the initial interview).

We followed up by asking what had happened to these friends, and how they were doing. The interview eventually turned to questions about respondents' own behaviors and adult life circumstances, including the central issue: "Would you say that the amount of things that could get you in trouble with the law is about the same, more, or less since the last time we interviewed you? Why do you think that is?" Probes/follow-up questions then elicited information about romantic partner/husbands, children, family, and friends and whether these had been a positive or negative influence. Because of the unstructured format of these interviews, we also learned much about sources of influence and other aspects of their lives that were not specifically prompted by the interviewer (e.g., the importance of spirituality). The interview transcripts that resulted from the open-ended interview often exceeded 100 pages, and were a primary resource for developing our ideas about mechanisms associated with criminal continuity and change. However, it was also useful that the structured data were available to explore associations across the sample more systematically. For example, while spirituality was an important dimension in many of the respondents' lives, we found that when viewed over the long haul, higher scores on perceived closeness to God and church attendance were not reliably associated with long-term desistance from crime (Giordano et al., 2008 and Chapter Seven, this volume).

THE SECOND FOLLOW-UP: PARENT AND CHILD INTERVIEWS

The third set of interviews conducted in connection with the OLS study was even more challenging logistically, as we focused primarily on the subset of respondents who at the time of the 1995 interview had reported at least one biological child, who would now be age appropriate for assessing a range of developmental outcomes, including delinquency involvement. We chose to interview a randomly selected child who was between the age of 10 and 19, but obviously not all respondents were living with their biological children. These included the incarcerated parents, those who had lost custody as well as some who had never resided with their children. It was sometimes necessary to return to a given location multiple times in order to secure both the child and adult interviews. When the child did not reside with the focal parent, we also attempted to interview the physical custodian or caregiver (this could be the child's other biological parent, a grandparent or other relative, or a foster parent). Most of the alternative arrangements were with family members; only six children resided in foster homes at the time of these interviews. In addition to the randomly selected "focal" child, we also interviewed additional siblings where possible. This was useful because we were interested in variations in child well-being, even under relatively similar family conditions.

The parent interview focused most parenting/child outcome questions on a randomly selected focal child, but the respondent was also asked an abbreviated set of questions about the other children in the family. It should be noted that some of the analyses that follow concentrate on these focal children (n = 96), while others draw on the total sample of children born to these respondents (n = 158). Parents, children, and caregivers completed structured interviews, about an hour in length, using preloaded laptop computers. In most instances respondents entered the information directly, except in cases where poor reading comprehension made this impractical. The parent interview contained scales and items similar to those administered at the time of the 1995 adult follow-up interview (e.g., the self-reported crime inventory, arrest information, and marital histories), but items were added that related to our interest here in intergenerational transmission, parenting experiences, and the nature of the respondent's relationship with the child. Some questions were tailored to the specific family circumstances we encountered (e.g., if respondents were incarcerated, the parent was asked about whether and how often the child visited). If the child did not live with the focal biological parent, a caregiver provided the information about the nature of supervision and other responses requiring daily contact with the child.

THE OLS CHILD INTERVIEW

The child interview included information about not only the nature of the relationship with the parent, but also multiple domains of the adolescent's life. Many items were drawn from the original adolescent interview in which the parent had participated, resulting in two generations of responses to identical items and scales. The child interview, similar to that completed by the parent, contained sections that were tailored to living circumstances (e.g., where the parent was incarcerated, the youth was also asked about visiting the institution; where the child lived apart form the focal parent, questions were included about whether and how often the child visited that parent and about the character of the relationship).

This sample of children is distinguished from typical youth surveys. Nationally, 90 percent of underage children live with their biological mothers and 66 percent live with their biological fathers. In contrast, in 1995, 49 percent of the OLS female respondents in the original sample had lost or never had custody of at least one of their biological children. Despite the instabilities in living arrangements that were common for many of the children born to the women in the sample, it was nevertheless more likely that the women compared with the men in the sample either lived with or at least knew the whereabouts of their children. A significantly larger percentage of the men did not reside with some/all of their biological children (as one male respondent put it:– "I've got children splattered all over the place"). Overall, 74 percent of the men did not live with at least one of his biological children. This finding is of substantive interest, but it made the locating process difficult and, in many cases, impossible. Thus, the total sample of children is composed of a much larger share of the children of the female respondents (the parenting interviews include 112 mothers and 46 fathers). This is a limitation of the 2003 parent/child interviews, and of the study as a whole, as we cannot include information on the well-being of children whose ties to the (more often male) parent were sufficiently tenuous that we were unable to locate them.

In addition to the structured interviews, a majority of parents, children, and caregivers also participated in in-depth interviews similar in form to the 1995 "life history narratives." And, as in the structured interview, the questions were directed toward issues of parenting and child well-being. During the adult interview, we updated the central question of how respondents had been doing since the last time we interviewed them. However, the addition of the child and caregiver interviews was extremely informative, as these made it possible to compare different family members' perspectives on family circumstances as they encountered them. For example, the caregiver interview often painted a more sober/critical picture of the focal respondent's life than that provided by the adult respondents themselves. The children's narratives were typically not as lengthy as those of the parents and caregivers, but a majority were remarkably candid about many aspects of their lives, including their feelings about parents' difficulties, such as their drug involvement or absence from the home. The interviewer used sensitivity and judgment during such discussions, generally gauging the child's comfort level about potentially painful family matters. For example, Jason told the interviewer that initially, he considered just making up stereotypical responses to the interview questions:

> I thought about coming to this thing and lying about stuff and acting like the Brady Bunch, acting like there was nothing going on. But then I was like, "well, they're just trying to help us." So, I wanted to tell the truth. I wanted to be clean about it. I want them to help us. I want to help people just like me.

COMPARISON SAMPLE: THE TOLEDO ADOLESCENT RELATIONSHIPS SURVEY

The TYAS was useful because it provided a basis for comparing a number of features of the OLS sample's lives as adults with results that are typical of a randomly selected sample. However, we did not conduct interviews with the children of the TYAS respondents. Thus, in Chapter Five, which concentrates on child outcomes, we rely on results of the TARS. This study includes interviews with 1,300 teens, contains considerable measurement overlap with the questions the OLS child respondents were asked, was carried out during the same time frame (2003), and was conducted in a similar geographic region.

This stratified random sample includes oversamples of African American and Hispanic youth. Although, like the OLS interviews, the sample design was devised from school enrollment records, the interviews were conducted in respondents' homes, and school attendance was not a requirement for inclusion in the study. Also similar to OLS procedures, the sensitive information was collected via preloaded laptops and generally completed by the respondents.[2] The parents of TARS respondents also completed a questionnaire while the teen was being interviewed, and these parenting responses provide another point of comparison regarding parenting experiences across the two samples (TARS vs. OLS parents).

[2] For a more detailed review of procedures used in the TARS study see Giordano, Longmore, and Manning, 2006.

CHAPTER FOUR

OLS Adult Respondents: Offending, Surviving, Parenting

I was makin' money, uh, living underneath the Wooster Street bridge ... there was a guy that was in the bar and he was flashin' around all kinds of money, I mean we're talkin' $100, $50's, $20's ... and he was lookin' for someone ... and uh, we set up there at the bar; we had a couple of drinks; we then left from the bar, went over to this hotel room, and he was he was a nice guy, and he took me out and he bought me brand new clothes ... make-up, new shoes, new bras, new underwear, bought me a stereo ... And bought me some tapes and everything, and I thought, well, you know, that's my payment, you know, and I went back to the hotel, 'cause I didn't have a home, went back to the hotel and everything and, uh, he, uh, took care of business, you know – [Q: So you guys slept together?] Yeah. And I got up and went in took a shower, put on my brand new pair of jeans ... brand new shirt, brand new panties, bra ... brand new hiking boots. [Q: You're all excited about that stuff.] Right. You know, I was like, man, I've never had anyone do this, you know.

This excerpt from her life-history describes an encounter that had occurred several years prior to the first adult follow-up interview we conducted with 30-year-old respondent Amber. It clearly depicts extremely marginal housing circumstances (living under the Wooster Street bridge) and involvement in prostitution as a means of supporting herself. However, the quote is especially evocative because of the manner in which the incident is narrated. The stranger's kindness reflected a level of [apparent] generosity that marked a distinct contrast with many of her prior experiences, and having access to an abundance of new clothing items was narrated, even at this later point, almost as a peak life experience. Although Amber's situation is rather extreme, the overall portrait that emerges from both the structured and in-depth interview data reveals many adult

problems associated with crime, drug abuse and violence, other
negative outcomes, and undoubtedly related to this, difficulties in
their children's own lives.

Our objective in this chapter is to develop an overall portrait of
the behavior and life-course experiences of these women and men
as they transition to adulthood. It is important to point out, however,
that considerable variation in "offending, surviving, and parenting"
exists, even within this selective sample of female and male respondents, all of whom are characterized by significant early backgrounds
of adolescent delinquency involvement. To illustrate, Lesa's adult
experiences were quite different from Amber's, as is reflected in this
description of her current family life:

> I couldn't live without them [her children] ... I love him [her hus-
> band] ... I've been married ten years. I've been with him since I was
> sixteen, and my marriage is great. I plan on having a future. I don't
> want to be poor. I want to buy my own house and you know have
> nice things for them ... my kids, I want them to have a great life.

Even though Lesa's life story does not include success along traditional economic lines (at the time of the 1995 interview she and
her husband lived in a poor neighborhood and could not afford to
purchase their own home), the narrative's tone is quite positive and
hopeful as she focuses on her stable home life, love for her husband,
and commitment to her children. It is consistent with this that her
self-reported crime score, drawn from the structured portion of the
interview, as well as her comments in the open-ended portion reflect
a consistent pattern of crime cessation: "If I were to find a penny, I
would return it. I am about the exact opposite [of her earlier delinquent behavior]. I have done a 180-degree turn."

We begin with the key issue of the *criminal persistence and desistance* of these young people as they have matured into adulthood.
We examine respondents' self-reports of criminal involvement, and
also discuss the trends we observed across the two adult interviews
conducted in 1995 and 2003, when respondents' ages averaged 29
and 38, respectively. To provide a basis of comparison, we contrast
rates of involvement we recorded at the time of the first adult follow-up with levels observed in the TYAS, the sample of similarly aged
adults described in Chapter Three. We supplement this portrait with

the results of an official records search, information about adult incarceration experiences of the respondents, and findings from our analyses of the life-history narratives that were also elicited from a majority of the respondents.[1]

We consider variations within the OLS sample, including those who evidence a continued pattern of criminal involvement (persisters); those who have apparently sustained a pattern of crime cessation across the period of time encompassed by both interviews (desisters); and those whose involvement in crime appears to be episodic (i.e., they report criminal involvement at one but not both adult interviews). Exploring the variability within the sample is of interest in its own right, but it is also intuitive to expect that the children of respondents who have consistently managed to steer away from crime as adults should fare better than those who are living with criminally active parents. However, it is also plausible that social learning experiences and poor social/economic circumstances combine to disadvantage even those children born to parents whose behavior profiles indicate a lack of adult criminal activity.[2] To illustrate the potential for "legacies" to transcend the parent's current behavior, we note that Angie, who evidenced a pattern of desistance in her adult years, nevertheless told the interviewer that she had already taught her daughter how to fight, starting at age four:

> I taught her how to defend herself. Because the kids around here are much bigger. And I've showed her how to defend herself if someone beats her up, or gets her pinned down, how to defend herself against men too. She's five now.

Angie's lessons for her daughter may be related both to the high-crime neighborhood in which she now lives, as well as to a world

---

[1] In these analyses, we generally rely on the most complete sample data available for each wave. For example, we present results for all respondents who participated in the adolescent interviews and then in each adult follow-up. A smaller number of respondents participated in the second follow-up as parents, but we also have a second wave of follow-up data on the larger sample, and this larger group is used to describe trends in persistence and desistance. Thus, the sample size for questions about parenting is smaller than that we rely on for the comparisons that focused only on adult outcomes.

[2] Although we cannot formally investigate this within the context of the current design, it is quite possible that genetic component may also be involved.

view that is influenced by her own early victimization experiences and delinquency involvement. Thus, the effects of Angie's and other respondents' early problems and delinquent lifestyles may connect to an array of indirect and direct sources of heightened risk to their children.

In addition to considering patterns of criminal involvement, we also explore how the respondents have fared on what are generally considered critical "basics" associated with the transition to adulthood – *marriage and marital stability* and *educational and occupational attainment*. Although these factors are often considered separately, we find it especially useful to consider the percentages of respondents within the sample who have attained what we term the "complete respectability package," namely, that they are both (relatively) happily married *and* have minimally adequate economic resources. Although each element has been described as a source of cultural, social, and economic capital, in our view it is the combination of these factors that is typically associated with the most favorable adult transitions. We also include subjective aspects of their lives, such as *emotional well-being*. The aggregate picture that develops from these findings is a useful backdrop for considering child effects; yet the in-depth narratives provide a more concrete way of illustrating some of the difficulties experienced by a large number of women and men in this sample. For example, in contrast to Lesa's optimistic, "I plan on having a future," Danika responded to a question about where she thought she was headed with an attitude of despair and hopelessness:

> Probably death – why not? I mean I don't care if I live or die ... I don't have anything to really to live for ... live today to get high, to not get sick. This kind of life is all I know, and to really change I would have to change my whole lifestyle ... my friends everything I know ... I don't have the knowledge, the intelligence to do anything else.

Against the background of the parents' objective and subjective life experiences, then, we conclude the chapter with an examination of the *childbearing and parenting experiences* of these respondents. We compare male and female respondents and also rely on both the TYAS and TARS (the parent questionnaire) as further bases of comparison.

CRIME: PERSISTENCE AND DESISTANCE FEDERAL BUREAU OF INVESTIGATION

Chapter Three described the delinquent-behavior profiles of these youths as teens, and revealed that during their adolescent years, a large percentage were involved in serious crimes, often at a high rate. However, considerable criminological research has documented a rather reliable decline in criminal activity (the so-called "age crime curve") that occurs as respondents mature into adulthood (Gottfredson & Hirschi, 1990). For example, traditional property crimes peak at about age 16 (Federal Bureau of Investigation, 2004). In addition to this general trend, however, criminologists have also documented that early delinquency is a strong risk factor for adult crime (Farrington, 2003; Glueck & Glueck, 1950). Thus, the themes of continuity and change that are emphasized in life-course studies also make sense for thinking about life-course patterns of criminal involvement (Sampson & Laub, 1993).

Using the identical self-reported delinquency-involvement index that we described in Chapter Three, we do observe an overall decline between adolescence and the first adult follow-up in respondents' reports of criminal activity. However, the data also reveal a leveling off: levels of involvement do not continue to decline between the first and second interview periods (when respondents averaged age 29 and 38, respectively). This distinguishes the OLS sample trends over time from the results based on general youth surveys (e.g., Warr, 1998) and even from studies focused on an earlier cohort of delinquent youth (Laub & Sampson, 2003). Further, the observation of a general initial decline does not fully capture the extent of the criminal and legal difficulties many of these respondents have continued to experience as they have traversed the adult phase of their lives. For example, almost 80 percent of the respondents self-report at least one adult arrest by the time of the first adult interview. This includes 86 percent of the men and 70 percent of the women.

Although our searches for officially recorded arrests in the various jurisdictions where the respondents were believed to reside cannot be considered a complete source of information (because of the lack of a statewide record-keeping system, among other difficulties we encountered), we were able to supplement the self-report information using

arrest data up to the 1995 follow-up period. Using three independent
raters and multiple sources of information – the self-reported crime
and arrest information, official arrest information, and information
from the life-history narratives – we classified individuals as desisters, persisters, or a less-clear-cut unstable middle category. A desister
classification resulted if we had no information indicating an arrest
(based on official searches and self-reports) within the two-year window prior to the interview, and if the self-report and narrative information did not include more than minor reported criminal activity
in the past year. Consistent with the self-report arrest information
described earlier, our analyses indicate that female respondents were
significantly more likely than male respondents to have desisted, and
within both gender categories, being African American was associated with a greater likelihood of persistence. Although these data thus
indicate that being female is somewhat "advantageous" or protective,
it is important to highlight that, based on these multiple sources of
information, 74 percent of the African American women and 57 percent of their white counterparts could not be categorized as desisters
upon reaching an average age of 30. Only 3.8 percent of the African
American and 10.4 percent of the white male respondents could be
so classified at the time of the first follow-up period.

   The availability of self-reported criminal involvement data collected
at the time of the second adult follow-up period allows us a longer
view of the criminal activity of the respondents. For this analysis, we
rely on self-reported crime and also on incarceration information: of
those who participated in both follow-ups (n = 153), 45 percent could
be considered desisters (no or only minor-offenses reported at both
waves, and not incarcerated at either wave); 26 percent persisters;
and 29 percent reflecting an unstable pattern. The unstable category consists of individuals who reported criminal activity or were
incarcerated at one, but not both follow-ups. Examining these patterns by gender, we find that 53 percent of women can be considered stable desisters, as contrasted with 36 percent of the men. Again,
when we examine this longer-term pattern, it is clear that the experiences associated with minority status continue to disadvantage these
respondents. Relying on both waves of adult data, we can classify 41
percent of the African American women as desisters, compared with

60 percent of the white females; the figure for the African American males is 25 percent, while 43 percent of the white males showed a pattern of desistance over the two waves. These methods for tapping desistance are obviously not ideal, since the long intervals between measurement periods can contain periods of high criminal involvement (or, conversely, at least some years free of criminal activity).

These statistics confirm that many of the respondents cannot be said to be free of criminal involvement over a sustained period of their adult lives. Yet the qualitative data are especially useful in capturing the nature/extent of these difficulties and in depicting the range of variability found within the sample. For example, shorthand titles were assigned by the project staff to each narrative account. Within the sample of women, titles from the 1995 narratives include "two manslaughters," "drink-drift-hit," "drugs, violence, crime," "unhappy, booze, poor," "heroin and prison," "struggling with alcohol," "terrible life," and "prison, killed partner." Interspersed with these were such titles as "very successful escape," "optimistic with plans," "Jesus saves," and "traditional success." Other respondents appeared to occupy the middle territory on the persistence-desistance continuum, as suggested by the following titles: "minor trouble," "just hanging on," "rule breaker but stable," "pretty clean but drugs," and "shaky future." Titles that refer to male respondents paint a similar but (consistent with the quantitative results), even grimmer portrait: titles like "three time loser-crack," "prison eight times," and "criminal lifestyle" were common. Nevertheless, there were also titles such as "clean family man," "financial success," and "doing well" reflecting the favorable circumstances that characterized the lives of a subset of the men, and titles such as "pothead," "job but drugs," and "successful alcoholic" depicting a group of male respondents who were "getting by."

One of the more unusual features of the OLS study is that we have been able to collect in-depth life-history data at two different stages of the respondents' adult lives. Typically, this sort of in-depth qualitative data are gathered at a single point in time. Consequently, an individual who has evidenced a pattern of successful desistance at a given point in time is forever a desister as far as the researcher is concerned. Thus, it has been especially useful to obtain the second adult interview in order to determine whether respondents who appeared to be doing well in 1995 had been able to sustain that pattern over an extended period of time. Individuals reflecting an unstable pattern are clearly represented by our classification scheme (described earlier), but the life-history narratives are much more revealing of what Laub and Sampson have called this zig-zag, or episodic, pattern.

For example, in 1995 Stacy (Jason's mother) was adamant about moving away from the criminal life, and her "turnaround" was critical to our thinking about desistance processes (Giordano, Cernkovich, & Rudolph, 2002). Stacy had accumulated an extensive arrest history by the time she was 30, for offenses ranging from burglary and theft to assault and drug-use charges, and had served three separate terms in the state's adult prison for women (eight years, which at that point constituted the bulk of Stacy's adult life). Stacy's mother's home, while located in a somewhat marginal neighborhood (e.g., there was a factory across the street), was a sturdy and immaculate two-story house. Stacy had recently constructed an elaborate Halloween tableau across the front porch of the house and appeared extremely pleased to be reunited with Jason. This respondent was likeable and had a good sense of humor. She had not, however, accumulated either of the elements of the traditional "respectability package." As a self-identified lesbian, Stacy appeared unlikely to benefit from a traditional good-marriage effect. Aside from a general societal tendency to marginalize nontraditional family arrangements, Stacy's mother's disapproval of her lesbianism may further inhibit the development of a stable intimate relationship. "I'll probably always live with my mom; we're just close. My mother's a Christian now, so like, if I was to become involved [romantically] I'll take it outside of here [her mother's home]." In addition, while Stacy expressed pride about her expertise and experience as a plumber, virtually all of this experience had been accumulated in prison. In spite of several attempts, she had been unable to make any inroads into the plumber's union in her area. Nevertheless, in 1995 Stacy appeared optimistic, indicating that other skills (roofing, home remodeling) should enable her to land a job in the near future. Stacy's family background (both nuclear and extended) was characterized by extensive drug use and criminality: "There was always drug abuse in my family. My father was a junkie ... He had been to a prison several times." Stacy's mother was also well-known to the local police (most of her arrests were alcohol related; however, during the adolescent interview, Stacy insisted on listing her mother's occupation as "professional shoplifter"). "I've always been raised by my grandmother and my mother and my aunt; we all lived together. And, when I was 13 my grandmother had a stroke. And that's where I started going bad ... my grandma was everything and she was a good Christian woman and when she took sick, I didn't know how to deal – I couldn't cope." Stacy started smoking pot at about age 10 or 11. In addition, she began to develop a reputation as "tough" and a fighter: "I had the reputation that I was real mean in school, where, the white people had to really be tough." Stacy eventually was sent to an alternative school "where the bad kids went, nothing but a dope – all the bad kids – dopefest ... from all over the city. But at lunch time there was an abandoned house ... so we all would run in there and get high. And I would stay so blitzed out in the school I would just lay with my head on the desk." Many of Stacy's problems with the legal system revolved around drugs and alcohol and assaultive behaviors: "I come out of the bar and they'd [police] be like 'hey Stacy how's it going' I'd just be, 'ah shut up and kiss my ass,' and pretty soon, I'd go to jail every time. I'd be just so zonked out I wouldn't even remember until I woke up." Even in prison, she continued to evoke this tough persona: "I was always taught, just take the biggest one [inmate] out and the rest of them will leave you alone."

Although she had thus accumulated an extensive criminal and incarceration history, was unemployed, and had no spouse or other stable intimate partner, during the interview Stacy provided a detailed account of changes in her life that can only be described as cognitive in nature: I'm through. You know. I'm really, really, really tired of that life. I don't want it no more, man. I laid it down. You know. I had to go to a group Thursday night. My parole officer – it's a parole-education group – and when I walked in, it's an old ex-cop that runs it, and he's telling the guy that's facilitatin' this new group I'm in, he's telling him, he's introducing me, and he leans over and whispers to him, he said "tell you one thing. Don't ever try to fight her 'cause she'll whip your ass'." You know, and I said "man, I said, I outlived that life." I said "I'm through with it" and we talked for a minute, and he's like "Stacy you've really grown up you know." Just things are different. You know

LEGACIES OF CRIME

the last time I was on parole I worked two jobs, and I was doing really good, but I would go to bars, right. I hadn't fully gave up the ghost. I was still trying to live both worlds. I told my mom the other day, I said, all my life I've had this reputation but [now] I'm gonna use it to my advantage you know. Because, like, people that come around, like I was telling you the one girl in my family that's still actively using [drugs], I was able to use it [leans in a mock-menacing manner toward the interviewer and yells] "GET OUT!!!" Before I was trying to do all the right things and my actions were doing good things, but I still tried to live both worlds. I mean, this last time I went back [to prison] you don't know what an awakening that was, because nothing happened [she felt that her parole violation was trivial] and I spent three years of my life, day for day and three years. Stacy contrasted this last prison experience with the previous two periods of incarceration: "I mean everything's different when you got a kid involved."

The disadvantages Stacy described in 1995 were considerable, including parental "legacies" (parental drug and alcohol abuse/ criminality; father absence due to incarceration) and those that accumulated within Stacy's own life (high school dropout, reputation as a troublemaker, drug involvement, and many years of institutionalization). In addition, we expected that her nontraditional sexual orientation would affect her entry into marriage and might negatively influence her employment opportunities as well. Nevertheless, Stacy had job skills and experience (e.g., roofing) and had been able to find work in the past. In addition, she focused on the stability her mother's residence provided ("she pays the bills") and could benefit from her mother's apparent reform (*she's a Christian now*). Thus, our view was that having access to some "rules and resources" (Giddens, 1984) positioned Stacy to benefit from the cognitive transformation she describes in such detail. Yet, in spite of our optimistic emphasis on the role of such cognitive transformations in the process of desisting from crime (see Giordano et al., 2002), the second follow-up with Stacy documents significant "derailments" that occurred in the years after the initial interview:

> I went to work for this guy, and I was doing great; I was clean, I wasn't doing drugs. And uh ...I had a car wreck and I wrecked and hit my sister's fence and the adult parole authority, the guy that is

the head of it, hates my guts ... it's really a beef that he has with my dad from 40 years ago that he carries on to me ... So, every chance he got he violated me. So, I had a car wreck and they got me for failure to control. And I went down, I went to prison, didn't come home until '99 for a traffic violation.

Stacy was again in prison describing the above incident and her current attitude:

I mean I live a very boring life. I mean I go to the movies and stuff like that, but for somebody that's always lived that fast life, that fast style, going to the movies and the ice cream parlor and out to dinner is a really boring life. You know, I've always been out in the streets living with thugs, you know, that fast money, fast style. That's always been my life. And now it's really ... it's losing its appeal to me, but uh ... the adrenaline is still there. I mean sometimes even now if I, if I'm in my room ... since it's getting close to my release, I've been dreaming about getting high. And it's like uh ... I really, I want to go out of here ... I would like nothing better than to have stability, have a roof over my head and be able to go back to school and have some kind of life. But the actuality of that really happening is far-fetched. You know? I mean I can ... my mom is almost unbearable to live with. The older she gets the worse she gets. [But] I knew I was loved. I never was beat or molested or raped or a lot of things that I see here. I mean it's really common here ... A lot of the women, their dads raped them, their uncles, their brothers. I've never been through that. I've always been loved ... I keep thinking "my God what will I do if something happens to my mother?" 'cause my mom is a safety net for me. Even when I was using, if I would use up my rent money I'd say "Mom, I need to borrow some money. you know, I fucked up the rent." And she would loan me the money. She would bitch and complain and [say] "I'm not gonna do it," but she always did. And I always, in my mind, I always knew that. But now it's like my mom's getting older; she's tired. And look. The older my son gets, the more I see things different. You know, the older I get ... It's ... and I realize how blessed I am.

[Stacy indicated that she needs to] get out of here and really get involved in his life ... I mean I don't care how nosey he thinks I am, but really get in and be a part of it and not just a fiction of it ... writing letters about it, you know, I just ... I've got to be a part of it, and I think that him and I were friends, but I never let him lose the fact that I am his mother...

Since Stacy was touted as a key example of the importance of cognitive transformations to the desistance process, her later "derailment" and subsequent incarceration strike a blow to this "provisional" theory. The details included in her more recent life history highlight a number of considerations that provide a more complete portrait and accord with a revised perspective on the subjective aspects of change that also takes into account emotional processes (Giordano, Schroeder, & Cernkovich, 2007). Even within the framework of our original theorizing about persistence and desistance, Stacy cannot be said to have a strong prosocial network that provides new definitions and support for the more conforming way of life. As Stacy noted, her mother has, in her later years, become more law-abiding and religious, but this element has always been in place – and thus did not prove to be a sufficient catalyst for Stacy's making/sustaining life changes. For example, in the more recent narrative she notes that her mother can always be counted on to give her the rent money if she has spent all her own funds on drugs. She also emphasizes changes that she associates with the birth of her son, but Jason could not, literally, provide all the elements of a more productive lifestyle. As she indicates, she has developed a street orientation and network ("I've always been out in the streets living with thugs ..."), and even within her own family, both drug use and violent behavior among cousins and other relatives are common. Indeed, her aunt Jennie, who had custody of Jason at the time of the second follow-up, pointed out that four other relatives had tried to take Jason but had been denied custody because of their backgrounds. In addition, the excitement that she associates with the "fast money, fast style" competes successfully with the routine "ice cream parlor and out to dinner" form of life that is foreign to her, and apparently not an easy fit. Stacy also has an extensive background of violent behavior, which has been associated with her more recent derailment experiences. Currently, Stacy remains in prison, with a release date of 2010.

Another way to illustrate the life-course difficulties of many of the OLS respondents is to compare their behaviors with those self-reported by respondents in the related TYAS adult follow-up. Since some respondents within the Toledo neighborhood study had also self-reported delinquency involvement during their teen years, we compared the OLS reports of levels of adult self-reported criminal involvement and similar reports provided by TYAS "offenders." Perhaps not surprisingly, results showed that OLS respondents, on average, self-report higher levels of adult crime than either the original nondelinquent TYAS respondents or their delinquent counterparts within this neighborhood sample (Giordano, Cernkovich, & Lowery, 2004). This pattern is consistent with the disparities characterizing their adolescent responses that we described in Chapter Three (see Cernkovich, Giordano, & Pugh, 1985).

The gap between the OLS and TYAS respondents is even larger for drug use. Almost half of the OLS respondents reported that they used drugs at the time of the first adult follow-up, while only 15 percent of the TYAS respondents reported drug use. Although the prevalence rate was higher for OLS males, 42 percent of the OLS females also reported recent drug use at the time of the first adult follow-up. Drug use was substantially higher among African American males who participated in the OLS study (64%) as compared to OLS white males (47%), and it was higher for African American female OLS respondents compared with their white counterparts (52% vs. 34%). All comparisons with TYAS figures indicate that OLS respondents in each race/gender subgroup reported significantly higher prevalence than their respective TYAS counterparts. Although statistics for the TYAS sample are not available in connection with the second adult follow-up because these respondents were not interviewed a third time, the drug-use patterns in the OLS sample are similar to those observed at wave two: at the latest follow-up, OLS males report greater use (43%); nevertheless 39 percent of the OLS females report involvement over the 12-month period immediately preceding this second interview.

Similarly, African American respondents who were located and interviewed at wave three report higher levels of drug use than do white OLS respondents (52% vs. 35%). At the time of the most recent adult interview, white males and females do not differ significantly in the reporting of drug-use, but the prevalence rate is higher among African American males than among African American females (59% vs. 48%). These drug-use figures are especially striking because during their adolescent years, white respondents reported higher levels of drug use than did African American teens who participated in the initial OLS interviews (see Cernkovich et al., 1985). The lower prevalence rates of alcohol and drug use among African American teens have been well documented in a number of studies (see e.g., Bachman et al., 1991); yet some research has shown that this early advantage dissipates with age: African American adults often report similar rates of drug/alcohol use and in some cases higher levels of use of the type of drugs (crack, heroin) that are closely related to continued criminal justice involvement. This pattern is also observed within this sample of serious delinquents. (For an excellent overview of these life-course patterns, see Doherty et al., 2008.)

For all respondents, drug and alcohol use is associated strongly with continued criminal activity and risk of adult arrest and incarceration. OLS respondents are also much more likely than TYAS respondents to be involved in some of the more serious behaviors linked to drug involvement, such as drug trafficking. Thus, disparities across the two samples in the levels of simple use are not as pronounced as disparities in some of the more serious concomitants of drug use. Further, in a previous analysis of the OLS data, Schroeder, Giordano, and Cernkovich (2007) documented that drug use is strongly associated with overall odds of criminal persistence, even after variations in early delinquency, sociodemographic characteristics, the character of adult life circumstances (e.g., marital happiness and job stability), and the criminality of the individual's network ties had been taken into account.

The effects of addiction to substances such as crack cocaine appear to be particularly debilitating as addiction is so often associated with high-risk environments and other risk factors (e.g., frequenting crack houses, residing in high crime neighborhoods, associating with antisocial companions, and finding it difficult to sustain meaningful employment). As one respondent interviewed in prison, speaking about the addictive properties of crack put it "there ain't no casual user on crack ... you smoke it, you own it." We believe that these drug-use patterns are related to the lack of decline in crime reports from the first to the second adult wave since many other general population studies reliably note steady declines with respondent age. And for those whose drug use careers span many years of this study, we see especially debilitating effects at the second adult follow-up. For example, at the time of the first interview (at age 30), Janelle was making money selling crack and living in her own apartment. Although this hardly constituted a prosocial lifestyle, the interviewer encountered an even more unfortunate set of circumstances as she attempted to locate and interview Janelle in connection with the second follow-up:

> Out of the house comes a woman [Janelle's sister]. I now know, because she had open warrants, that she was as scared of me as I was leery of her ... It was obvious that she was high and that I was clearly interrupting a perfectly good Friday afternoon buzz ... She starts to take me to every crack haunt in the area in an attempt to locate Janelle. For nearly three hours, we rolled through the neighborhood, and I saw car after car meander down the street, stop, look, trade, and go. It was mind boggling. We then started going into "secondary areas" that were much worse. It was funny, Janelle's sister actually told me to lock the door, because we were in a bad neighborhood! We continued to drive up each street, looking down each alley ... I stopped counting crack haunts after 14, because we started to go to new houses, but began doubling back ... I watched women, who walked by, looking emaciated, drawn, and sunken and cracked out – no more than 75–100 pounds. They strolled the parking lot, heads up when they saw me, like if they walk straight and look ahead, maybe no one would notice how "lit" they were ... I was growing weary that we'd find Janelle. It was becoming later and later. Finally, at one of our stops, Janelle's sister got her on the phone at a friend's. I talk to her, and she's high. It's clear ... When we arrived, I noticed a young woman soliciting; it turned out to be Janelle's daughter Tonia. Tonia was very pregnant and her eyes were ice cold. Although we were unable to interview her (because she exceeded our age range), Janelle's sister told me that Tonia was so deep into the street life, that she'd take your clothes off you for dope without any thought.
>
> I was not prepared to see Janelle in this condition – she was sunken, drawn, walked with a cane and looked 25 years older than she should have. She looked nothing like my memory of her or even her inmate photo from the Web (this photo was taken in 1999 – Janelle was interviewed in 2005). Instantly, I recalled the '96 interview, in which she was hard, flying high, running a flop house. She told me when to leave and demanded to see the money order first. This time, she never asked. In '96 she was spunky, rude, interesting. She was pitiful now.

Long-term involvement in drug-oriented lifestyles is undoubtedly
deeply implicated in the lengthy criminal careers of many respondents and reflects unique cohort experiences that provide a stark
contrast with the circumstances Laub and Sampson (2003) described
as characterizing the lifestyles of many of the Glueck respondents.
Likely also reflecting a cohort shift, the focal respondents' life-history
narratives document an extensive family component to drug use,
another factor that serves to marginalize and encapsulate individuals
in drug-oriented environments. Although we will describe these family dynamics in much more detail in Chapter Six (where we examine
the children of the respondents and their exposure to drug-involved
parents), it is important to highlight that in many instances such family processes predate those relating to the parent-child pairs that we
concentrate upon in our study of intergenerational mechanisms.
Rhonda, age 30, describes her early exposure to crack cocaine:

> **Q:** How did that make you feel to have to get your mom from the crack
> house? Like how many times do you think you had to do that?
>
> **R:** About three times out of the month … 'cause she'd only do it
> when she'd get her check … or some extra money; she'd say "You
> don't rush me … I'm your mom … I tell you what to do." And I
> said, "You've been sitting up in here cracking for days …" And
> I would just recall myself sitting out in the living room. She'd
> be in the bedroom with the door shut. And I'm sitting, making
> sure don't nobody take advantage of her while she's smoking this
> crack… She comes out there with a stem, and she said, "Here
> Rhonda, hit it." And I said, "No, I told you I ain't going to be
> smoking that." Then I said to myself if I hit it, if I hit this then
> she, she'll leave, I'll get her to leave. So I got ready to hit it, and
> she said, "You don't even …" She said, "You're going to waste the
> dope." She said, "You don't even know how to do it. You've got to
> melt that on there." So she melted it on there for me, told me to
> hold the lighter. I held the lighter, and kept holding it down like
> this. If you hold it down like this, the dope will run … and you
> don't want it to run, cause the dope will get oily. You got to keep
> it held up. So she showed me how to inhale it and everything
> … [but] we don't crack no more in a crack house. We just start
> doing it at her house … I got my own stems and stuff now.

In the OLS, substance use is clearly associated with criminal continuity, and for respondents who have evidenced a pattern of sustained

desistance, avoiding drugs is central to their efforts to sustain a more conforming lifestyle (see Uggen & Thompson, 2003). However, the structured data and narratives reveal that the respondents' lives often include much experience with violence (both as victims but also as perpetrators), and many were involved in property crimes as well.

EXPOSURE TO VIOLENCE

The violence that permeates many women's life-history accounts is particularly striking in light of the fact that a lot of criminological theorizing has highlighted the degree to which it is the socialization of boys and young men, which rewards toughness and – especially in disadvantaged contexts – violence itself, as marks of masculinity and a means of enhancing image/status (Anderson, 1990; Messerschmidt, 1993; Wilkinson, 2003). Because male violence has garnered more scholarly attention, from both the theoretical and the empirical standpoints, it is especially important to explore the OLS women's experiences in this regard. We again need to note the difference between members of a sample such as the one we have followed up here and the individuals who make up the bulk of randomly selected youth surveys. In the latter, the rates of violence among girls and women are indeed reliably low. Even when the focus is upon adult women offenders, it has often been suggested that many women can be considered "compelled to crime" by virtue of their victimization at the hands of male partners (Richie, 1996). Consistent with this idea, Ogle, Maier-Katkin, and Bernard (1995) argued that women generally are not socialized early for violence; thus even extreme acts of violence committed by women may involve distinctive social and psychological processes. These authors suggest that because women lack early training for violence, in stressful situations (again, typically involving abuse) women may erupt in a sudden manner. Many incidents of homicide of husbands and male partners can be traced to a lengthy sequence of victimization events followed by a single act of explosive behavior on the part of the female spouse/partner.

Although this theory undoubtedly captures the experiences of many women, including those who are serving prison sentences for the manslaughter/murder of intimate partners, the life-history narratives of women in the OLS sample often reveal an extended, and in some instances, lifelong exposure to a violent way of life. The respondents' discussions of the early childhood and adolescent years do include numerous instances of victimization, however, such as the serious sexual and physical abuse Chantell recalls:

> **Q:** Okay, you are eight years old and you said your dad molested you? And you said he had sex with you?
>
> **R:** He didn't penetrate me [graphic description of what occurred]. He did it that time and he told me never to tell nobody and I didn't. But I told some teacher at school and I got in big trouble when I got home.
>
> **Q:** You got in trouble? What did you tell your teacher?
>
> **R:** I told, um, that my dad did some stuff and he told me not to tell nobody and I didn't think that was right and that I thought my mother was in cahoots with him because she didn't believe me.
>
> **Q:** She didn't believe you? You told your mom?
>
> **R:** Yeah [respondent starts to cry]. Sorry –
>
> **Q:** That's all right. Did you tell your mom before you told the teacher?
>
> **R:** I told her, I don't remember if I told her that night [the night it happened]. And he did it again when I was 13. [The first time] I got in a lot of trouble when I got home. She, uh, she said I was lying and she whooped me. Yeah, and put me on punishment, too, along with my dad. My dad whooped me. He tied my hands to the table and beat the hell out of me .... he beat me all the time. And I guess because he thought he was whippin' me on my butt that he wasn't doing no damage to me, but he was doing more damage to me than he ever know.

Although Trina, quoted below, indicated that she had not been abused, she recalls her parents' violent marriage, a level of exposure that was also highly stressful and traumatic:

> **Q:** What kind of relationship did he and your mom have?
>
> **R:** Oh! They had one rough relationship. He used to beat her up.
>
> **Q:** In front of you guys?
>
> **R:** Uh-huh. I used to break it up.
>
> **Q:** How old were you?
>
> **R:** About, about 11 or 12. That is when I started to get my little attitude.
>
> **Q:** Because you would have to break up your mom and dad?
>
> **R:** Yeah.

Q: You got an attitude?

R: Yeah. It was a difficult situation. It was really difficult. My mom used to run to the battered women's shelters and she used to take us with her ... I tried to break them up and they just kept fighting, so I called the cops on them.

Q: How did you know to do that?

R: My mom.

Q: She was screaming, call the police, call the police?

R: Uh huh.

Q: And the police would come, and what would happen?

R: They would take him to jail.

Although such experiences involving victimization have long been considered central to understanding women's involvement in delinquency and crime, such narratives highlight what might be considered even more direct socialization that may also be important to the process of learning a violent repertoire. Recall Widom's (1989) research documenting that even when young people have experienced physical and sexual abuse, a majority do not go on to commit juvenile and adult offenses. And, of these abuse cases, girls in the Widom study were less likely than males to gather juvenile and adult arrest histories. Thus, even though many victimization experiences are clearly gendered (as reflected in higher rates of sexual victimization), these experiences, although often traumatic and life altering, do not fully explain the criminal offending evidenced by serious offenders such as the OLS respondents. In many instances it appears that a *combination* of early experiences of abuse and direct socialization, often by family members, fosters violence in this small but problematic subset of female adolescents. The two examples below illustrate the more general level of socialization toward violence that female OLS respondents indicate that they experienced:

R: I got a whoopin' when I was a kid for not fightin'. I got beat up and every time I ran home, my mama beat my ass.

Q: For not fightin'?

R: For not fightin'. So I learned how to fight and I start beatin' everybody's ass that said something to me, and I got suspended from school and I got my ass whooped.

Q: So you got your ass whooped for not fighting and then you got your ass whooped for fighting, is that what you are saying?

R: Exactly.

Q: How old are you when this is going on?

R: I was, uh, between the ages of, let's see, from third grade, I didn't fight. I got my ass beat. When I got to fourth grade I start fightin' and I started beatin' up people really bad, hurtin', um, and mama had to go to court and stuff and she didn't like that very well. I got into a lot of trouble; I almost, I almost killed this girl ... But at fourth grade I started fightin' back and, uh, in fifth grade I got suspended from school. That's when I started really getting suspended from school. I was hurtin' people. I was doing really, really, really mean things.

Q: Why?

R: Because my mother said she was gonna kick my ass if they got me first, so my best bet was to get them first so they wouldn't get me.

Q: And then your mom would kick your ass anyway.

R: Yup.

In the following exchange, Susan's mother becomes involved in an altercation with a teacher that escalated into violence and resulted in Susan being expelled from school. Note that Susan's account of her mother's response teaches a number of lessons about the appropriate way to handle such situations:

R: Well, I got in a fight with this girl and then the teacher, Miss McCaghy. I remember her ... she said I was getting suspended and I ended up getting into that fight with her and arguing with her, the teacher ... and she kicked me ... the teacher.

Q: The teacher kicked you?

R: The teacher kicked me, and she still had her footprint on my pants where she kicked me. And I went home and I told my mom and my mom came back to the school, and my mom said you want to see what its like to get kicked? And my mom kicked her butt, period. She hit ... my mom fought the teacher and ...

Q: In front of the class?

R: No outside. And said, "No one touches my daughter." And they took us to court, and they kicked me out of school and I had to go to a different kind of school.

Early exposure and socialization toward violence may also heighten the risk for later violence within the context of marital or other romantic relationships. Indeed, rates of relationship violence (reports of both victimization and perpetration) reported at the time of the first adult follow-up are on average significantly higher than those reported in the young adult comparison sample, TYAS. The OLS women in particular evidence higher rates of both victimization and perpetration of relationship violence relative to their TYAS counterparts, and this disparity is greater than that revealed in a comparison of men's reports (Lowery, 2001). Further, whether we focus on the TYAS or the OLS sample, those young adult women who scored higher on self-reported delinquency during their teen years report a higher level of intimate-partner violence as an adult relative to those in each sample who scored lower on delinquency involvement (see also Giordano et al., 1999; Moffitt et al., 2001; Capaldi Kim, & Shortt, 2004). One explanation for this is the tendency, as documented in prior studies, toward "assortative mating," that is, the tendency of individuals to choose partners who are similar to themselves on a number of characteristics, including antisocial behavior (i.e., a young woman with a history of drug and alcohol use or other delinquent behavior is more likely to become involved with a similarly inclined romantic partner, whose repertoire in turn includes violence against women) (Krueger et al., 1998). However, this statistical association also likely reflects that women's backgrounds of exposure to violence result in a greater likelihood that they will resort to physical violence as one response to conflict situations.

The narratives accord well with the statistical results on partner violence, as can been seen in the numerous descriptions of violent altercations and outright abuse they contain, such as in Michelle's account of difficulties with her husband:

> **R:** Oh yeah, he had, uh, chased me down in my car and I was going down a back road trying to get away from him, and the football field is right in front of us and he starts pushing my car into the football field. So the first thing I do is I go straight to the police department and I jump out of the car, and I am in front of the police department and he's trying to jerk me into his car. So, just as I am banging on the police window, he reaches out and is hitting me across the face, as the police see it.
>
> **Q:** Okay.
>
> **R:** And so they talked me into pressing assault charges and I did. I got a restraining order on him, and that is how it ended.
>
> **Q:** And yet they still had to talk you into it?
>
> **R:** 'Cause, oh, we had been together for, oh, so long. Honestly, I think it was the security. Scared of just going out on my own

again. And he was taking care of all the bills and stuff and I
had, I had a job, you know and I was just worried that I wouldn't
make it on my own, and you know, we had a brand new house
and it never been lived in, we was the first ones to ever have lived
there. I got a $500-a-month house, and life was nice. I knew he
had a girlfriend ...

These stories of abuse are quite commonplace within the narratives
and are critical background for understanding the kind of environment the children of OLS must navigate; however, our analyses of
the narratives also indicate that many OLS women were involved
in relationships characterized by mutual or reciprocal violence. For
example, one respondent noted that she and her partner often hit
one another with rolled up magazines; another indicated that her
boyfriend no longer bothered her "after the second time I shot him."
Jackie described a fight with her partner, Joe, that demonstrated significant violence on her part:

But the last worse thing I did before I came here [prison], a month
before I came here, me and Joe was arguing about drugs or whatever, and I cut him with my box cutter all the way down. And he was
like, "Help me. Help me." And I'm like ... I just took a board and
started beating him, and I left him in the back for dead. [Note: This
is not the incident that resulted in her incarceration.]

The life-history accounts also contain frequent references to violent
altercations that are not related to romantic-partner conflicts, thus
depicting an even more multifaceted learning environment to which
children may be exposed. This eclectic mix of stories about violence
is consistent with Kruttschnitt and Carbone-Lopez's (2006) recent
detailed analysis of the violent experiences of a set of women who had
actually been incarcerated for violent offenses. Their analysis documented that although domestic-violence disputes were common, they
were not the only situational context that resulted in violent responses
and, in turn, increased the women's legal difficulties. The violent sce-
narios described by OLS respondents often reference incidents that
did not reach the attention of official criminal justice agencies; thus the
self-reports and life-history approach draw attention to an even wider
array of violent incidents. A number of women in the study describe
a worldview that includes a readiness for violence if the situation calls

for it. This worldview, or "anger identity," may have been deeply influenced by past experiences, but it is a feature of the self-concept that women recognize, one that appears to limit their chances to effect a completely prosocial way of life (Giordano et al., 2007). Below we quote first Janice, who succinctly depicts this type of worldview:

> I'm not gonna go out there and look for trouble ... and try to pick up a fight with someone, but if I'm pushed to the point that, you know, like backed in the corner or, you know ... [someone's] running their mouth when they shouldn't be ... I've just gotten to the point where, you know, its hey, I'm not lettin' people run over me no more, and if it comes down that I have to fight, then so be it. I mean that's not really a good way to feel, but the lifestyle that I had to live, I mean it come to the point of, you know, if it comes to me or someone else, you know, then it's gonna be somebody else; it ain't gonna be me.

Thus, even though many of the women had been victims of violence, their views of self and the narratives of their actions sometimes transcended the "victim" role. Monica, quoted below, describes a fairly routine situation (being asked to babysit by a friend of hers) that nevertheless escalated into a set of violent confrontations. In the first incident she appears reactive and defensive; in the second less so:

> I was babysitting her little girl. She was going to go get her income tax check cashed. She never came back. So I took the little girl over to my aunt's, and I told her she could watch her, you know that I watched her all day and half the night. And she [the little girl's mother] approached me in the bar and was calling me all kinds of names and shoved me, ripped my necklace off my neck, plowed me in the nose. [Q: For not being there with her kid?] Yeah she was drunk, and I just couldn't take it anymore ... and then I went, after we fought the first time, I went back to her apartment and kicked the door in ... and beat the hell out of her.

Tisha's narrative, quoted below, contains similar themes. It is interesting to note that traditionally gendered social processes are evident in both Monica and Tisha's life histories and in these particular "slices of life." In both instances, for example, the women talk about providing caregiving to other women's children. Perhaps not surprisingly, this caregiving theme (and, indeed, references to issues involving the care of their own biological children) is much less prevalent in the narratives of the men who participated in the OLS study. And yet, the conflict-solving method both women describe seems nontraditional when considered in light of traditionally gendered behavioral proscriptions. Tisha's prior background includes extensive fighting and a tough self-image, which increases the odds that she will draw upon this repertoire and identity when new stressful situations arise. It is also important to note that the episode Tisha describes depicts an apparent derailment from the pattern of progress that she has been able to sustain over the last several years. For example, at the time of this interview she reported involvement with a stable/law abiding partner, and no problems with drugs or alcohol:

R: I was always with somebody, always, school, something, neighbors ... I just liked to fight ... but now I've found I got a lot more self-control than what I used to, though.

Q: But you think you have ... if somebody provoked you, you could unload on them?

R: Oh yeah. I did right here. It was last year ... My ... ex–sister-in-law come down here. She's got two kids, and me and my husband has took her two kids three different occasions, and took care of them because she just didn't want them. She come down in here doing that shit [drugs] again, so I took them again. and then she come in here, telling me what to do ... cause I cashed her welfare check, just to get these boys some clothes for school. I was clothing them, I was sending them to school; that check in my opinion belonged to them ... she tried to have me throwed in jail. I told her, no, it ain't happening. I done told welfare all about it. You're screwed, man. You ain't getting no drug money. Your young'uns ... go look at them ... Don't they look good? Too bad, you can't have them, and then one day she was out here and commenced slapping the hell out of her boy ... the oldest one ... And I'm watching her through the kitchen door ... and Morris, my boyfriend, he said, you're not getting in it. I said no I'm not, I said it's none of my business. He's trying to walk away from her, to keep from hitting her is what the boy was trying to do and I could see it. So I met them here at the front door. I said what the hell's going on. She said it ain't none of your business. I said bullshit. I said, thanks to you, HUD and Welfare and everybody else is making me have you stay here ... whatever pertains in your life pertains to mine. I am head of this household, whatever's going on ... it is my business, 'cause he's in my temporary custody, not yours. ... I've had a 12-year problem with this woman ... for 12 years she has did nothing but intimidate me, and I've always been scared of her. I mean, because she's a bulldog (laughs) and I'm just a little thing. I mean, she's a big old girl ... she's mean ... I've seen her knock men out bigger than her. You know, she just pushed me one too many times in my doorway, and I flew into her ... and by the time we got in the house in the kitchen, I commenced then to beating the hell out of her on my kitchen floor ... and she just laid there ... flopping ... just a flopping ... flopping ... and I wasn't going to quit. I mean, I'm not the kind of person to hit somebody that ain't going to hit me back, you know ... when they're just laying there, I'll walk away ... I'm not that mean, you know, but on that woman ... yeah, I was going nuts. I was just ready to lose it. I backhanded my boyfriend ... knocked him down clean over here into the other side of the wall onto the couch from my kitchen ... told him you get the fuck away from me, I'm killing this bitch ... I've had it with her .... she'll not intimidate these children no more or me ... I've had it.

While most discussions of women's violence include attention to negative influences from a male partner – if not outright abuse – in this instance Tisha's boyfriend Morris plays a minor and essentially prosocial role as he tries to dissuade Tisha from "getting in it." In addition, as part of the violent situation, Tisha winds up backhanding Morris, knocking him "clean over here into the other side of the wall onto the couch from my kitchen." Numerous incidents described within the narrative, then, do not correspond to the idea that women only aggress "in defense of self and children" (Dobash et al., 1992: 80), but a more complex picture emerges from the life-history narratives taken as a whole.[3] Many of the women have been victims and also participated in a range of violent situations – some of which clearly reflect traditionally gendered inequalities of power as reproduced at the couple level – but other incidents that may involve a range of social dynamics and other kinds of stressors. And, as with drug involvement (and its attendant relapse periods), violent eruptions such as the one Tisha describes limit the respondents' abilities to put

---

[3] On one level, Tisha is acting to protect a child in her care. However, the situation is more complex because the threat is not a male partner but a drug-addicted mother who was slapping her son. In addition, the narrative comments make clear that both women have backgrounds that include previous violence (e.g., when she notes that she has seen her ex-sister-in-law "knock men out bigger than her," and describes herself as someone who "just liked to fight," and also as one who, "when they're just laying there I'll walk away...")

together a convincing career as a completely prosocial individual. Because a significant number of the respondents – male and female – have not completely discarded the idea of resorting to violence, nor given up drug use in a sustained way, their actions necessarily intrude into and, in multiple respects, shape the lives of the children we have followed-up in this investigation.

PROPERTY CRIMES

Most of the OLS respondents are not professional thieves. Violence and drug use, as described above, are two areas that figure prominently in both women's and men's adult lives and, in turn, increase the odds of continued contact with the criminal justice system. Yet property crimes such as theft are also represented in the respondents' arrest histories and contribute to the criminal portfolios of these respondents. And as Farrington recently noted, theft offenses occur much more frequently than is reflected in official statistics (Farrington, 2003). It is consistent with this notion that the respondents' self-reports of criminal activity and the life-history narrative data reveal more involvement than is reflected in the arrest and incarceration information. For example, 63 percent of the OLS respondents reported engaging in one or more property offenses at the time of the first follow-up, and 60 percent reported at least one such offense at the second follow-up. And, as we have argued in reference to violence and drug use, there is evidence of a social-learning component, as reflected in the respondents' narrative descriptions of their early years:

> Q: So you kind of knew how the system worked? How did you know that?
> R: 'Cause my brothers got sent off before I did. And they got put on probation and stuff ... so I knew I'd have to have a chance on probation, so ...
> Q: Who introduced you to cigarettes?
> R: My brother.
> Q: Did you ever get in trouble with the law ... besides truancy as a kid?
> R: Yeah, stealing bicycles with my brothers ... We'd take them across the bridge (into Kentucky) and sell them. When we'd get done

riding them, we just walked until someone, ask everybody if they wanted to buy them.

In some instances, it is not that the children commit such acts with family members, but that the messages they receive did not actively discourage these theft behaviors:

> **R:** I was stealing then. From J.C. Penney's and Sears and all them stores like that. Boosting ... but not for no one, but for me. Like I'd steal my, for my babies ... I stole their clothes.
>
> **Q:** What would happen every time you'd get popped for stealing when you got ... when they would take you home to your mom? What would happen?
>
> **R:** She wouldn't say anything ... 'cause they would even put they little bids in when I went to the store ... "Get me this and get me that." I'd be, like, I ain't going to steal nothing for nobody but me ... If I'm going to the store, it's for me ... I'm not ... trying to steal something for them.
>
> **Q:** Your mom would tell you to ... steal stuff?
>
> **R:** She was, like, uh ... get her some ... couple sweater ... (laughs) my mother figured if you going to do i t... do it, I guess.

Another way in which early family circumstances figured into the life-history narratives and, in turn, to references to stealing and other acquisitive crimes involves respondents' focus on the conditions of economic and social marginality that characterized their early childhood experiences. The substance use and legal problems of their parents resulted in periods of neglect for the OLS respondents and their siblings. Perhaps not surprisingly, we describe analogous circumstances when we consider the living situations of the children of the OLS respondents (Chapters Five through Seven), but again, it is important to note that in many instances these patterns did not originate with our focal sample:

> **Q:** When you started stealing, you said initially you stole food because there wasn't any at your house?
>
> **R:** Yeah, but she [her mother] used to make just enough to pay the bills and the rent.
>
> **Q:** Okay, so was it obvious, like to neighbors or whatever, that you guys didn't have any food or ... when you would come home with food, would anyone question where that was coming from?
>
> **R:** Yeah, my mom did.

Q: Okay.
R: I told her not to worry about it.
Q: And then she didn't?
R: She did, but she didn't dare (say) anything to me.

Other respondents described blended-family situations that were associated with economic difficulties:

Q: Why would you steal clothes?
R: When I first went to Cleveland, I didn't have any clothes and my dad was never around – it [was] always just me and my step-mom over there. And I didn't want to ask him [her dad] for any money so I just went and got them on my own.

Donnell described similar circumstances:

Q: Okay. How old were you when you started stealing?
R: About ten.
Q: And you were stealing what?
R: Stealing clothes and whatever.
Q: Okay, what would happen when your stepmom would call and say, Donnell is stealing and come get him? What would, what would your dad do to you?
R: Uh, he would come and get me. And whoop me.
Q: Okay, so he would come and whoop you, and did he ever ask why you steal? Did he know that your, your stepmom wouldn't buy you anything?
R: … I had told him.
Q: Okay.
R: I guess he had got into it with her about it, but then he would still do the same thing. Give her the money and she wouldn't give any to me.
Q: Okay, when you say, you weren't getting nothing, are we talking that you weren't getting anything? At all?
R: Nothing at all. I just … since I was 10 years old I got everything on my own.

EDUCATIONAL AND OCCUPATIONAL ATTAINMENT OF THE RESPONDENTS AS ADULTS

The early marginal living circumstances described above fit well with the adult educational and occupational attainment levels the respondents report at the time of the adult follow-ups. Overall, 83.2

percent of the females and 82.7 percent of males failed to graduate from high school. Only 6 percent had advanced educational experience, and the majority of these were either associate degrees (4%) or other types of technical training (1.5%). These educational levels stand in sharp contrast to the academic achievement levels reported by the TYAS respondents, and it is important to note that even a majority of the neighborhood "offenders" reported that they had graduated from high school. These are traditional objective indicators of lack of success/attainment, but the narratives also effectively highlight that the respondents themselves clearly understood where and how they had missed out in this regard:

> I always, that's why I cry a lot, I do; certain things I cry about, you know, I cry about, you know, not gettin' a high school diploma. I can even cry watchin' *Grease* ... [At this point the interviewer tries to pick up on the *Grease* theme, and begins talking about the John Travolta/ Olivia Newton John love story; yet Alicia eventually steers the interviewer back to the original point:] The end part, where everybody got their diploma and everybody was friends, and everybody graduated all at the same time ... I'm talkin about the end, what really got me was when they got their diploma, their high school diploma, and they were all friends and then they do that part, we'll always be together and stuff like that. [Q: And that's the part you never had.] No – never, never, never.

Some of the original participants in the study have earned GEDs or been involved in other educational experiences, but these often take place in prison or in connection with rehabilitative efforts. Here, too, the respondents recognize at this point that such credentials are not likely to dramatically alter their living circumstances:

> **R:** Yeah ... I (have) regrets. A lot of that.
> **Q:** Yeah ... anything in particular?
> **R:** Ah ... not finishing school.
> **Q:** High school?
> **R:** Yeah.
> **Q:** But you're in school now.
> **R:** Yeah ... a GED. But it's not the same as graduating ... It's suppose to be just as good ... but it's not like actually doing it.

These low levels of educational attainment are important as descriptors of the parents' circumstances, but also are potentially consequential for understanding the later lifecourse experiences of the children. For example, Hagan and Parker (1999), in connection with an intergenerational study carried out in Toronto, hypothesized and found support for the idea that early educational "disinvestment" has significant consequences for the later delinquency involvement of the children of their original sample members.

Employment and income figures coordinate well with these low levels of educational attainment. For example, household incomes were divided into quartiles, with the lowest quartile represented by the 0–$14,000 category. Overall, 52.7 percent of the men and 54.8 percent of the women fell into this category, and only 7.6 percent (8.6% of men, 6.7% of women) listed household incomes higher than $40,000. Gender differences were not significant, but African American men and women were more likely than their white counterparts to be in the lowest income category: only 1.5 percent reported incomes over $40,000.

Although income data did not differ dramatically across gender, men were significantly more likely than women to report full-time employment at the time of the wave two interviews (65.6% vs. 32.7%). Since women are somewhat less likely to be employed full time, we also compared this group to the TYAS women, and found that the latter were significantly more likely to be so employed. The life-history narratives reveal that the OLS respondents, whether male or female, rarely garnered "above the table" wages. Men were more likely to describe construction or roofing work, whereas female respondents frequently listed service-sector jobs, such as nurse's aid or waitress.

Clearly, for those in the "persister" and even "unstable" offending categories, selling drugs and prostitution often added to these meager income levels. Recall, for example, Amber's quote at the beginning of this chapter in which she described her involvement in prostitution. Tim, another currently incarcerated OLS respondent, contrasted for the interviewer the periods when his children had to sleep on the couch, and his drug-selling days, when both children had their own rooms. The children's sleeping arrangements are likely not the sole motivation for Tim's drug-dealing behavior (and their well-being has undoubtedly been negatively influenced by Tim's lengthy prison time, during which he is unable to earn income). However, Tim and many other respondents' low educational attainment levels, lack of marketable skills, and early criminal histories are clearly implicated in their erratic employment histories as adults and their frequent returns to illegal sources of income. Referencing her involvement in prostitution, Tasha, another respondent, put it quite simply, "It's all I know."

Mary focused on her previous system involvement as a major impediment to her repeated attempts to secure legitimate employment:

> I can't get a job because of my record; don't fucking nobody want to hire me! Oh you got this, this, and that; I was arrested over twenty-seven times and put into juvenile hall as a minor, and then arrested as an adult and got two felonies. So how can I explain to you [her children] that the reason that I can't live in [nice suburb] is because nobody wants to hire me because of my record? People don't believe in giving you a second chance. I have been out there, and those doors that I have knocked on get slammed in my face constantly. That right there is enough to make somebody not want to go. Okay. I'm honest on my applications, I have been arrested for this, that, and whatever. And they're always "Sorry we can't help you" over and over and over again for a year or two years straight. You go looking for a job and people tell you no because of your past. I have changed and I'm walking with God and I'm a different person ...
>
> As far as where I live and where I raise my kids, I chose not to raise them here but I have no choice. That is what I am telling you. I have no choice in ... employers won't give me a job and I have no choice in those things, those are the things that I pay for everyday. But I don't quit, I'm not a quitter, I'm not ever going to quit as long as I have breath in my body, and I can get up and go, then I'm going to keep on trying.

MARRIAGE AND OTHER INTIMATE PARTNERSHIPS

While a majority of the OLS respondents were not married at the time of the first adult follow-up, and an even smaller number within the sample had been able to put together what we called the complete respectability package, which included a full-time job (8%), it would be erroneous to conclude that intimate relationships and marriage were of little consequence to these respondents. Indeed, taking into account information from both waves of interviews, we found that 62 percent reported being married at some point in their lives, and a majority of respondents reported at least one and more often multiple cohabitation experiences. Some criminological theories depict juvenile delinquents and adult offenders as uninterested in or incapable of forming intimate ties because of their selfish orientation and inability to bond with others (Gottfredson & Hirschi, 1990). Although this is undoubtedly characteristic of a subset of those with criminal experience, the life-history narratives we elicited from these respondents reveal that intimate partnerships and other close relationships were often important and meaningful to them. However, this did not always translate into a stable, long-term relationship with outstanding "desistance" potential, with spillover effects on the children's stability and well-being.

Liebow (1967) observed early on that for disadvantaged individuals without a strong foothold in the occupational arena, the world of interpersonal relationships may loom especially large. Lacking a diversified portfolio of interests and concerns, intimate relationships may be accorded a high place in the individual's rank ordering of what matters most, what Stryker (1980) labeled the individual's "hierarchy of salience." Yet Liebow also cogently observed that the very forces of disadvantage that heighten the meaning/salience of such ties also act as destabilizers and increase vulnerabilities within the interpersonal realm. The social positioning of these respondents also tended to foster frequent contact with other individuals with drug use and other criminal experience, factors that further limit the prosocial potential of marriage and intimate partnerships.

Control theorists have suggested that it is the quality of one's intimate ties or "bonds" that exerts a positive influence on the individual. This presents a problem for understanding changes in criminal involvement over the life-course; delinquents have previously demonstrated their antisocial tendencies and hence are theorized as incapable of relating intimately to others. Laub and Sampson modified some aspects of the control theory position, arguing that although delinquents as a group may be less likely to go on to develop strong bonds (particularly marital ties), to the degree that they do so, this offers a key social mechanism through which "desistance" is accomplished. Social learning approaches focus more heavily on the criminality or prosocial orientation of the individuals to whom one is attached, arguing that strong ties may either work "for good or ill," depending upon the attitudes and behavioral proclivities of these intimate others (Cairns, 1979). Although researchers differ in theoretical emphasis, most would probably agree that strong bonds to a prosocial partner represent the "ideal"; yet this is a life-course development that has been difficult for many of these respondents to achieve.

Karla's narrative, quoted below, is striking as a strong contrast to many of the stories of relationship changes/difficulties woven through the various life-history accounts. Karla reported a very happy marriage to Edward at the time of both adult follow-up interviews. Edward was a solid family man and someone who offered Karla continued love and social support:

> He means a whole lot to me, he's like my own little comfort zone. We have a real good understanding, a real good relationship with one another. He's a wonderful father, not perfect yet, but I'm working on it. What I love about him most is his warm heart. He's got a huge heart; he cares about everything and everybody. He helps me out when I'm down by just allowing me to share with him whatever I'm going through, it means a lot to me because I know, even if he can't do anything about the situation, he'll listen. Lots of times that's all it takes for me is to just talk something through, to come up with a solution. So him just being there to listen does so much for me.

Karla nicely illustrates the subtype "happily married to a prosocial partner," but three other logically possible intimate-partner situations make frequent appearances within the life-history narratives: miserable with an antisocial partner, miserable with a prosocial partner, and happy with an antisocial partner. Based on the content of the narratives and subsequent quantitative analyses, we must conclude that the unhappy-but-connected-to-a-prosocial-partner respondents are in a favorable position from a desistance point of view. But these relationships lack the long-term stabilizing potential of the loving, affectionate relationships such as Karla describes. This creates areas of vulnerability for the individual as well as for the children in these family environments. For example, the effects of marital discord on a parent's mental health or that result in changes in the child's living arrangements undoubtedly have the potential for negative effects on various types of child well-being.

The family contexts that clearly exposed the OLS children to espe-cially high levels of risk, however, were those in which respondents were involved with antisocial partners and enmeshed in highly con-flictual relationships. The child in these situations has ample oppor-tunity to learn about drugs, crime, and violence from the partner as well as from the parent, whose desistance efforts are often com-promised by continued contact with this type of romantic partner. Further, prior research has shown repeatedly that witnessing paren-tal violence has negative effects on children, and in these families the level of domestic discord is sometimes very severe. Dianne describes her long-term relationship with Gerald, a partner who clearly reflects this nexus of negative influences:

> [Why'd he get locked up?] Um, he's just ... he's a criminal ... (Laughs.) He's just always at the wrong place at the wrong time. He's always, uh... the accessory to it ... someone else is breaking in somewhere, and he doesn't have the good sense to leave. (Laughs.) So he hangs out with them quite a bit. Basically, he got caught with some money, doing something ... they were breaking in people's houses. He just helped them and he didn't know he was helping. He said he didn't know he was helping them. [Do you believe that?] Honestly, I don't, I don't ...

Dianne later described a period of time when she became romanti-cally involved with Gerald's uncle:

> I didn't sleep with him... and knowing my checkered past ... he just believed the opposite. He just thought I did ... he confronted and beat the crap out of him, and beat the crap out of me too ... and that's when it really started getting bad. He started beating me up. He started physically abusing me. He started verbally abusing me. He's tried to kill me on several occasions ...

PARENTING EXPERIENCES

The basic findings outlined above (criminal persistence on the part of many respondents; nontraditional family structures; unstable, often violent intimate partnerships; economic marginality) provide a general basis for expecting that parenting may be far from opti-mal in many of these families. However, the interviews we conducted also include specific details about the respondents' experiences as mothers and fathers, including custody arrangements, and direct questions about parenting practices.

Comparisons to the TYAS adults show a pattern of early and high fertility on the part of OLS respondents (Lowery, 2001), a finding that accords with prior research indicating that teenage childbearing is often linked to other problem behaviors, including delinquency and drug/ alcohol use (Pogarsky Lizotte, & Thornberry, 2003). It is interesting to note, however, particularly in light of the early and later difficulties that these respondents faced, that the OLS respondents scored higher than the TYAS young adults on the "wantedness" of their children.[4] The qualitative data do typically reveal great concern for and attachment to children, but observed rates of custody loss and the content of the life-history narratives indicate that the birth of children was not an automatic route to desistance and instead often compounded the respondents' difficulties. It is a stark illustration of this lack of an automatic parenting effect that, as we indicated in Chapter Three, almost half of the female respondents did not have physical custody of at least one minor child at the time of the first adult interview. This finding is in contrast to the TYAS (12%) and national figures indicating that 10 percent of all U.S. children do not live with their biological mothers (Kreider, 2007). An even higher percentage of the OLS male respondents (55%) did not live with at least one as contrasted with 24 percent of TYAS men and statistics indicating that 34 percent of U.S. children do not live with their biological fathers (Kreider, 2007).

While there has been an increased appreciation of the father's role in child development (Harper & McLanahan, 2004), day-to-day caretaking of children often remains a highly gendered activity. These findings thus have implications for the well-being of the children born to women within the sample, particularly those who have continued their earlier pattern of antisocial behavior as they have matured into adulthood.[5] Another complicating factor is that societal sanction of women who have not fully engaged with the press of "nurturant role

---

4 Wantedness was measured with an item that asked respondents, "Thinking back to each of your pregnancies (or partner's pregnancies), how would you say you felt about each one? Would you say you..." Responses ranged from "wanted to get pregnant at that time," to "did not want her to get pregnant at all."

5 Certainly, the children of male offenders also face numerous difficulties, as we will show in subsequent chapters.

obligations" (Robbins, 1989: 119) is also much stronger than that levied against comparable males. Thus, there are undoubtedly strong social desirability elements in the sections of the life stories relating to the respondents' children, as well as a nearly universal interest on the part of the women in their children's well-being. Women's stories were, in fact, more likely than men's to emphasize children as a positive force in their lives. But we observed considerable variability in the way respondents perceived the influence of children on their antisocial lifestyles. Delia is one who made a clear connection between the birth of her child and lifestyle changes she has sustained over time:

> Having a baby, that changed a whole lot of me. I knew I had a responsibility, and I mean, if I did this wrong they would come and take him. I couldn't imagine getting in trouble. I mean, even spending the night in jail and having him know about it. Him growing up and saying, oh, my mom has been in jail. You know my mom drinks, she's been in jail and this and that ... I think that if I wouldn't have had him, I probably would have gotten in trouble. Honestly, that really settled me down.

Another group within the sample appeared to embrace wholeheartedly the good parent role but managed to disassociate their experiences as a good parent from their own deviant behavior:

> All my kids are on the honor rolls. My children have been through counseling ... Family Focus. My kids will complete school. My kids will not be like I was. I am real strict. I might be a drug addict, and I may not get up but even if I'm not up, they will get up for school, dress proper for school, don't disrespect any teachers or anything like that. My children don't do that. Don't break the law. My girls don't even leave the back yard unless I take them.

In her study of the transition into motherhood, McMahon (1995) found that a majority of the middle-class respondents in her sample experienced motherhood as a time of life-enhancing personal growth. For example, many of the women were surprised at the depth of their feelings after they had given birth, indicating that they were often "overwhelmed by their emotions ... as totally absorbed by their children; as though they had fallen in love" (McMahon, 1995: 135). She contrasts this sense of personal transformation with themes of obligation and "settling down" encountered in interviews with working class respondents. Nevertheless, in both groups the women emphasized the rewards of their new status, including the feeling of "loving and being loved," and enjoyment of the opportunities to "watch them grow and learn."

In contrast, in this sample many respondents' stories that focus on children are often dominated by negative themes. Both women and men comment on the importance of being a good parent largely as a kind of disaster-avoidance strategy, rather than as an intrinsically rewarding experience. As we describe in more detail in Chapter Six, respondents recognize the potential for their children to experience the kind of negative family climates that almost universally characterized their own upbringing. Particularly as their children matured, they became more aware of the potential for the intergenerational transmission of negative outcomes:

> That's why I've went all this time and not worked. I just didn't want nobody else to have them. They're too little and can't tell for their self, and once the damage is done it's done and you can't … you can always say you're sorry but you can't fix it. [Lynette]

> I don't want them to have a father that's not working, that's on drugs, that's a bum … can't do anything for them. I know how living through that, I know how that makes me feel about my father. I didn't want to do that to my kids. [Jeffrey]

> I didn't want her to have to go through anything that I had to go through. [Edna]

The above quotes are from the first wave of adult interviews with the respondents, when their children had not yet become adolescents. By the time of the 2003 interviews, the hopeful narrative was more difficult to sustain, especially when respondents continued to have drug and alcohol or other types of problems and their children often began to exhibit behavioral and/or emotional problems themselves. Gina, interviewed in the state prison for women in 2003, begins to describe her commitment to parenting in a positive light, but could not sustain this theme, as she reflects on her drug involvement and periods of incarceration:

> We always did agree I was going to be a stay-at-home mom. I never had a problem with that. I believed that my children probably fare as well as they do now because I was at home, you know, maybe not

so much in the last six years. … I'm really ashamed of myself, actually, because I have not been a great big influence on my children. It
doesn't mean I don't think about them every single day …

Men in the sample also experienced regrets about absences from their
children or having negative effects on them. For example, Jeremy's
second interview was conducted in a state prison. When asked about
his parenting experiences and relationship with his daughter Jenny,
he replied:

It's kind of hard for me to talk about that … because so many times
where I wasn't in their life, you know, being incarcerated, not being
able to watch them grow up … I had a problem with Michelle once,
and she was like, "How are you going to get out and try to tell me
something. And you ain't been there for me." I've asked her, you
know, "How do you feel, you know, I'm your father, right?" It's like
a blank stare. And then when she comes back, "Well you know you
wasn't there for me. Blah, blah, blah, blah." I don't want to, I don't
want to have to go through that … I don't want her to feel no badder
than she already does. You know I'd be hurt and I, I'd just feel that,
you know, damn, look what I did now, like alright, it's my fault. I'm
paying for it now. She has no one to turn to … She doesn't like it.
You know, she's having problems with it. I'm not there to help raise
her. It's hard for her like that. Not being there, not being a father
figure in her life, period 'cause I'm in prison.

Although a number of the men expressed such regrets, others were
sufficiently removed from the children's lives that these narratives
lacked the immediacy/intensity of the women's accounts. As noted
above, while the women were less likely to have physical custody of
their children than is traditionally the case in the general population, they were nevertheless more likely to live with, or at least have
intermittent contact, with their children than their male counterparts in the OLS sample. As research has shown, individuals typically
possess a strong desire to see themselves in a favorable light (see, e.g.,
Bradley, 1978), but these positive views of self were often difficult to
sustain in the face of child-endangerment charges or their involvement in behaviors that they recognize clearly compromise their children's well-being. Angelina discussed her repeated attempts to point
her children in a different direction, even as she reveals the toll her
lifestyle has taken on all members of her family:

We talked about everything that is going on, about their life and their future. I told them, "Wouldn't it be nice, do you think this is fun for me to sit here and get high? Do you think its fun for us to get drunk and drink beer and smoke weed? I don't know a lot, but I know it's not a lot of fun." I said "How much fun do you think it is if I can't get up tomorrow because I'm hung over from the night before and I sleep all day until you get home from school and haven't done shit. I haven't cleaned up or nothing, how much fun do you think that was?" I said "How much fun do you think it is to take all your earnings and spend it on dope, and when you really want to do something nice, you don't have no money to do it?" I said "I want to take you to Six Flags, I want to take you to Disney World, I want to get in my car that I don't own but I want to own and drive you to a basketball game, a football game; I want to do these things for you that I cannot do. And this is what dope is doing to me. This is what drinking and smoking and partying every night does to me. I cannot do the things I want to do with you because I'm addicted to something that I cannot control. Fun is being able to go in your life, take out a credit card or take out some money and say Mom, we're going to fly down to Florida to see Robin this weekend, I already purchased the tickets, would you like to come?" [But] This that we sit in here and do or when everybody come over and we're drinking beer and smoking weed, that shit ain't fun. All this shit is fucked up because we've been doing it for so long that we're addicted to this kind of fun, but this shit ain't really fun. And I tell them this every day, when we get into something about something going on in our lives, which is almost every day, about something that you should be doing and that you should not be doing. "So is that what you want to do, smoke until you're sick, drink until you're sick? It's not fun. And then pray that you get better?"

They don't sell drugs out there in [nice suburb]. You know you're not going to see those dope boys pulling up in your parking lot asking you what's up. And this is the life we live because we have to live it because I can't get out of it. I don't have the money to get out of this [crying]. So I believe in my heart truly that if I wasn't around it all the time, I wouldn't be doing it. If I wasn't faced with it everyday when I walk out my door, like the dope man living around the corner and the weed man living right there; my sister smokes, you know what I'm saying? If I wasn't living with these people all the time, I wouldn't do it. That's why I tell them don't be a follower, be a leader because I'm a follower.

Some of the respondents, recognizing the potential harm to children, emphasized the positive steps they had taken to make sure their children were taken care of by other relatives or indicated that they always refrained from taking drugs in front of their children (*I take it outside*). And certainly some OLS respondents, such as Delia, quoted above, did alter their lifestyles in a more prosocial direction.

While these narratives provide a general indication of how the respondents have experienced the parent role, the structured interview questions provide a systematic assessment of the day-to-day monitoring and care that the OLS children have received. Here, we rely on data from TARS parents for the purposes of comparison. This obviously represents a somewhat primitive depiction, since the OLS sample families encompass a range of living arrangements and levels of criminal activity, and the TARS families are also heterogeneous. With this caveat in mind, we do observe significant differences across the two samples on a number of specific parenting practices. Interestingly, OLS youth actually score higher on a general monitoring scale relative to the TARS youth, who provided responses to identical questions. This scale *asked* teens such questions as: "how often do your parents let you make your own decisions about ..." "the time you must be home on weekend nights," "the people you hang around with" and the like.[6] And, relying on parent reports, no significant differences between OLS and TARS parents were found in the percentage who say that their child often/very often stays home alone, after school, all day, when there is no school, or at night. However, perhaps reflecting a more serious lapse in monitoring, OLS parents were more likely than TARS parents to report that the child had often/very often stayed home alone overnight.

Other questions about follow-through on parenting rules reveal a mixed portrait. For example, OLS parents are more likely to indicate that their child gets away with breaking the rules and that they don't always follow-through to enforce the rules they do have. However, a higher percentage of OLS parents reported calling to check to see whether their child is where she/he said she/he would be. We also asked the children to agree or disagree with the statement, "My

[6] If the child does not live with the focal OLS biological parent, we relied on interview data from the physical custodian of the child for these assessments. Higher scores reflect higher levels of monitoring, based on the child's report.

parents are clueless about a lot of things I do." Consistent with the parents' reports on a lack of follow-through on basic rules, a higher percentage of OLS youths agreed with this statement.

We also observe consistent differences across the two samples on parents' responses to questions that index the parent's active involvement in specific aspects of the child's life – from friends to schooling and extracurricular activities. For example, the OLS respondents reported less involvement in the child's extracurricular activities and greater likelihood of missing meetings or other activities at school. OLS parents also reported less involvement in academic matters, from checking on whether the child did homework or other school assignments to actively helping the child with the assignments, to simply talking with the child about school activities and events. OLS parents were also less likely to have met the child's friends or the parents of the child's friends; however, the basic pattern is similar across the two samples – a majority of parents had met the child's friends, but a minority had met the friends' parents.

Most of the questions about parenting described earlier can be considered indices of either monitoring or involvement. Particularly when we consider specific indices (rather than the general monitoring items), there is ample evidence that parenting is likely to be an important mediator of intergenerational effects. However, as we describe in more detail in Chapter Six, parenting involves an even broader array of communications and behaviors that fit comfortably under the umbrella of social-learning theories. As one way of gauging differences in the normative climates within these family settings, we asked parents, "regardless of whether or not your child has done them, how serious do you feel the following things are," and then listed teen behaviors ranging from dyeing [his/her] hair and getting body art (e.g., tattoos or piercings), to cutting class, dropping out of school, getting someone pregnant/getting pregnant. As shown in Table 1, OLS parents on average do score lower on this scale, reflecting less perceived seriousness – although it should be noted that no differences were observed for items about dropping out of school or cutting class, having sex with someone the child does not know, and getting someone pregnant.

TABLE 1: *Parent Reports of "Seriousness" of Various Forms of Deviance: TARS vs. OLS*[1]

	TARS (N = 1,314)	OLS (N = 127)
Dropping out of school	4.792	4.575
Dyeing her/his hair	2.298	2.236***
Failing a test	3.723	3.315*
Mouthing off (cursing/being rude)	4.356	4.173
Cutting class	4.431	4.283
Getting body art (e.g., tattoos or piercings)	3.756	3.433*
Refusing to attend church	3.284	2.566***
Having sex with a boy/girlfriend	4.554	4.150***
Having sex with someone she/he does not know	4.843	4.614*
Getting (someone) pregnant	4.839	4.709
Using birth control	4.404	4.095*
Having an abortion	4.697	4.500*
Getting HIV or another STD	4.894	3.315***
Total seriousness score	4.22	3.95***

Notes: *$p<.05$: **$p<.01$; ***$p<.001$
[1] Referent is the child's (hypothetical) involvement in each of the behaviors
Mean differences are tested with between-person t-tests

Finally, as we argued at the outset, social learning in general and intergenerational mechanisms in particular are not affectively neutral affairs. Subjective feelings and emotions are important concomitants. While our theoretical perspective (Chapter Six) emphasizes the child's subjective response to the parents' deviance and other aspects of their living circumstances, it is also important to consider the emotional lives of parents as they attempt to navigate the parenting role and do what is best for their children. Perhaps not surprisingly, given the total set of adult circumstances described in this chapter, both male and female OLS respondents score higher on a depression scale than their TYAS counterparts. Their rates of psychological distress are also higher than levels reported by TARS parents in connection with these more recent interviews. However, we also asked questions about the stresses associated with the parent role specifically, and the OLS respondents score higher on this "stress of parenting" scale as well. This scale includes items such as "raising my child can be a nerve wracking job," "I feel on edge or tense when I'm with my child," and "I'd like to be able to do a better job of communicating with my child." As the results of the Chapter Five show, the parent often has reason to be concerned. Thus, the child's own difficulties, including moodiness and acting out, which may have origins in the parents' problem circumstances, undoubtedly contribute to a lack of parenting confidence, inconsistency in rule enforcement and additional stresses associated with the parenting role.

How Have the OLS Children Fared?

We would stand on the side of the hill and she would hold up her sign saying, you know, "my daughter is sick and we need money to get her some medicine to help her feel better." And I just had to sit down and curl up in a ball and cough all the time. That's what I was told to do. And her boyfriend, Derek, would sit on the block and make sure because [if not], I would get punished.

We lived, we lived in a trailer. It was me and mom, Derek, and his mom and his brother ... we had dust storms there all the time. I was constantly locked out. I had to sit out in the middle of the dust storm on picture day ... And I wore my favorite purple dress. We had a windstorm that day, a dust storm, and I was locked out and tried to climb through a window, and Derek's mom slammed the window down.

It is difficult to sketch a straightforward portrait of the lives of the children of the original OLS respondents, not only because there is much variation across families, but because each youth's own life history frequently included so many different "eras." For example, at the time of her interview, Jana, quoted above, was actually living with her stepfather (not the Derek mentioned in the quote) and stepmother. Jana indicated that currently she had *no idea* where mother Denise was, and recounted a virtual panoply of living arrangements across the short span of her life. After Denise initially "took off for Colorado," Jana's stepfather raised her for another year, but then "she called for me, and I lived with her for a year or two." Out in Colorado, the trailer was small and crowded. When asked about the incident described above, Jana indicated that Derek's mother had diabetes, wasn't always taking her medicine, and also was on drugs: "They were all on drugs – my mom, Derek, his mom and his brother."

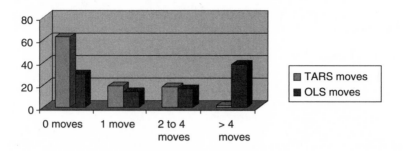

Figure 1: A Comparison of OLS and TARS Youths' Histories of Residential Moves

Eventually Jana returned to her stepfather's house, but when Denise moved back to the region, Jana and her younger brother would generally stay with their mother one night a week:

> So we started spending time with her ... the next thing you know she's back in the county jail in Springfield again. She did this, she did that ... she disappeared for another year. Then she reappears.

Jana's longer narrative also includes references to time spent with her grandmother, and even a period of independent living in an apartment that was in a very marginal neighborhood that she described as "full of crackheads."

To illustrate this concept of residential instability more systematically across the sample as a whole, Figure 1 presents a comparison of the percentages of TARS and OLS children who had experienced no residential moves to one, two to three, or four or more. As these statistics indicate, about twice as many TARS as OLS youths had not experienced any changes in residence. In contrast, the data on OLS youth indicate that approximately 38 percent had four or more moves. And as Jana's story indicates, these moves are often not a simple matter of finding a more desirable house or apartment, but represent fundamental shifts in custody arrangements and are linked to an array of other stressful circumstances.

Table 2 presents results of comparisons across the two samples in other forms of instability in household circumstances. The OLS respondents are significantly more likely to have experienced all

TABLE 2: *Parent Reports of Various Forms of Instability in Housing/Custody Arrangements: TARS vs. OLS[†]*

	TARS (1,316)	OLS (104)
A relative (other than a parent or sibling), friend, or boy/girlfriend moved into your child's home.	37.35%	70.19%***
Your child went to live with her/his other parent (if parents not living in the dame household) or another relative.	13.18%	35.58%***
Your child was placed in a juvenile detention facility.	7.06%	29.81%***
One of your child's siblings moved to her/his own home or went away to school.	33.67%	37.50%
One of your child's parents spent more than a week in a hospital or treatment facility.	20.12%	46.15%***
Child welfare officials took your child away from her/his parents.	4.34%	30.77%***
Your child moved in with a friend's (or boy/girlfriend's) family.	2.51%	11.54%***
One of your child's parents was sent to prison.	10.86%	72.12%***
Your child ran away.	5.79%	24.04%***
Your child moved into her or his own apartment.	2.21%	13.46%***

Notes: *$p < .05$; **$p < .01$; ***$p < .001$
Differences in proportion are tested with a chi-square
[†] OLS parent with custody

of the changes included in the list (with the exception of a sibling moving out of the home – arguably a normative or expected family change). An important instability on this list is the percentage of OLS youths who have had the experience of a parent being incarcerated (72%). It is consistent with this that the narratives include numerous references to the child's experience of the parents' arrests and periods of incarceration.

> I've went through raids, I've went through ... Where people ... a bunch of cops come in your house, and they throw you down on the ground, tell you "freeze." And stuff like that. Seeing dad get arrested ... it's really hard. My first time, I was like eight. And then one time I was getting off the school bus and the detective was bringing him out and I started screaming like, "Get off my dad!"

And my grandma made me get in the house because they were taking him to jail. Right when my bus pulled up they were bringing him out in handcuffs. It kind of embarrassed me, but I was just like, "You know, whatever." My dad didn't say nothing. He just got in the car. And I hate cops to this day. Because I seen them take my dad away. In prison I was, like, "I don't like the po po's." And they were, like, "Why is that?" "Because they take my daddy." I think my dad made the choice like ... but the way that they arrested them was ... it wasn't right. They didn't have to stun him with the stun gun ... not like that. That was not right. [David]

While much time has passed, David remembers the first time his father was arrested, and vividly recalls the details of the "the school bus incident." The narrative communicates effectively that these events are not merely something his father has lived through, but also something David has lived through. Both the memories about the specifics of the arrests and the experience of recounting them thus continue to be linked with strong emotions. It is also noteworthy that David references a prior discussion about this incident that took place during the time when he himself was in prison. David's reference provides a clear example of intergenerational transmission within this particular family, but it also foreshadows our larger perspective on the importance of including emotional reactions and responses as key dynamics of the entire process. Another respondent, Emily, suggests that she is no longer bothered by her father's incarceration, but she believes that her brothers are having a more difficult time:

He was in ... like prison. He's been in prison almost my whole life. He went to prison when I was like ... I was like ten or nine. And he went to prison for seventeen months. For selling drugs. And he had a warrant. And he went to jail before that. And he's been to the county a bunch of times. And then he went to prison this last time. And that's the last time he's been in jail. But he's been to prison a lot. So, it don't bother me 'cause I know what it's about, like drugs and stuff. But I know it bothers my little brothers because I know what it was like when I was little, because that's like the main things that you remember. So, I just know that it bothers them. It don't bother me no more.

Although Emily declares that her father's problems no longer bother her, her narrative makes clear that these experiences have been a traumatic part of her childhood, and some of the "main things you remember." The statistics on experience with parental incarceration shown in Table 2 are striking because data we gathered on the original OLS respondents indicate a lower percent reporting adult jail or prison time; thus a reliance on those figures would result in an underestimate of the child's actual exposure to parental incarceration experiences. In short, these reports undoubtedly incorporate the other parent's incarceration history. One of the most critical areas of the child's development to be influenced by unstable living arrangements is school attendance and performance. Jana forges this connection explicitly:

> Lived with my grandma, lived with my dad, lived with my mom. I never went to school. That's why I have problems now with multiplying and dividing. I never was in school for the basics. [Later on] I was in school for all that because then I went and stayed with my [step] dad, and stayed permanently because she went to prison.

Jana connects her unstable life circumstances and her inability to learn in school. Her quote also provides an initial example of some of the limitations associated with the idea that incarceration is the primary negative life event to which these children have been exposed. For Jana, the period during which her mother was incarcerated was one of relative stability and more consistent school attendance.

SCHOOL PROBLEMS

Across the entire sample, results indicate that about 46 percent of the OLS children interviewed had been held back a grade, compared with 23 percent in the TARS sample. It is even more evocative of intergenerational transmission processes that the data show that 69 percent of the OLS youths had been suspended or expelled from school (as contrasted with 39% of the TARS youth). Dropout rates are difficult to estimate because many of the respondents were interviewed prior to an age when their dropout status could be firmly established. Yet among the older respondents nonattendance and dropping out of high school were frequently referenced in the life-history narratives:

> When I lived there she was always out every night with different guys, in and out. And I didn't really have time to concentrate or to study or anything. So I just lost interest in it. [Betsy]

[I dropped out in] sixth grade. I got removed. When we first got taken from our parents, it was because my mom said that my father raped my three-year-old sister, which he wouldn't. I had just started the school year; my aunt's daughter came to get me from school, and she dropped me off in Toledo and that was it. [Cathy never went back to school, wound up at age 13 being a "totally nude stripper," as she described it, and eventually turned to prostitution.]

These quotes from Betsy and Cathy add to the statistical portrait of parenting practices discussed in Chapter Four, indicating that the youths often lacked even parental basics, such as an adult in the household to ensure that the child got up for and was attending school, or the continuity of attending the same school for several years.[1] Adding to this picture, the parents' low socioeconomic standing was often associated with living in very marginal neighborhoods, a pattern we described in Chapter Three. In turn, the schools in such neighborhoods frequently lacked adequate resources, were characterized by high dropout rates, and were more likely to grapple with problems such as violence, drug use, and other forms of delinquency. Results of the structured responses to a "neighborhood environment scale" corroborate this notion. Parents of OLS children were more likely than TARS parents to report that their child attended a school where "fights between students, robbery/theft, vandalism, students using alcohol and drugs, and students having weapons" were a problem. The children's own narratives also frequently include references to the quality of the neighborhood ("you see how ghetto it is over here"), and difficulties posed by the broader school climate:

[And how do you like the school that you go to?] I like it, I just don't like the people there. They start trouble a lot. I don't talk to nobody in school anymore because I got a month left until I graduate, and they're all trying to mess it up for me. So I just mind my own business. I only to talk to Haley and Izzy in school. And, like, she said something that I supposedly said this, and I know it was my old friend Nikki because we don't talk no more. And she's like "Oh yeah, if you going to stand up and hit me," and I stood up and grabbed my stuff, and I walked off. And she's like "Yeah, walk away like a bitch" and I

[1] Recall that the parental involvement in school items focused on more traditional indices, such as participation in school activities or programs, or helping with homework.

said "Yeah, I'm going to walk away like a bitch." I said "Yeah, I'm not going to sit there and get into an argument with you and mess up my graduation just for you." And I walked out of class.

DELINQUENCY INVOLVEMENT

Janice, quoted above, appears to be trying very hard to avoid the kind of trouble that characterized her mother's early years and that she confronts daily at her school. Although the desire to avoid repeating their parents' problems is a common refrain among OLS youths, results of both the quantitative and qualitative analyses suggest that many of these children have nevertheless participated in delinquent acts, used drugs and alcohol, and had encounters with the criminal-justice system. A common offense that links in a straightforward way to the family difficulties we have described is running away from home or other unruly charges stemming from family discord. Diane, for example, said that she moved out when she was in the eighth grade: "She just threw me out – we started arguing and stuff a lot. Kicked me out."

Prior research on runaways and "throwaways" amply demonstrates the association between family discord and running away (Powers, Eckenrode, & Jaklitsch, 1990; Whitbeck & Hoyt, 1999); in our view parents with a criminal and/or drug-using background represent a singularly risky environment in this regard because these backgrounds bring together and concentrate a whole host of family dynamics that render running away or moving out virtually a considered, rational response. The statistics on delinquency involvement show that the child's behavior problems frequently extend beyond such clearly reactive offenses as running away, however. The findings reported in Table 3 are thus central to this investigation of the nature of intergenerational transmission of delinquency and crime. The table presents responses of OLS and TARS youths to a 10-item scale that indexes the youth's own report of delinquency involvement. The OLS respondents score significantly higher in total self-reported delinquency relative to their counterparts who participated in the TARS. Although comparing individual items on the scale shows that differences are not uniformly significant (e.g., the prevalence of

TABLE 3: *A Comparison of Mean Levels of Self-Reported Delinquency: TARS vs. OLS*

	TARS (1,304)	OLS (119)
Total Delinquency	.29	.62***
Drunk alcohol	.99	1.27
Stolen (or tried to steal) things worth $5 or less	.20	.47*
Carried a hidden weapon other than a plain pocket knife	.15	.33
Damaged or destroyed property on purpose	.18	.36
Stolen (or tried to steal) something worth more than $50	.11	.16
Attacked someone with the idea of seriously hurting her/him	.22	.75**
Sold drugs	.15	.59**
Been drunk in a public place	.29	.65**
Broken into a building or vehicle (or tried to break in) to steal something or just to look around	.10	.08
Used drugs to get high (not because you were sick)	.50	1.23**

Note: Restricted to 12- to 19-year-old respondents
*$p < .05$; **$p < .01$; ***$p < .001$

alcohol use and petty theft are not significantly higher than the rates of these acts reported by TARS youth), the OLS respondents were more likely to report involvement in serious offenses, such as using and selling drugs and violence (attacking someone).

A similar pattern is evident in responses to items in a scale designed to index the "problem use of alcohol and drugs." For example, the two groups did not differ significantly in what might be considered the "hangover" items ("not felt so good the next day," "felt unable to do best job at work or school because of drink or drugs"), but OLS youth were more likely to have had problems with a romantic partner, hit a parent, or gotten into fights because of drinking or drugs. Overall scores were also higher on the problem-use scale.

These findings suggest generally elevated risks for OLS youth. Nevertheless, a comparison of prevalence rates for offenses

TABLE 4: *Percentage of OLS Parents Involved in Delinquent Acts as Teens Compared to Prevalence Rates Reported by Their Teenage Children and TARS Respondents*

Delinquent Behaviors	OLS Parents as Teens	OLS Children[†]	TARS Respondents
Damaged or destroyed property on purpose	61.16	12.71	11.12
Carried a hidden weapon other than a plain pocket knife	59.50	7.56	4.52
Stolen (or tried to steal) something worth less than $5	57.02	15.97	5.91
Hit or threatened to hit someone	94.21	54.24	NA
Attacked someone with the idea of seriously hurting her or him	53.72	25.21	11.27
Broken into a building or vehicle (or tried to break in) to steal something or just to look around	61.16	4.24	4.14
Sold marijuana or hashish ("pot," "grass," or "hash")	41.32	8.47	NA
Stolen (or tried to steal) something worth more than $50	72.03	5.93	4.37
Gotten drunk in a public place	69.75	19.49	11.66
Used drugs to get high (not because you were sick)	78.51	24.37	16.15
Drank alcohol	84.30	44.92	41.64

Note: [†] Restricted to respondents aged 12 to 19

reported by OLS parents in 1982 indicate that this subgroup on average reported significantly more delinquency than the OLS children. Table 4 provides prevalence data on offenses common to both interviews and also provides figures for the TARS sample. As is evident in this data, the OLS youth are more delinquent than the TARS respondents but not as delinquent as their parents were at a comparable age. This is consistent with prior research on intergenerational transmission and with other prospective studies of growing up in a risky environment (e.g., Widom's [1989] finding that while abused children faced elevated risks for later delinquency and adult arrests, a majority in her sample did not go on to exhibit these conduct problems).

However, one limitation of this comparison is that the self-reports elicited from the original OLS respondents referenced the 12-month period immediately prior to their incarceration, a time that would almost by definition constitute an active delinquency period for these youths. Conversely, the 12-month period we reference in our assessments of their children's behavior does not capture all the difficulties these children have faced. This becomes clearer when we examine the most recent life-history narratives of these parents and their children. Thus, the narrative accounts are a particularly useful adjunct to the structured data because they convey the context and level of seriousness of their delinquent acts more fully than the straightforward delinquency and drug-use items referenced above does, and also provide the longer life-course view of their past difficulties. This idea is well illustrated by Danielle, a 19-year-old who told the interviewer that she was now determined to stay away from crack: "It's not, it's not like it's gonna take me drug rehab to get over it, you know. I don't need that ..."

Excerpts from the narratives of a large number of respondents highlight the seriousness of their behavior problems and illustrate that these are not isolated cases within the OLS sample:

> I did aggravated robbery. But I'm about to get off [probation] because he don't ever get no bad reports from me. I was doing real good, so he was, like, you're going to be off real soon. When I was 8 I used to live with my auntie. I was, like, a little gangster, like, running dope to people and stuff and weed. I used to hang around the wrong group. [William]

> [Don has a felony record for driving a stolen car and has also been a drug dealer but is trying to change his life for the better.] I mean I was out there real hard, looking for people to sell drugs ... and people will come to me and I give them what they need ... [Don]

I dropped out in 10th grade.'Cause I went to jail. Never enrolled back. Domestic violence. It was my sister. Me and my sister got into it. They said I pulled a knife on her. She pulled a knife on me ... [Johnny]

[Ellen spent time in county lock-up for shoplifting at a flea market, and also references her involvement in violent acts.] I can fight. I can handle my own. I can take care of myself. I don't need nobody to help me.

So I've been smoking cigarettes since I was in the fourth grade. [When did you start doing coke [cocaine]?] Sixteen – this year.

I had to go to West Central. It's like a jail. My mom and dad sent me there ... Because I was getting in trouble at school. [Eric]

[Jason, age 19, went to jail for assaulting his sister:] I punched her and threw her over the couch.

These quotes reveal that illegal-substance use frequently meant more serious drug involvement than using alcohol (e.g., cocaine use; drug dealing); self-reports of violence included references to injury and weapon use, and some of the property crimes (aggravated robbery, auto theft) exceed in seriousness the petty thefts that in population-based surveys make up the majority of affirmative responses to these types of general delinquency questions. Some of these incidents did not involve the official system; however, other references within the narratives suggest that the offenses reached a threshold of seriousness that did involve system contacts (I went to jail; I'm about to get off [probation]). Because narrative accounts are potentially subject to "self-serving biases," it is perhaps not surprising that the comments of parents and other caregivers evoke even more strongly behavior problems on the part of many children in this sample group:

I told her to quit doing what you're doing because it could end up you being in here. [Laura is currently in prison herself.]

They searched his room; they found everything underneath his bed. That's when we all got put on house watch. This lady was coming every week to see us, to see how things were going. Uh, Adam and I had to go through a drug court every week and take a test and all that crap that they were putting us through. And then they busted me for drinking because I wasn't supposed to be drinking. [Dina]

[Although Loquisha, the core respondent (mother), is currently incarcerated in the Ohio state prison for women, she laments that her oldest daughter is selling drugs, has written bad checks, and is in a gang, the Crips. (Dad is currently in prison on a robbery charge.)] She's already stolen. I stole. She likes to fight, and I fight. I mean, she fights; she fights in school; she fights on the bus. She's already stole, she's already been in jail.

Well, the most difficult thing I had to deal with was Robert and his pyromaniac. [Danny, a repeat offender, contends that his son is much more advanced with his own delinquent activities than he was when he was his son's age.] He's headed [down the same path] because he wants to be like Pops. He wants to, you know, he wants to run the streets and carry guns and drink and all that …

[Dave is serving a prison term and contrasts the situation of one of his children who is doing relatively well with his other daughter Michelle] … Michelle is more rebellious. She's a hot head. She's the one that fights and throws the first punch and cuss you out, get in your face and that. My concern for Michelle is the lifestyle she's leading, she's gonna end up dead. She has two kids. She's been … She had eighteen arrests by the time she was 12 years old.

He went to, um … to this boys' institution for like nine months. And that really straightened him out. 'Cause I told my mom, "Don't send him no pocket money, no boxes or nothing. No visits or nothing." [Nancy]

I know my child. 'Cause I know when I had him on track and doing good. I know the tone of his voice when he's doing good. Or the way he carry himself. He's not doing good now. I know he's lying. [Diane]

[David no longer speaks to his daughter because they had a falling out over her problems] She's come out to visit me and stole money from me and stole cigarettes from me and stole pot from me.

And it's kind of scary because Jonathan has been caught with a gun too … [Elise]

I was on the telephone … my daughter's school. She gets in trouble all the time … She's a fighter. [Q: Get suspended a lot?] Yeah… detention, oh, bad grades … bad grades. [Yvonne]

I don't know about him selling [marijuana] … Of course sometimes he comes in here and he has money. He just helps. I don't think he's a runner. I think he just helps every now and then. And they caught Anthony driving the [stolen] car. He didn't have no license … They took him over to county. Oh, he had um … a ankle bracelet on. He cut that off. So, they finally came back and they caught him and they took him over there [to a more secure facility]. [Vanessa]

Then they grow up, they want to drink, they want to get high, they want to fight and kick my door in, fight me. I know my kids good. I know my kids. They're out there getting high. [Keisha]

We took these quotes from a large number of families who participated in the OLS in order to highlight how extensive problem behaviors are across the sample as a whole. Yet another way to illustrate effects of the parents' experiences on the next generation is to consider how these experiences have influenced all the children within a single family. Adaptations on the part of the children vary, but the narrative accounts of Daniella Wilson and her children suggest that there are multiple legacies associated with this one parent's own difficult life. We interviewed Daniella as a 16-year-old and again at ages 30 and 39. In connection with the last interview, we also interviewed her six older children, aged 18, 17, 15, 14, 13, and 10, as well as 15-year-old Rickelle's foster mother. Two other children, aged 5 and 4, live with Daniella's sister.

DANIELLA WILSON

Daniella was a 17-year-old when we first interviewed her in the library at the state institution for delinquent girls. Although we did not conduct in-depth qualitative interviews during this early phase of the project, Daniella's responses in the structured interview indicate a pattern of extensive delinquent behavior. The self-reported delinquency index revealed gang involvement, drinking and using drugs, selling marijuana and hard drugs, major theft, attacking someone with a weapon, and auto theft. Responses also detailed numerous official contacts prior to her institutional experience at Scioto Village. Daniella had previously been sent to the principal's office for disrupting class and threatening teachers and fighting. She had also been suspended for being high and drunk at school and expelled for possession of drugs. Daniella had been picked up by the police eleven times for running away and assault and had appeared in court eight times for the same offenses.

We located Daniella again and interviewed her at age 30, and at the time of this first adult follow-up it was clear that she had continued to have numerous problems as an adult. Indeed, her case and abstract were labeled, "more jail, violence, drugs, misery." At the time of this first adult interview, none of her six children, then ages 10, 9, 7, 6, 5, and 2, was living in the household with her. They lived with either Daniella's mother or their aunt, Daniella's sister. Her apartment was small, and as the interviewer described it, "roach infested and filthy. It has a bed, two plastic chairs, an ottoman, and a color television with Super Nintendo, and a telephone." Daniella reported the annual household income as "less than $7,000," and told the interviewer that she and her boyfriend spent much of their time playing video games and talking on the phone.

We wish to focus here primarily on the experiences of her children, but it is important to highlight that difficulties within the family did not commence with Daniella's problems and difficulties as a parent (a pattern that is also reflected in several examples in Chapter Four). Indeed, Daniella's life-history narrative includes descriptions of her own early years that included references to serious trauma and abuse. For example, she described physical abuse perpetrated by her stepfather and a very traumatic incident when she was 8 years old in which she was sexually assaulted by the leader of her Girl Scout troop. Daniella also spoke at length about her negative feelings about having the darkest skin of any person in the family and her belief that her mother treated her lighter-skinned sibling with more love and care ("she wouldn't have let my sister get shocked with an electrical cord"). In addition, Daniella mentioned the impact of delinquent companions, noting that some had continued their behavior patterns into adulthood: "Some of my friends, some of my friends are still doin' the same thing ... Uh, well, I just saw one last week, and, uh, she was in jail for prostitution ... And sellin' drugs ... And she still doin' it." Daniella had also been arrested as an adult, on charges of domestic violence, probation violation, and disorderly conduct, and had been in jail five times and on probation twice.

When we again located and interviewed Daniella in 2003, she had become severely diabetic. She needed a new kidney (she was on dialysis) and had developed a much more negative attitude about drugs and alcohol: "I'm sick of it ... ain't no fun being high. I guess because I'm ... I've got older you know. I don't like the feeling of it no more. I ain't down with it." Since the initial follow-up interview, Daniella had had two more children (Christian, aged 5, and Chelsea, aged 4), both of whom lived with Daniella's sister ("I'd like to get to know the two youngest, I don't hardly know them").

The interviews with Daniella, the children, and her daughter Rickelle's foster mother document several years in which Daniella did not have physical custody and, accordingly, much fluidity in the children's living arrangements. It is important to note, however, that the narratives also reveal extensive contact between this mother and her children and a number of positive aspects to her relationships with them. At the time of the 2003 interview, Daniella did have custody of her oldest daughter, Lyneice, and oldest son, Maurice, who was, nevertheless, living with his biological father. During periods when Daniella was unable to care for them and/or Children's Services had removed them from the home, Daniella's sister, mother, and various foster families took custody of the children. It is also important to point out that for each child, this often meant shifting among caregivers, and not a more stable situation in which each of the children lived on a continuous basis in one of these other households. For example, Maurice, who was 17 at the time of the interview and living with his father, had also lived with his grandmother, aunt, and Daniella herself. He also told the interviewer of plans to live with his mother again after he graduated from high school and turned 18.

How are these children faring? What do the narrative and other data reveal about delinquency involvement and other problem outcomes for the siblings in this next generation? A superficial reading of the narratives would lead us to focus our attention primarily on 15-year-old Rickelle, since everyone seems to agree that she is the "problem child" in the family. Indeed, it is noteworthy that Rickelle had already been incarcerated and released from the same juvenile institution in which we first met her mother in 1982! Although her story provides perhaps the most dramatic example of intergenerational transmission, it is also important to highlight some of the challenges the other children have faced as they have matured, including periods of emotional difficulties and the ways in which they too had "acted out."

LYNEICE

Lyneice, at 18, is Daniella's oldest child, and her worldly wise demeanor and life-history narrative deeply reflect this sibling position. Although she currently lives with her mother, she also lived with her aunt for a number of years, during which time she apparently shouldered much of the burden of caring for her younger siblings. Lyneice expressed resentment for being placed in this position:

> My auntie she said that since I was the oldest, I had to do everything for 'em. The mother figure. To keep track of everything. I'm even working; I had a job working at Burger King. Come home from work, change the diapers, feed them, clean them, everything. She [aunt] was either gone or she'd be out or she say she have to work overtime at another job, but we already know she actually be out of town with some dude. I felt like, okay, I'm in this, too, and I do need to finish my education. I was still in school. I was only eighth grade. And I felt that I shouldn't have to be in school, try to take care of myself also, and she ain't doing [it], and now I got to take care of two kids. I know they're my brothers and sisters, but that's your [her aunt's] responsibility.

Lyneice's comments illustrate a larger point about the alternative living arrangements OLS respondents typically relied upon, a pattern that is consistent with other survey data. Prior studies have shown that caregivers for the children of female offenders are most likely to be relatives of the offender (Seymour & Hairston, 2001). Although it is well intentioned and even heroic that grandparents, sisters, and other relatives have been willing to assume caregiving roles, this does not automatically translate into an ideal set of living circumstances for the children. For example, these relatives may themselves live in highly marginal neighborhoods, lack stable housing circumstances, have drug and alcohol problems, engage in harsh discipline practices, or simply lack a full investment in the children's lives. The family link to the focal respondent increases the likelihood that at least some of these risk factors will be present in the alternative household-living situation, and these problems obviously add to the stresses that relate directly to being separated from their biological parent.

At the time of her interview, Lyneice was again residing with her mother. The interviewer noted that the apartment building was the site of former drug raids and that things "still needed to be fixed." The apartment itself was tidy but sparsely furnished. Daniella enforced some rules and structure within the household. For example, the interviewer noted the quasi-institutional practice of insisting that everyone turn their chairs upside down on the table when they were finished eating, a household ritual that may stem from previous periods of incarceration. Although Lyneice lived with her mother, she appeared to maintain a prominent position within the family and reflected on the "role-reversal" aspects of this position:

> I spend most of my money right after I help my brothers and sisters out and my mother. She asks for money and I give it to her. It be, like, she just senses I have money, and I be telling her I don't have none, she be like "come on Neecy, come on." Okay so, here, just take it. Get out of my face; here, go. She senses all the time. I could come in here looking like a bum. Like today, I was about to go to dance practice, came in; she knew I had money. She just "Neecy let me borrow $5. Come on, let me get a ten." [Q: How does it make you feel, giving your mom money?] Happy because I don't need her. She needs me (giggling). It's like … like, if she really need it, yes, she asks me.

Although Lyneice thus shoulders much of the responsibility, she is still in school and references involvement in a prosocial extracurricular activity (dance practice), and her current self-reported delinquency score is low. It is also interesting to note that, while an outsider might consider Lyneice's life to be extremely difficult, Daniella herself argues that in some respects Lyneice's childhood had been more normal and fulfilling than her own:

> She's 18, and I mean, she goes skating, she be with her boyfriend. Goes to parties. I ain't never been to my prom. Lyneice, at least been to one of her proms. I ain't never been to a prom. Never, ever, ever, you know, and I kind of misses that. You know what, I don't even remember why I left school. I know why. I was having problems at home. My education, I can always go back and get that but … I didn't really want to wait this old, you know what I mean, to … when I'm damn near 50 years old, not look like a fool, you know,

going back to school but little things like that. Like they have the
OWA [Occupational Work Adjustment program] and stuff like that.
I ain't ever been through that. I mean it's a lot of things I … I wish
that I … that's why I cry all the time. I always cry. I always cry when
they get their diplomas and stuff. I be boohooing and Brandon be
like "what is wrong with you?"

Although these sections of the narrative combine to create the impres-
sion that Lyneice is doing well, the other narratives (particularly
those of Lyneice's siblings) contain references to Lyneice's involvement in behaviors that would appear to qualify as delinquent acts.
For example, Maurice says that part of the motivation for his striving
in school is that he doesn't want to end up "like his sisters." Although
Rickelle, the sister who has spent time in Scioto Village, represents
the most striking example of involvement in delinquent behavior
within the family, Maurice provides a different lens on Lyneice and
her life circumstances:

You know, I hate to say it but I really don't like her because of the
things she did to me … I feel like, I'm your own brother. I ain't
never did nothing wrong to you. She did things to me that was just
uncalled for. Like, you know, she done stole from me … . Bringing
her little boyfriends all up in the house, you know. Just … just all
types of stuff. Stealing from Target, you know. You know, like I
said, it's people's own decisions. If you want to go out there acting
silly and be stupid and always want to party and all … Don't get me
wrong, I'm the type of party person too, but I know how to control
myself and all that stuff, and stuff like that.

MAURICE

Maurice's life history and comments his siblings and mother made
about him in their interviews reveal a similarly complex portrait. Like
Lyneice, Maurice described problems and resentments during the
time he lived with his aunt.

Just a lot of things. It was like the way she use to treat me and stuff
and things she wouldn't let me do. Yeah, she wouldn't let me do no
sports or nothing. Because I wouldn't have no transportation home
and she … and she wouldn't even come and get me or nothing …
I wanted to play football; that's what I wanted to do when I was my

freshman year. And, you know, she wouldn't let me do anything, basically, I wanted. Anything I had to do, I had to sneak and do it.

I mean, the only time I went to CSI ... went to CSI one time, when I was with my auntie because I got fed up with her stuff and the stuff she was doing, hitting me with pool table sticks and stuff and, you know, I wasn't with that. So I fought back and I went to jail that one time but [other than that]; I ain't never messed with no police.

Maurice's story did not begin with problems he encountered at his aunt's house, however. Note the dizzying array of household and school moves he references in the excerpt below:

I went to Jefferson my whole freshman year. My sophomore year I went to Jefferson first semester; second semester I went to Fairview. And then, for like the first quarter of my junior year, I went to Central, and then I went back to Jefferson my whole junior year. Because I was moving with my mom. See, when I was going to Fairview, I was staying with my auntie, and I moved with my mom my sophomore year right when I switch. So I was still staying on the west side and going to Fairview. And then the next year, my junior year, I started off at Central because she ... she's in Central's district. So I went there first quarter, and then I moved with my dad that same year, and then I went back to Jefferson the rest of my junior year.

Maurice is now living with his father, who bought a house in yet another school system:

Walnut Grove. I really don't like it that much. I don't know. It ain't my type of school. I think it's because there aren't a lot of blacks there. I just feel like I don't fit in, I just ... the people there are nice but I just feel like I don't fit in. [Q: And why couldn't you just stay at Jefferson?] Because ... I got suspended so many times my freshman year. When you're a senior you can go to any school you want to, but my freshman year I got suspended thirty times so they wouldn't let me back, so I got to finish my senior year off at Walnut Grove. I was just a clown. Talking back to my teachers and stuff. It's ... clowning in class, being disrespectful, things like that. Yeah, just like if you come down there a lot of times like they'd ... Its called demerits; they all add up.

In spite of these problems at school and his short stay in the juvenile-detention facility, Maurice does not consider himself a delinquent. He describes his "cognitive transformation," and the positive influence of his father as factors associated with his turn-around:

> It was my ... after my ... my sophomore year, I started turning off (no longer getting in trouble). I was being cool and I stayed out of trouble, and ever since my sophomore year I ain't never been suspended from school. I mean, because ... I mean because people looked at that stuff, I mean. I want to graduate from school and stuff; that's why I put my head on straight. I don't want to continue to be in trouble. It was, basically is, my decision. My dad, you know, he leaded me in the right direction and lead me to do the right stuff. I mean, because he just moved back from ... he moved back from Tennessee. He just told me to do the right stuff, and I wanted to be like my dad and stuff like that.

Although Maurice thus seems determined to stay on track by both avoiding fights and doing well at school, and his father is a positive influence, his life now is not problem free. For example, he is currently experiencing stresses chiefly related to his father's financial difficulties:

> After I switched to Walnut Grove, then I stopped [playing football], because I wanted to work instead of playing football because I, my dad, he got problems with money ... with his money problem, you know, and I had to get my own money, so I decided to work, to keep working. I had to quit playing football so I could work on Fridays ... Yeah, I help him a lot. Uh ... I give him just about anything he asks for but ... I let him know there are things I want, too, and that's why we bumping heads now... .

RICKELLE

Although Maurice spent time in the local juvenile detention center and was suspended numerous times, and Lyneice had apparently stolen things (she was, according to Maurice, a partier and had cut Rickelle's face with a knife the previous summer), it is Rickelle who is the agreed-upon delinquent in the family. The interviewer asks her about her experience at Scioto Village:

> [Q: And tell me, uh ... your mom was in Scioto when she was a kid. Uh ... tell me what ... what's it like to have been exactly where your mom was?] Nobody [there] that, it's like one person that would remember my mom. They was like new staff, [but] it's like she go to Lincoln when it first came [the school for behavioral problems that Rickelle now also attends]. It's like, dang, I'm following in my

mom's footsteps. It's the same stuff that my mom do. So I'm trying to get myself right back on the right track for do something good with myself instead of before I turn out, like, my mom's lifestyle because I ain't trying to follow her lifestyle. [Q: Because?] Because I don't think she's leads a very good life. [Q: How so?] Because. I don't know. She don't got none of her kids and, I don't know. I couldn't explain it. She always ... she's sick. She has ... she made some bad choices and, like, I made some bad choices.

Even though their interviews took place at different times and locations, Daniella develops an argument similar to Rickelle's, emphasizing the degree to which problem behaviors are a result of individual decision making. In addition, however, she highlighted that Rickelle's living arrangements had been less than ideal, and even considered Rickelle's peers a negative influence. Note that there is only an oblique reference to her own role in relation to her daughter's current problems:

Because she made her own decisions, I mean, I make my own decisions, too. Everybody makes their own decisions. [But also involved are] foster homes and, you know, hanging with the wrong people and stuff like that. And don't got nobody to, you know, to head her to the right direction. I mean, I'm not saying that my mom dumb, but she ain't going to listen to my mom. She going to try and run over her. Because she know that my mom can't really do nothing.

While the objective data corroborate the views of other family members that Rickelle is a problem youth, Rickelle's narrative nevertheless reveals what appears to be a sincere desire to distance herself from this pattern of behavior. Thus, we observed positives in this problem narrative, even as we saw troubling undercurrents that surfaced in the narrative accounts of her more successful siblings Maurice and Lyneice:

R: I go to two schools, Lincoln and Harrison.
Q: Why do you go to two schools?
R: Because Lincoln is the behavior [problem] school and you've got to go through those programs to get back into regular school. I've been there ever since I was in the seventh grade. It's like you got to get on a certain level to get out of there with good behavior. All you have to do is show good behavior and stuff and you get, we call it mainstream. Like, then you get half days. If you continue to do good, then they'll put you, uh ... all day at your regular school.

Q: What kind of behavior problems do they say you have or do you think you have?

R: That I did have? I, uh … I had anger problems and getting along with others. In, like, how to deal with other people and how to control your anger and stuff. They just teach you.

Q: What's the most helpful thing they've taught you?

R: They've taught me a lot of things, but the most helpful thing they've taught me is how to control my anger. Like, when I'm really mad, you know, and about to go off and stuff all the time and stuff they just take … they taught me a lot of things. And they just told me, it's not worth it to have trouble and stuff and trying to get the last word in the argument. Leave it go for another time.

I've done matured, I think … All this running around, beating up people and just wild like I was … that life I was living before I got in. That stuff is behind me. I don't look at that stuff. I'm above all of that. I'm more mature than that. I'm … I'm a lady. That don't look cute. I don't look cute, like, running around the town all the time.

Q: And who taught you that it didn't look cute?

R: Me. I just decided to teach it to myself that I … and I'm not getting younger. I've got a whole another year and I'll be eighteen, and that will be it … I like Harrison. I'm embarrassed to say I go to Lincoln.

Q: Why's that?

R: That's the behavior school. I ain't got no behavior problems.

Q: You don't think you have a behavior problem?

R: Because I'm more mature than that. I don't … I don't act up in school. I don't know [why]. I just started when I was in boot camp. I got a boyfriend, and I know he ain't going to want a girl that keep running in and out of jail. How can you experience things like having a job? Going to college? Being like that. You can't do all that stuff.

Rickelle, like Maurice, emphasizes that she simply decided to change her behavior, but Maurice, in addition to this "cognitive shift," simultaneously acknowledges his father's good influence. Similarly, Rickelle's boyfriend, Jeff, appears to provide beneficial social reinforcement for staying on this new prosocial path. While romantic partners have often been described as a major impetus for girls' and women's involvement in drug abuse and crime, the quotes below underscore that the nature of this influence is not universally negative or deviance amplifying:

He help me with school. He help me find a job. He's keeping me out
of trouble and stuff. Like, when I be thinking about doing something that I know that it's going to get me in trouble he ... he tries
to help me see, uh... the consequences that going to help ... that's
going to get me in trouble. [Q: Like, give me a "for instance." What
does he help you with?] Like, I wanted to leave, and my first time I
was going to be running away and, uh ... he just talked me into staying. And when I was skipping school, he use to always go up to the
school and try to see was I there or come to my house and tell my
foster mom I wasn't at school. Yeah, he's trying to see me do something with my life instead of just go run in the streets and not doing
nothing with my life.

In spite of these positive developments, Rickelle suggests that her
life can be very stressful. And, other than Jeff, the lessons learned
in anger-management class, and the desire to change, she feels that
she has limited support for coping with negative events and emotions
that may continue to occur. She mentions a fight with her older sister
during the summer that required her to get seven stitches, getting
in an argument with her foster mom, and arguments between her
mother and brothers:

It's nerve wracking and just my family I would ... I would like for
everybody to quit arguing and just get together. My mom to quit
arguing with my brothers and my brothers to quit arguing with her.

Rickelle's foster mother agrees that Rickelle is making some progress,
but effectively describes some of the continuing stresses for foster
care youth and those attempting to care for them:

[Q: What's, uh ... what are some of the difficult things of being a
parent ... a foster parent.] The most difficult thing being a foster
parent is that the foster kids kind of blame you. Sometimes I think
they be mad at you for something you didn't do or something you
didn't cause, and it's just that way. Even though you might be nice
to them, they still take it out on you because they don't want to be
with you. They want to be with their mom and they just can't, so
then they take it on you. [Q: Has she ever pressed you about wanting to go and stay [with her mother] permanently?] Oh, she let me
know it everyday she don't want to be here. She want to be with her
mom. And I think it don't have nothing to do with me; it's just that
she just want to be with her mom, which is natural. [Q: Do you think
she's going to avoid contact with the law or do you think that she'll
be back in trouble again?] I know she tries hard not to go back that

way and she don't want to go back that way, but if she's out there and she don't learn how to, uh … control her anger. She let her anger go too far and it could easily put her back, yeah, because that's what anger do.

The three younger children we interviewed are all still in school, and their levels of self-reported delinquency are low; yet some parts of their narratives suggest that they, too, have already experienced their share of difficulties. For example, Brandon, 14, indicates that he is no longer delinquent in any way. He notes that he would like to play football professionally, "instead of being out in the streets," but then indicates that he and his sister are "always getting into fights." His narrative is hopeful, but he also describes problems on the way to his current perspective:

BRANDON

People say I'm kind of like … me and my sister Rickelle, we some-times have the same problems. We usually always getting into fights. People just, they be just push me too far … They always, like, talk-ing about me, really. They like start cracking on me and stuff. Like, mostly the clothes I wear and stuff. So, and then … really, I usually start fighting 'cause they always be thinking I'm scared of them. And then they keep saying I'm scared of them, and then I end up fighting them. And then just be, like, anybody that want to fight me, I don't care. We just gonna fight then, get it over with. They want to fight me, they can go ahead and do it. Do what we got to do. I haven't got in that many fights in a while. I got kicked out of a couple of schools. Because of, um … my behavior. I just be being disrup-tive, like, yelling and, you know, just not following directions. I don't know. That's how I was back then. I don't know. I just changed. Just a change. I was young then. I don't even know what I was doing. I was at elementary. I'm at high school now. I mean, I've got good grades in school now.

CURTIS AND ASHLEY

Brandon is close in age to his brother Curtis, but Curtis has more difficulty expressing himself and, according to the interviewer, seemed to be developmentally delayed. Although in his open-ended narrative he tended to give one-word answers, Curtis said he has been in trouble before, "getting arrested and stuff. Fighting and stuff." He notes that he is also currently in a group dealing with anger problems.

Finally, the youngest of the six children we interviewed, Ashley, is a self-described (fifth grade) bully. Initially, she stresses that the school she attends is very tough, but then gives the interviewer an account of her own violent and disruptive behavior:

> Mostly everybody in my class is bad except for one person. Our school is crazy … One boy was carrying a gun. A lot of people have guns. We always having police up there. Mr. Simons, he always arrests somebody. And you, we can't even slap nobody. We can't just poke them. We can't pinch them or nothing, or we get charged …
>
> Sometimes me and my friend be messing with people on the bus, on the Metro. Like, bothering them. Just messing with them and stuff. Like, starting stuff with them. We just play around. Like, we like talk and make fun. Then we just start messing with everybody on the bus except for the grown-ups and the older kids. I can't control what's inside of my mouth. I just got to say it. No, like, if I'm playing around I get really hyped up and stuff, and then I just start saying things. Like, talking about them and stuff. Like, tell them how ugly they is (laughing).

Even though she is only in fifth grade, Ashley understands that she has built up a reputation at the school:

> It all started when I beat up this girl named Taylor at lunch. But it wasn't my fault. She started it. I was walking and I accidentally bumped into her. Right? So, she pushed me. Then I pushed her back. Then I swung her by her hair. And then I punched her. And then they said that I started it first and all that. And first they said that I was suspended for a month 'cause I did the worst damage that ever been in the school. Like … Like I made her face, like … Oh, her lip was. [Q: You gave her a fat lip is what you're saying? How'd that make you feel?] Fine. At least it ain't me that got a fat lip. She don't go to this school. Nobody didn't like her in the class. Sometimes just people be like, "You're the girl that beat up Taylor?" And I, like, "Yes."

Compared with some other OLS respondents, Daniella's criminal history is quite unremarkable. For example, Denise, another respondent, had already been in prison for two different manslaughter convictions by the time of the initial adult interview, and Shana was a homeless prostitute who lived in her car. Yet, while Daniella's crimes were not of a spectacular sort, the effects of Daniella's continued drug involvement and violent behavior were nevertheless keenly felt by all her children; intergenerational effects are apparent in the numerous references to the school suspensions, fights, 'getting off parole,' alternative schools, and anger-management courses that have been integral to the life histories of these young respondents.

PARENTAL PREDICTORS OF VARIATIONS IN CHILD OUTCOMES

As we have analyzed the data in connection with this study of child behavior and well-being, the difficulties experienced by the entire set of young OLS respondents are, in our view, the most compelling findings we uncovered. Nevertheless, we also systematically explored variations within the sample based on gender of the original OLS parent, living arrangements, and other parental factors (e.g., incarceration experience, drug involvement).

We begin by considering basic features of the children's family situations as potential sources of systematic variation in child well-being. We first examine the child's risk of experiencing traditional forms of victimization based on whether the child was born to OLS female or male respondents and current living arrangements (whether or not the child lives with the core respondent). As shown in Table 5, regardless of whether or not children born to female offenders were living with their biological mothers, these children report high rates of any abuse (one or more instances of physical or sexual abuse). Over 75 percent of the children living with their mothers reported abuse, and about 72 percent of children who did not live with their biological mothers reported abuse. It is likely that the children living in alternate placements may have experienced abuse or neglect that was directly associated with the decision to place the children in a different household, but it is interesting to note that these figures are similar across living circumstances.

Examining the reports of children of male offenders shows that 80.77 percent of those who did not reside with their biological fathers reported any abuse, whereas only 30 percent of the children currently

TABLE 5: *Percent of OLS Child Respondents' Experience of Any Physical or Sexual Abuse by Gender of Parent and Living Arrangements*

Children of Female Core Respondent (N = 112)		Children of Male Core Respondent (N = 46)	
Mother has custody	Mother does not have custody	Father has custody	Father does not have custody
75.34%	71.79%	30%***	80.77%
N = 73	N = 39	N = 20	N = 26

Note: ***p < 0.001 Chi-square indicates significant difference between fathers with custody and all other subgroups

living with their biological father (the core respondent in the original survey) reported abuse. It is important again to highlight that we were unable to locate many of the children of male offenders. Nevertheless, among those we could locate, living with the biological father seemed to offer a level of protection or, at least, to diminish the overall likelihood of experiencing one or more forms of victimization. Across the study as a whole, the rates of victimization appear to be significantly higher than those observed in population samples. For example, Costello et al. (2002) found a low overall prevalence of sexual abuse in a population sample of youth (3.4% of girls; 1.8% of boys) . In a nationally representative sample of 2000 children aged 10 to 16, Boney-McCoy and Finkelhor (1995) found that 11 percent reported experiencing attempted or completed sexual abuse at some time during their lives, and Kilpatrick, Saunders, and Resnick (1998) found that 8 percent of ninth grade students in the Midwest reported sexual assault and 17 percent physical assault. Although variations in the instruments used and in locales influence these prevalence estimates, limiting the bases for comparison, it seems conservative to conclude that the rates of victimization reported by OLS children are very high. These statistics, with the exception of the lower rates for respondents living with biological fathers, again support a focus on central tendencies within the data (i.e., high vulnerability for a majority of children).

In our initial examination of the child's problem behavior, we first examined the parent's self-reported criminal involvement as a predictor of the child's delinquency. Whether we relied on self-report scores as reported in 1995 or 2003 or the persister/desister classification described in Chapter Four, the parent's level of involvement was not a significant predictor of variations in the child's self-reported delinquency score. One explanation for this, again, relates to the central tendencies within this sample (i.e., a high percentage of parents report current criminal involvement or experienced significant involvement at various points in their life histories). However, variations in criminal-involvement scores were related to the odds of experiencing child abuse, and also emerged as a significant predictor of a more general index of violent victimization (e.g., whether the child respondent had ever been jumped, shot at, stabbed).

Based on our analyses of both the adult and child narratives, we reasoned that it might be important to consider effects of the parent's drug involvement on children's behavior problems and that the drug involvement of romantic partners/spouses should also be taken into account. Thus, we subsequently estimated models that included a composite index of parent and spouse/partner's drug problems as well as measures derived from control theory (attachment to parents and supervision/monitoring) and a variable focused on whether or not the parent had ever been incarcerated as an adult. These models controlled for child age, gender, and race/ethnicity. The results, as reported in Table 6, do indicate that even within this relatively disadvantaged sample, this composite index of parents' drug involvement is associated with the child respondent's self-reported delinquency. Lower levels of attachment to parents is also significant, but monitoring is not a significant predictor. Similarly, parental incarceration is not significant in these models. The results shown in Table 6 are reminiscent of prior research on offender populations indicating that drug use is associated with the length of criminal careers or returns to illegal activities (Uggen & Thompson, 2003); these findings show that the drug involvement of parents and their partners also figures into cross-generational continuities. This is also amply demonstrated by the qualitative data reviewed in this chapter and is explored in more detail in Chapter Six.

TABLE 6: *OLS Youths' Self-Reported Delinquency: The Influence of Parental Substance Abuse, Attachment, Monitoring, and Incarceration (n = 158)*

	Zero-Order		Parents' Drug Use and Demographics		Attachment and Monitoring		Incarceration (Full Model)	
	b	SE	b	SE	b	SE	b	SE
Parental substance abuse problems (2003)	.172**	.062	.161*	.063	.148*	.062	.145*	.063
Male	.542**	.200	.547**	.197	.542**	.195	.536**	.195
Age	.038	.030	.032	.030	-.002	.033	-.003	.033
Minority	.225	.203	.076	.200	.019	.197	.014	.198
Parental attachment	-.360**	.124			-.340**	.122	-.335**	.123
Parental monitoring	-.164*	.077			-.111	.084	-.118	.085
Parent incarceration	.219	.232					.131	.223
R-square			.10		.15		.16	

Notes: *p < .05; **p < .01; ***p < .001
Beta estimates are unstandardized
Some variables are logged due to overdispersion in the raw distributions

CHAPTER SIX

The Intergenerational Transmission Process

I don't talk to her. Because I'm mad at her. She smokes something she shouldn't be smoking. I call her a crackhead all the time. I should be living with her right now if she wasn't smoking crack.

The preceding chapters document that the original OLS respondents had numerous problems as adolescents, and our follow-ups indicate that many continued to have legal difficulties well into their adult years. Chapter Five details results indicating that many of their children had been victimized and also exhibited problem behaviors, with the severity of delinquency, drug/alcohol use, and violence often exceeding the types and levels we observe in a random sample of adolescents. We found a significant effect of the parents' substance-abuse problems on the variations in the children's self-reported delinquency, providing a general indication of intergenerational transmission processes at work within these families. In this chapter we describe in more detail the family and individual-level processes that we believe are important to a comprehensive understanding of the mechanisms underlying these cross-generational continuities, and also provide a framework for understanding variability in child outcomes. We outline a symbolic interactionist approach that can be conceptualized as a revised social learning perspective on intergenerational transmission, and illustrate with material drawn from the narratives of the children and adults who have participated in the OLS study.

Recall that much of the research we reviewed in Chapter Two emphasized the importance of poor/inept parenting as a key mediating mechanism linking the parent's behavior and the child's risk for problem involvement. The multivariate results did not indicate a strong relationship between monitoring and delinquency involve-ment within the sample itself, but this may have been due to limita-tions of the monitoring scale that we relied upon. Nevertheless, the differences in parenting practices we presented in Chapter Four do provide support for the general emphasis on effective monitoring, supervision, and involvement (in the aggregate, OLS parents scored lower on certain types of monitoring and, especially, involvement relative to TARS parents, and the rates of loss of custody provide an objective indicator of the presence of inadequate or neglectful par-enting within some families).

As we argued in Chapter Two, however, a focus on inadequate super-vision and other aspects of parenting "style" does not present a com-plete picture of life within the families we studied or of the dynamics involved in intergenerational transmission. As we suggested at the outset, social learning mechanisms are less well researched but are, we believe, also key to an understanding of both what occurs within these families and of the social forces that present a formidable cul-tural press toward intergenerational continuity. Hirschi and other scholars developed an essential critique of this idea, however, sug-gesting that social-learning mechanisms are of little import. As stated in the literature review, the premise underlying Hirschi's (1969) argument is that parents, even if deviant, tend to shield their deviant activities from their children and thus can hardly be considered as models for the negative behaviors the children may eventually take up. And, while recognizing that some social learning mechanisms may be involved, West and Farrington (1977) also concluded that this may not be commonplace because (i) most parents express a strong desire for their children to avoid the circumstances that have caused so many difficulties within their own lives and (ii) research indicates that parents and children are rarely arrested as co-defendants.

We explore the issues raised by scholars such as Hirschi, high-lighting the need to develop a conceptualization of the content of life within such families that goes beyond family structure or par-enting styles. A critique of social control theory in general and this perspective on intergenerational transmission in particular is that it emphasizes only what is absent or lacking within families, rather than giving attention to specific attitudes and behavior patterns to which the child is exposed. The emotional lives of children and families are also potentially important and are integral to our perspective on intergenerational transmission.

A NEO-MEADIAN PERSPECTIVE ON INTERGENERATIONAL TRANSMISSION

A straightforward way to understand intergenerational transmission from a social-learning perspective centers on the idea of modeling or imitation. Being in close proximity to an individual who is engaged in criminal acts increases the likelihood that the child will *observe* and later enact a similar behavioral repertoire. However, differential association theory and the symbolic interactionist perspective more often emphasize language and communication as central to human behavior and the learning process. It is thus useful to distinguish the notion of "simple" imitation from *interactions* between parent and the child that foster delinquency. An obvious complication from the outset is that, as Farrington and other scholars have pointed out, most parents do not set out to teach their children delinquent acts. Indeed, most parents express a strong interest in ensuring that their child avoids contacts with the police and other difficulties that they know firsthand are associated with serious negative consequences. It is more intuitive to conjure up an image of same-aged peers "coaching" a teen about various forms of delinquency, actually encouraging this behavior, and participating jointly in such activities. These considerations may underlie the continuing focus on peers rather than parents in studies of social-learning effects. However, in our view, the parents' overarching hopes for the child must be distinguished from life's smaller everyday lessons, which can communicate in multiple ways "definitions favorable or unfavorable to the violation of law."

We use the term "direct transmission" to refer to those instances that most clearly evoke the central thrust of differential association theory, that is, when the parent directly communicates attitudes and other information that supports criminal behavior by the child. It is useful to deconstruct the generic label "crime" in order to highlight that the behaviors that fall under this umbrella often involve hurting others, getting high, or taking things. These domains of criminal activity obviously vary in the degree to which parents will play an active role in teaching attitudes and techniques related to such behaviors. For example, while the parent may communicate attitudes that support violence under specific conditions (don't let people push you around, the best defense is a good offense) and even teach the child to fight, instruction in the finer points of robbery is undoubtedly less common.

Opportunities for indirect transmission are potentially more commonplace. For example, upon entering the house the parent may say to the child or partner that it's been a terrible day and immediately open a 40-ounce can of beer. Such a learning opportunity can well be labeled as modeling. However, more complex language and thought processes are involved; here, the parent communicates to the child that stress and a particular coping strategy are intimately related. This is different from the less common instance in which the parent gives the child a beer, an action that uncritically endorses and hence directly "transmits" the behavior. Indirect transmissions are more commonplace, not only because most parents know that it is inappropriate to give alcohol/drugs to a child and therefore refrain from doing so, but also because they have so many more chances to communicate attitudes as they reflect on their own actions and those of others in their social networks.

It is also important to highlight that whether we focus on direct or indirect communications, the parent imparts knowledge/attitudes about an array of noncrime behaviors, which together with those that are crime-related, constitute the full roster of definitions involved in intergenerational transmission. The idea that there are definitions favorable or unfavorable to the violation of law has tended to place most of the conceptual attention on the parent's attitude toward illegal acts; yet the parent communicates about a range of noncrime areas of life that also figure into the child's orientation and behavioral repertoire. For example, the parent may hope the child does well in school, but communicate a dislike of teachers and principals or show little interest in the particulars of their son or daughter's science project. Prior research has established significant connections between poor academic performance and risk for delinquency involvement, and these attitudes and actions thus may be considered as potentially delinquency amplifying.

Akers' (1977) version of social learning updates this theory with attention to principles of reinforcement. Thus, whether focusing on criminal or noncriminal actions, indirect or direct transmission processes, it is also important to consider the parent's reinforcement of the child's actions. The child who skips school learns much from the parent's response. If the parent does not react strongly and negatively, it can be considered a case of inept parenting from a control theory perspective. However, more nuanced understandings are often being transmitted. For example, the child may learn that it is acceptable to skip school to care for younger siblings when the parent wishes to visit some friends or relatives in another city, at any time, or under no circumstances.

AGENCY

Learning theories have been criticized for their conception of individuals as passive actors whose behavior is based on a particular mix of definitions they have received from others. Although our overarching objective is to highlight the key role of these network others (particularly parents), symbolic interaction theorists also emphasize that humans are thinking animals, continually exercising selectivity of attention (i.e., paying more attention to some objects and individuals than others) and foresight (planning future actions and then aligning behavior with these ideas):

> The human animal is an attentive animal, and his attention may be given to stimuli that are relatively faint. One can pick out sounds at a distance ... Not only do we open the door to certain stimuli and close it to others, but our attention is an organizing process... . Our attention enables us to organize the field in which we are going to act. Here we have the organism as acting and determining its environment. It is not simply a set of passive senses played upon by the stimuli that come from without. The organism goes out and determines what it is going to respond to and organizes that world. (Mead, 1964: 138–139)

The symbolic interactionist theory thus emphasizes that individuals are constantly sifting and weighing the information that is received and have agency with respect to actions that may relate to others' definitions. As Emirbayer and Goodwin (1994) and other theorists have pointed out, the individual typically has a strong role in choosing the very networks that will "nevertheless influence them in turn." This uniquely human capacity is often overlooked by researchers with interests in social-network effects (where the conceptual attention is placed on the social network → actor connection) but is consistent with a symbolic interactionist social-psychological perspective.

This point has been made often with reference to peer and romantic partner effects: since at least in part individuals choose friends and partners whose behaviors/attitudes are "in sync" with their own, this makes it difficult to conclude that social networks have exerted a powerful influence on the actor's behavior. Indeed, this has been the basis for the control theorists' argument that the specific attitudes and behaviors of others in the network do not increase the likelihood of a given individual's involvement in delinquent behavior. It is, in Hirschi's (1969) view, simply a "birds of a feather" phenomenon, rather than a case of "real" influence. However, children do not choose their parents, making the nuclear family particularly interesting for studying network effects (because the observed similarity between parent and child cannot be due to selection or the tendency for actors to affiliate with others because of their own behavioral tendencies).

Stipulating that family membership is not a choice behavior and is potentially constraining in ways that other associations are not, it can be said that the symbolic interactionist focus on agency nevertheless has utility: even in this ascribed context, the actor may align with some family members more than others or even reach out to those outside the immediate family circle. The symbolic interactionist perspective, particularly Mead's version, makes clear that an individual is more than a bundle of received definitions, as one might surmise based on a literal interpretation of Sutherland's excess-of-definitions hypothesis.

IDENTITY

In addition to focusing attention on agency, the symbolic interactionist perspective highlights the importance of identity concerns. In childhood and adolescence, individuals begin to develop identities that reflect but also provide a higher level of organization and coherence to the attitudes or "definitions" gleaned from the various social experiences to which they have been exposed. This includes the possibility of being similar to or different from one's parents. As children mature, then, identity itself becomes consequential as a cognitive filter when individuals think about the past, act in the present, and construct future plans. The basic ideas within differential association theory fit well here; Sutherland stressed that associations do not all carry the same weight – the idea of the "intensity" of the source clearly encompasses the notion that the child may identify strongly with the parent, giving the definitions parents provide potentially more impact (Mead's idea of "selectivity of attention"). Not as well specified by Sutherland but explicit in symbolic interactionist theorizing is the notion that the child can identify with other models (see, e.g., Glaser, 1956) or engage in behaviors designed to present a strong contrast to those of their parents. Even where identification is strong, the child's identity is never an exact replica of the parents'. The life-course perspective supports this idea, highlighting that each generation comes of age during a unique period in history with its own opportunities and constraints (Elder, 1996). Further, the child inhabits family, neighborhood, and peer contexts that may be influenced by the parents' circumstances but are nevertheless distinct from those that influenced the parents' identity development. And, as development proceeds unabated throughout the life course, this also continually offers up new situations and social experiences that may serve as catalysts for redirecting one's initial start within the family.

A focus on identity adds to the idea that the definitions parents provide are influential, and it provides a conceptual focus for later discussions of intergenerational differences (Chapter Seven) as well as for the continuities we emphasize in this chapter. We focus primarily on identity's content areas rather than on global evaluative dimensions such as self-esteem or self-efficacy. Matsueda (1992) showed, for example, that adolescents who believed that others saw them as delinquents or troublemakers were more likely to evidence higher levels of delinquency, even after the initial levels of delinquency had been taken into account. And, as we argued with respect to the concept of definitions, self-views encompass many more domains (e.g., the academic self, the sexual self, the emotional self) that also influence the likelihood of delinquency involvement.

The children of criminal parents do not begin development as a blank slate, however; they face an identity "legacy" in the form of judgments or attributions from the wider community, parents' concerns that the child will face similar problems, and so on. Following the symbolic interactionist's view of identity, these "reflected appraisals" of others have consequences or weight in terms of the child's developing views of self. Each individual nevertheless represents a unique combination of personal assets and social experiences that can permit them to develop in a more favorable (from a crime standpoint) direction. Once identity begins to take shape, these self-views can either encourage behaviors that solidify continuity (choosing delinquent friends) or differences from one's parents (joining a church youth group). In turn, others may react to the child's identity-relevant actions by labeling the individual as "just like her mother" or "the only one in the family who is trying to do something with her life." Within the logic of the symbolic interactionist tradition, these attributions are not mere labels for an emerging behavioral repertoire; they link to differential treatment by others and a more fully formed self that acts as a guide to the child's own behavioral choices.

BRINGING EMOTIONS IN

To summarize, the symbolic interactionist perspective adds to traditional treatments of mechanisms involved in intergenerational transmission by explicitly foregrounding interaction and communication as central to the learning process. This differs not only from the focus on inept parenting found in much of the literature, but also from some treatments of learning that conceptualize the child's behavior as a simple matter of imitation. In addition, however, the symbolic interactionist perspective fosters a more conditional, less passive view of mechanisms by focusing attention on the actor's agency in selectively filtering information and acting in accord with emerging identities that serve as guides to action.

A potential limitation of the resulting depiction is that the various components of the traditional symbolic interactionist perspective (the focus on definitions or 'meanings,' identity, agency) and treatments of the learning process itself have been conceptualized as largely cognitive in nature. This contrasts with the recent flurry of scholarly interest in emotions as a legitimate object of inquiry and basis for human action (Collins, 2004; Massey, 2002; Pacherie, 2002; Turner, 2000). And, as we have recently argued, emotions have an especially intuitive connection to behaviors such as violence and drug abuse (Giordano, Schroeder, & Cernkovich, 2007). It is somewhat ironic, then, that with some notable exceptions (Agnew, 1992; Braithwaite, 1989), theorists have not focused heavily on ways in which emotions are linked to criminal behaviors. We recently developed a life-course perspective on emotion-crime linkages that has implications for understanding intergenerational mechanisms as well. Recently, symbolic interactionist scholars have developed what has been called a neo-Meadian approach to emotional processes that we believe has much potential in this regard. Mead, consistent with many other theorists, concentrated heavily on cognitive processes; yet Engdahl and other scholars have highlighted that Mead's basic insights can usefully be extended to cover the emotional realms of experience (Engdahl, 2004).

EMOTIONS ARE SOCIAL

Early on Schott (1979) pointed out that some emotions are highly social in nature. For example, it is difficult to understand the experience of shame and embarrassment outside some attention (imagined, actual) to the reactions of others. More recently, Engdahl (2004) expanded on this idea, arguing that virtually all emotional experience is fundamentally social in origin. Engdahl stressed that we learn what emotions are through our interactions with others, and the actual experience of emotions is situated within particular social experiences (*what are you lookin' at?*). This is consistent with Mead's emphasis on the social origins of meanings, but here the referent is the character of feelings and emotions. Finally (and more conventionally argued), the ways in which emotions are displayed, regulated, or managed is also socially constructed (Collins, 2004; Massey, 2002; Pacherie, 2002; Turner, 2000). Hochschild, for example, famously developed the notion that organizational imperatives influence the display of emotions (stewardesses must remain cool, calm, and collected no matter what), and gender socialization can also deeply affect how a given emotional experience, such as anger, is "handled" (e.g., the idea that while both women and men experience anger, women are more likely to become depressed, whereas men may externalize anger by lashing out at others).

EMOTIONS HAVE RATIONAL OR "COGNITIVE" UNDERPINNINGS

Another recent trend in theorizing moves away from the idea that emotions and cognitions are fundamentally in opposition and instead forge a variety of interconnections. As Seeburger argued,

> Cognition is obviously not the same thing as emotion. Judging or believing is not identical to the feeling of being moved ... Nevertheless, cognition and emotion are not two substantially separable things either. Instead wherever judgment is, there is feeling also; and whoever is moved, believes. (Seeburger, 1992: 52)

This idea has been explored both philosophically and in laboratory experiments demonstrating that emotions influence cognitive tasks and that cognitive processes affect emotional experience. Mead (1934) argued that both emotions and cognitions arise from "problematic situations," that is, instances in which the actor cannot move ahead on the basis of past habits. By virtue of the new situation, actions are blocked. In contrast, habitual actions are so routine that no special thought is required, no heightened emotions are occasioned. This provides a Meadian rationale for considering emotions and cognitions as interconnected phenomena (since both unfold – or not – under similar circumstances).[1] This is an important point in relation to the present focus on intergenerational transmission because we argue not only that emotions are involved in what

---

[1] We are grateful to Ross Matsueda for suggesting this connection.

goes on within the family, but also that the feelings engendered have a rational or cognitive basis. This contrasts with the idea that emotions and the way they are managed derive solely from personality traits/characteristics or that they represent a kind of external force that "takes over" (Katz, 1999), rendering useless one's thoughts or rational faculties (i.e., as reflected in popular phrases such as "flying off at the handle," "losing it," and the like).

EMOTIONS ARE AN IMPORTANT PART
OF THE SELF'S CONTENT

While Matsueda and other researchers have focused on self-views that foster delinquency (notably the delinquent or troublemaker identity), the individual develops a range of other identity-content areas that round out one's views of self and act as a filter for decision making (Giordano, Schroeder, & Cernkovich, 2007). For example, the maturing adolescent who is highly confident/engaged within the heterosexual world may be more likely to attend parties and be drawn to other social settings that increase exposure to alcohol and drugs (Seffrin et al., 2009). Engdahl (2004) argues that the individual's developing emotional repertoire forms another important aspect of the individual's self-concept.

Drawing on Engdahl's theoretical framework, we recently documented that anger identity and depression were systematically related to adult criminal involvement, even after taking into account lifestyle factors such as marriage, employment and the prosocial/antisocial characteristics of the individual's network affiliations (Giordano et al., 2007). To illustrate several aspects of our argument, we quote from a short excerpt from one of the life-history narratives we elicited from a 30-year-old respondent, Pamela. In connection with her 1995 interview this respondent, who is a "parent" for the purposes of the current study, stated quite simply: "I've got an anger-control problem. I think men are dogs – I'm real violent toward men." In her longer narrative she describes a number of negative social experiences that appear to have fostered this world view (buttressing the notion that emotions are social). Even in this short excerpt Pamela outlines specific cognitions that link to her angry feelings ("I think

men are dogs"). Subsequently she forges the connection to behavioral consequences ("I'm real violent toward men"). Finally, and consistent with a neo-Meadian viewpoint, the narrative makes clear that
her angry emotions are a recognizable, and apparently stable, feature of her identity. This illustrates Mead's (1934) contention that the
individual has a unique capacity for thought, including the ability to
view the self reflectively, or as an object. Thus, cognitive and identity
processes are involved, but here they reference the emotional realms
of experience.

EMOTIONS ARE IMPORTANT TO AN
UNDERSTANDING OF THE INTERGENERATIONAL
TRANSMISSION PROCESS

If we accept the idea that parents strongly influence a range of other
attitudes and behaviors (with reference to school, dating, crime, and
so on), it is intuitive that they also play an important role in the child's
experience of emotion. As part of the defining or meaning-making
process, the parents will also, through recurrent interactions, specify
links to cognitive processes (e.g., this is a situation that righteously
evokes an angry response). And the parent can also be expected to
provide a particular template of an emotional self that the children
may draw on as they begin to craft their own. Again, it is useful to
focus on specific content areas.

Agnew (1992) made an important contribution to the criminological literature by highlighting the role of anger in the genesis of delinquent behavior. He argued that while a number of different sources
may produce a condition of strain, delinquent involvement is more
likely when negative life circumstances have elicited an angry reaction. Agnew has suggested that crime is conditional on anger, but
in most of his theorizing has not fully elucidated the origins of the
angry response. In a recent analysis, however, Agnew et al. (2002)
link the tendency toward anger to the individual's personality traits,
a viewpoint that contrasts with our neo-Meadian perspective. The
symbolic interactionist perspective suggests that both definitions of
specific situations as aversive and angry reactions themselves emerge
through a process of role taking with others. While some definitions

undoubtedly derive from social interactions outside the family, as we noted previously, "the family is likely to be an important site for the initial development of an angry repertoire and over time an angry self" (Giordano et al., 2007: 1610). This also differs from self-control theory, which treats emotion-management either as a matter of effective, timely supervision or as a lifelong characteristic of the individual (see also Horney's [2006] critique). Thus, while a number of theoretical perspectives may theorize a link between anger and criminal behavior, the symbolic interactionist perspective ascribes a social origin to these aspects of the self and emphasizes their potential malleability in response to subsequent social experiences.

Katz' (1988) phenomenological perspective adds to this depiction of emotion-crime linkages in his focus on the positive, sensate qualities of crime. The idea that crime is associated with various thrills is consistent with many delinquents' accounts of the excitement they associated with their criminal exploits (Shaw, 1930). These positive emotions are undoubtedly part of the process of constructing a self-concept that provides a sense of worth, albeit of a particularistic sort (e.g., as someone who is always up for a party or a fight). In this regard, parents play a potentially important role in their direct and indirect transmission of what counts as thrilling or exciting. Drug use, a critically important dimension of offending in the contemporary era, provides a ready example of a behavior that is intimately connected with both negative (anger, depression) and positive (search for excitement, inexpensive vacation) emotions.[2]

The above account suggests that children may be more likely to use drugs or become violent not just because their parents do, but

---

[2] Katz' basic insight is important and fully consistent with theories of symbolic interaction; individuals engage in behaviors that have meaning for them, and thus even negative outcomes such as delinquency or violence are viewed by the actors involved as providing some benefits, perks, or identity-enhancing elements. Thus, for example, Erica explained her initial thoughts about using drugs, "Well I'm not having that much fun not doing things that I'm not supposed to be or whatever. Maybe I'll just try the drug..." But while more positive emotions are implicated in the respondents' behaviors, our analysis focuses heavily on negative emotions such as anger as central to the intergenerational transmission process. This emphasis is consistent with the central place of these emotions within the children's own narratives, and more general theorizing about anger as a key factor associated with delinquent outcomes (Agnew, 1992).

because the latter have taught them even more fundamental lessons about emotions and their management. This draws on basic principles of learning and social influence but applies them to the emotional realm. Yet in order to complete this discussion of intergenerational mechanisms, it is important to focus even more directly on the particulars of being the child of a criminal or drug-using parent. First, the parent's behavior and lifestyle often exposes the child to an array of victimization experiences that evoke strong emotional responses and heighten the child's risk for delinquency involvement (e.g., a mother's romantic ties with antisocial partner may link to a daughter's risk for sexual abuse). Importantly, the more "basic" emotional and behavioral lessons sketched above are in place to guide the child's choices with respect to possible coping strategies.

Second, many aspects of the parents' actions are likely to be experienced as demoralizing and alienating from the child's point of view. Thus, it is also potentially very useful to conceptualize parental criminality itself as a victimization experience that engenders strong emotional reactions and potentially adds to the child's risk. As described in connection with the literature review, children may be depressed, upset, or angry that they are unable to be with their parents when the latter are incarcerated. However, as the quote that introduced this book suggests (and we will demonstrate in more detail below), fear, anger, and other emotions may accompany family life with an actively criminal parent, one who is very much present within the home. Here children's other social experiences and associated cognitive processes come into play, as they, for example, contrast their own experiences with those of friends whose parents lead more predictable, conventional lives. In short, the child's emotional reactions do have a rational basis (*why do I have to be the one whose mom is on crack? why can't we keep this apartment?*). Yet because these emotions unfold within a context that has already provided more "basic" lessons (e.g., supporting antisocial behavior, demonstrating nonproductive emotion-coping strategies), a delinquent adaptation to these experiences becomes all the more likely (*To hell with it, I'm outta here*). The parent's lack of effective supervision (Thornberry et al., 2003) in combination with the learning mechanisms we have outlined (cognitive, behavioral, emotional) together form a formidable social basis for expecting intergenerational continuities in the expression of delinquent behavior.

In the rest of this chapter we use quotes and examples from the life-history narratives to illustrate key aspects of our theoretical perspective. In Chapter Seven we rely on this same symbolic interactionist perspective to explore variability in child outcomes within the sample and, in particular, to examine the lives of young people who have marked out a path that is distinct from that of their parents.

PARENTS, EVEN IF DEVIANT, RARELY REVEAL THIS TO THEIR CHILDREN

The strategy of interviewing the children rather than relying solely on parental reports is particularly informative, because the children's narratives often indicate a keen awareness of the parent's involvement in antisocial behaviors. This contradicts one of Hirschi's (1969) key assumptions: parents, even if deviant, generally hide such activities from their children. Some examples of this awareness are evident in sections of the life-history narratives quoted in earlier chapters. For example, recall the quote from Bill, who described the experience of seeing his father being taken away in a squad car as he alighted from the school bus. Although it is possible that very young children do not have a completely accurate understanding of the nature of their parents' problems, the pre-adolescent and adolescent respondents we interviewed indicated familiarity with the reasons a parent has been or was currently incarcerated or why they had been removed from their parent's custody:

> [Dad was in prison because] he almost killed a lady. Attacked her. It was his girlfriend and he attacked her. On purpose, because he was drunk. [Tim]

> [Q: Why are you living with your grandma?] ... because my mom has an addiction. [Megan]

> Well my mom she didn't have no electric or nothing. My mom hasn't been paying bills. [Q: What do you think your mom has been doing?] Drinking. A lot. [Caroline]

> [Shanisse got harassed at school by other kids] "Your mom's a murderer."

I've been in fifteen [foster homes]. As far as we know, it's because of drugs. [Samuel]

[Delia recently started writing letters to her incarcerated father]. I wanted to get to know him. But he was always locked up. For stealing and doing drugs and stuff. I just started writing letters.

Dad deserves to be in prison: he deserved it because he used to sell crack to get his money. I felt bad because he was changing other people's lives by selling the crack to them. It was hard because he was, he was messing other peoples lives up with it. [Kimberly]

[Alisa has been living with her grandmother since age two]. 'Cause my momma had a problem with drugs. I just feel like ... I mean everybody in this world has their purpose whether it's to be an addict or to take care of their business and to be successful or whatever. And I just feel like that she personally feels that's her purpose.

These children's comments reference parental absence due to incarceration, but also a general knowledge about why they were not living with one or both of their biological parents. The narratives make apparent that this awareness is not based only on second hand accounts (e.g., where a grandmother explained the reasons for a parent's absence), but often derives from closer observation of at least some aspects of the parent's behavior. This underscores our view that the life-course perspective on children's experiences adds to the traditional focus on the parent's incarceration as the singularly stressful life event with which the children must cope. The incident narrated below is of interest because on one level it reveals that James' father has neglected his son, but it also indicates that James is well aware of his father's involvement in deviant activities. This is the case, even though James' contact with his father has been sporadic at best:

Q: Now how old were you, you said the only time you ever went to visit your dad?

R: I was like thirteen or twelve. He put me and my little cousin in the closet while [he] went out and shot up or deal or whatever he had to do. He didn't come back until the next day. My aunt actually came into the house and we were banging on the door and my little cousin Drew; he younger than me, he's eighteen now, so if I was twelve then he was ten. No bathroom, no food, no nothing. Over night, I don't know how many hours, I don't even know how we got in there. But my aunt opened it up and we were in there.

Q: And he locked you in the closet to go do drugs?

R: I guess. That's probably what it was, I mean, he stole cars and he did drugs.

While James was unclear about the particulars that sent his father out of the apartment, he was aware that his father stole cars, did drugs, and was possibly dealing them as well. Although clearly James was not properly supervised, this incident highlights that the concept of "lack of supervision" is insufficient to capture the totality of the child's experience, including traumatic feelings of victimization and knowledge about and exposure to his father's antisocial lifestyle. Other OLS children's life-history narratives included even more direct evidence that they routinely observed their parent's actions. It is possible that parents who steal may be able to effectively hide this behavior from their children, but drug and alcohol abuse (the centerpiece of many of the OLS respondents' continued adult difficulties) are more difficult to hide from family members, including the children we interviewed:

> I kind of get mad at her because whenever she comes over or we talk she's usually drunk and she'll start to cry. [Amanda]

> [Q: How old were you when you first remember your mom on drugs?] Seven. She'd just stay out all night. This has been going on since I was seven years old, and I'm twenty one. [Kiersten]

> She drinks and she gets nasty when she drinks and abusive and things like that. [Kelli]

> I was using marijuana. She [mom] was using crack. [Ivonne]

> I really don't want to picture my mama using because she had this side where she would look, like, so good when she was clean. But then when she got, when she used, she just looked so tore up. [Josie]

> I think she drinks way too much and she's too old and she needs to slow down. [Shannon]

> These last couple months we haven't got our allowance. Because she spent 'em. At first, I thought she gave it all to my older brother [but realized his mother spent it on drugs]. [Kassandra]

> [Rob's sister Natalia concurs that her mother's drug use draws money away from needed resources:] Because we don't ever have enough money to buy stuff that we need. I don't know … I guess my mom being all messed up and stuff like that.

> She doesn't drink that much, but when she does it is bad. I see them stumbling around and all passing out everywhere, can't walk, can't

hardly talk, and I just [look] at them disgusted, like, why would you want to be like that? [Steven]

'Cause when she drinks she gets mean and she's disgusting when she drinks. Just the way she acts. She acts immature. She's embarrassing. [Josh]

In addition to frequent references to drinking and drug use, the children's narratives accord well with other findings reported in Chapter Four, indicating higher than average rates of intimate-partner violence. Such violence is another readily observable behavior that most often occurs within the home:

[[Stepdad] threw her [mom] down the stairs and broke her foot. He sliced her hand open with a knife.] So I started staying around when they were together, and a couple of times I've thrown him down the stairs for just raising his hand to my mom. [Joseph]

Joseph's story also highlights that children who witness violent acts or other criminal behaviors in the family home are not always silent observers. In many instances, the children become a part of the immediate situation and may actively intervene. Robert, quoted below, takes it upon himself to find out more about his father's antisocial activities, snooping that was intended to influence what was taking place within the family. He told the interviewer that he searched for his father's crack, as a way of forcing him to be more honest about what he was doing. Robert's father's interview corroborates Robert's suspicion that his father was a dealer, a reality that influenced not only Robert's life, but also his older sister, Elayne's:

Yeah, I've seen it, pulled it out. Because I had snuck in the kitchen. Because ... so I could spot him. So he would quit lying about it. This is how my sister would get it. She would sell, her boyfriend would sell stuff to get crack. You could smell it on her. It just smells weird. It just smells like smoke. Like you can just tell because when you smoke it your eyes get red and her eyes were always red.

Another window on the child's awareness is provided by details from the parents' narratives. Although some respondents do emphasize ways in which they have attempted to shield their children from their drug use or other activities, these efforts are not always successful. Other parents describe children's questioning or their concerns about what the parents have been doing. This, too, indicates a level of awareness on the children's part since it is only possible to be concerned regarding a behavior about which one has some knowledge. Anthony, interviewed in prison, describes conversations he remembers having with his 15-year-old daughter Morgan: "'Dad, have you been smoking pot?' 'No.' Yeah, of course I've been smoking pot. I'll just sit there and tell her a little lie. She knows I'm doing it."

In the Carter family, sisters Anna and Meg vary in their reactions to their father's drinking. Their mother describes the contrast:

> Anna say, "Dad, you don't need to be drinking." And Meg would say, "Shut up, Anna, Dad's over 21. He's not bothering nobody. This is his house, and if he wants to drink he's gonna drink." [In her interview, however, Meg indicates that she does worry about her father's drinking, and the discussion reflects that she has intimate knowledge of his behavior patterns. For example, she is quite aware of how much is "too much" liquor for her father.] So a six pack to you is not a lot of beer? No, he can't, like, get really drunk off a six pack, but if he drinks a twelve pack then he can.

Another indication that the child is often keenly aware of the parent's problems is provided in accounts of instances when the child specifically asks the parent to stop the behavior or engages in behavior designed to make them stop. We saw this in connection with attempts to interrupt violent incidents, but it also occurs when parents have alcohol and drug problems. Anna appears headed in this direction in her statement, "you don't need to be drinking," but other children have made more impassioned pleas for their parents to stop their involvement in these activities. For example, Rodney, also currently in prison, was asked by the interviewer whether his son Gerry had ever asked him to stop: "Yeah, and I stopped it. When I was dealing. I just recently started back dealing [though]." Paul sounds a similar theme:

> He says, well, I'll stop and then he stops, but then, you know, it's like he goes back to it sometimes. I remind him that he promised he would stop and then, like, he's like "I know." And then he stops for about four days.
>
> [Francine has taken an even more active role:] She just can't stop. But I'm making her stop. 'Cause every time she picks up a beer I'll

just throw it outside. The weed issue is [different, more difficult] …
my mom will not like it if I throw it out.

Jason also describes a well-developed (if largely ineffectual) set of
strategies he uses to deal with his mother's drug use:

> I've seen her pass out and stuff fall out of her pockets and hands
> and stuff. I flush it down the toilet and I throw it as far as I can.
> And, like, I spit on it and, like, I do every … like if it's weed or stuff,
> I flush it down the toilet. If its pills and stuff I put them in hot water
> … then I put it down the sink 'cause I know she'll drink it. I've put
> her pills down and alcohol … she's so messed up on drugs … she'd
> take … she does the stuff like take pipes off the sink and start suck-
> ing on them to get drugs and stuff out of them … that's why I always
> flush them down the toilet … 'cause if I put them down the sink she
> always, like, she thinks about getting in the pipes, and she always
> looks for wrenches and stuff.

The quotes above provide ample evidence that children are aware of
their parent's violence or drug involvement. It is likely that the parent would have preferred that the children had not observed those
behaviors; yet the all-encompassing nature of drug addiction and the
typical context of intimate-partner violence inevitably increase the
likelihood that the child will be exposed to these behaviors.

DIRECT TRANSMISSION

The life-history narratives also reveal situations and contexts in which
a more direct transmission occurs, however. As described above,
direct transmission occurs when parent-child interactions provide
the child with both definitions favorable to the violation of law and
"techniques" for engaging in these behaviors:

> My dad. He taught me to fight like a guy, fight like he does. I don't
> smack, pinch or pull hair. I fist fight. No, he's taught me how to fight
> my whole life. [Amanda]

> Um, how old were you when you first started drinking? 13. I drank
> with my dad, but I never smoked pot with him. [Drew]

Viv, an adult respondent who had some legal problems, told the interviewer that her husband was even more heavily involved in criminal
activities:

My husband, at times, he would make my son ... he'd throw a pound at a time and he would go to Texas, he'd get pounds. And a lot of times he would make my son clean them. And clean the bits out, extend them and everything ... I don't want my son doing that. You know 10, 11, 12 years, no. He knows, he's seen the smoke, but you don't sit there and teaching him how to clean it and bag it ... He's teaching him, teaching him the business. You know, he was going to start teaching him the business ... His job was selling pot ... He didn't sell a little. I mean, he sold pounds.

These incidents are face valid as instances of direct transmission, but because of the parent's hierarchical relationship to the child and the child's young age, it seems appropriate to label them as victimization experiences as well as learning experiences. Amanda, for example, seemed rather proud that her father taught her to fight "like a guy," but the content of many other narratives indicate a significant amount of ambivalence or outright resentment about what has occurred. Becky, as the more prosocial parent in the family, telegraphs her negative reactions to Mark involving her son in his drug-dealing activities. Although she indicates that her son has seen the smoke (a passive kind of transmission, more akin to the modeling notion), she finds it unacceptable to involve Daniel in illegal activities so directly. These dynamics lack the straightforward qualities implied by Sutherland's descriptions of the learning process because they carry this affective, evaluative component. In our view, this is a potentially important feature of intergenerational transmission processes, particularly where criminal behavior is the referent.

Emotional reactions are often even more central to the children's accounts. Jason, who had tried to control his mother's drug use by throwing the drugs away, expressed negative emotions not only about her drug use but also about her tendency to steal:

Little things will come up missing. Sometimes like $5 or maybe like $2 will come up missing. Like if I have a bunch of quarters, like, half of them will come up missing and stuff ... I've got Game Boy pieces like my Game Boy Advance I bought. I bought all those games and they just keep coming up missing. And she, like, comes up and she just can't, like, walk and stuff. It's just so weird ... like, why would she steal off me? If she was gonna steal off anybody why would she steal off me? Why her own son? Like why her own mom? Why her own cousin? Why wouldn't she steal off a stranger? You don't steal off somebody ... you don't steal off somebody you know. [Jason]

Again, the above quote makes it clear that Jason is aware of his mother's illegal behaviors, but it also conveys that the meaning of her actions is more complex than simply providing the required "excess of definitions." This respondent knows that the lost quarters or Game Boy pieces are "little things," but his mother's actions have meaning for Jason as a violation of the interpersonal trust that he believes should characterize family relationships.

In other instances, the child discusses the parent's criminal behavior in a more straightforward, less obviously emotional manner. Nevertheless, the narratives often include a strong evaluative component:

[Q: Have you guys (mom) ever done drugs together?] Oh yeah. We've done 'shrooms together. One night we tripped on 'shrooms so bad she ... she started screaming and crying because [she thought] there was a troll underneath the porch. Never, never was ... We ... we've done acid together. We use to go out ... she would take me to the bar. I'd get drunk with her, and I thought it was okay because she was my mom. You know other people with their moms would never do that ... Smoked pot with mom, and then I got close to my mom and she just kept giving it to me. I was like "cool shit." Started selling it. Making money. Started smoking it and I was like "whatever, she didn't care."... and when I first had the abortion, the first thing she gave me was a fat bud. She was like "smoke this you'll feel better." And that's all I did. That's what I started doing, is laying on the couch everyday after school just smoking weed and I didn't care. That's how we bonded. Drugs ... [we had this big party and] she actually was the only adult here. Partied with a bunch of 18-, 21-year-old kids. Got drunk with us and supplied us with hundred a quarter. Like some really good ass weed. Supplied us all with hundred a quarter. [Kaley]

Kaley thus indicated that she had learned about the details of smoking marijuana, taking mushrooms and dropping acid from her mother. Along with exposure to drugs and learning to view them as a method for coping with stressful life events (as when her mother provided her with marijuana after her abortion), Kaley's narrative reflects that while she "thought it was okay 'cause she was my mom," she simultaneously recognized that "other people with their moms would never do that." These expressions of ambivalence suggest that Kaley's exposure to these learning opportunities has not unfolded in affectively neutral ways. While we do not have direct knowledge of all of Kaley's other social contacts, it is likely that she contrasts her own situation with that of neighbors, friends' parents, classmates' parents, or even media depictions of families. Recall that Jason pointed out that he had considered giving the interviewer "Brady Bunch"– type answers, but decided it was more important to be honest about his family situation. This reveals that he finds many aspects of family life to be far different than the idealistic portraits he has seen on television programs.

A LIFE-COURSE PERSPECTIVE ON PARENTAL INCARCERATION EFFECTS

As we have stated in previous chapters, in our view the focus on parents' periods of incarceration does not provide a comprehensive portrait of children's experiences, which often include extended exposure to definitions favorable to the violation of law and the complex emotions these family dynamics engender. Again, it is important to highlight that the parents' periods of incarceration are not universally viewed as the most stressful circumstances with which these children must cope. Jason feels that he must constantly be "on guard" about Stacy's tendency to erupt violently, especially when she is high on drugs or alcohol. In the past, Stacy has not typically been aggressive toward Jason; nevertheless he feels that he must always be prepared, lest her angry moods result in harm to other family members. Recall our quote from Jason in Chapter One:

> Every time she comes she always gets mad at my grandma ... like she choked my grandma before she went to jail. I'm always, like, I don't want to hit her and stuff but like I have a hammer and I sit it right next to my bed 'cause I know if my mom comes in messed up on drugs she gets real violent ... and she always comes up and rips the phone jack out of the wall and stuff ... I just have to be ready ...

When asked what was the best thing that had happened in the last six months, Jason replied, "my mom came home from prison." When asked what was the most stressful thing that had happened in the last six months, he replied, "my mom came home from prison." Thus, it is important to consider the parent's incarceration as multifaceted in meaning and effects and to juxtapose these periods against the (typically) more extended periods when the parent is not in jail or prison. Even though he loves his mother, Jason concludes:

> The best place for her is in jail. And that's the only place I know where she ... I know where she is, I know she ain't trading, stealing off of ... even drug dealers call the police on my mom 'cause she tries to kill them. And they put their drugs ... they hide in alleys and stuff.

His aunt corroborates this notion:

> When she is locked up, they do communicate. She does send him letters and she draws him pictures and she does things like, uh ... crafts and things and sends them to him. They actually communicate more when she's locked up than when she's out ... I, I feel that it does more damage to him by seeing her in this shape every four or five days than it did him going seven or eight months without seeing her. It's not a healthy situation.

Dawn indicated that, like Jason she actually communicated more with her mother when she was in prison than when she was actively using drugs and out on the street:

> As soon as she get in jail she want to write and call and say all this stuff. But when she out she don't do nothing. She just hit the street. Like she can't get no drugs in there and stuff and at least she has some kind of friends and she get contact, like letters, phones, anyway. Even though I don't see her I get to talk to her and stuff.

Other children noted that they were happy that as a result of incarceration or jail time, the parent might now get help for their problems:

> But then when she got her act together and she went to jail and stuff I was glad because she wasn't on the streets and stuff. She wouldn't have the drugs. And she'd be off the streets, get herself back together. [Amy]

These complex emotions undoubtedly increase children's feelings of stress, including guilt about feeling personally safer or less apprehensive about what is happening to their parent. It is important to highlight that while many young people grow up in impoverished, dangerous neighborhoods, there are added stressors for those whose parents contribute to its categorization as a high-crime neighborhood:

> I got to worry about, uh ... seeing in the newspaper that they found a dead body and stuff. Like, when there were shootings down, two miles from our house, I thought it was my mom [was] one of them three people. I thought, "it's my mom. I know it is." 'Cause I know my mom's like that ... I seen my mom the next day. I cried all night thinking it was my mom and stuff. It's just, it's heartbreaking really ... [Jason]

That Jason finds the entire situation "heartbreaking" is central to our argument that emotional reactions to these circumstances are critical to an understanding of both contemporaneous and later child effects. Some youths within the sample, however, attempted to develop a narrative stressing that their parents' criminality or associations did not affect them. Nevertheless, close readings of their accounts and those of other family members do not accord with this conclusion. The adult respondents themselves often highlighted emotional costs and the possibility of negative effects on child well-being. Consider Mitchell's discussion of his parents' problems:

> I don't care really. To tell you the truth. They can go in and out all they want to. When they first went in, it didn't bother me at all 'cause I was too little to be [bothered] then. I didn't know she was on drugs. It didn't even bother me. I told you, it doesn't bother me. I don't even think about it. It's her life, she can do what she wants to. I don't really care.

Although this quote suggests a letting go or disinterest, Mitchell's comments appear to be a case of "protesting too much." Indeed, later in the narrative he contradicts the above statements, telling the interviewer: "I just want them to get cleaned up. Not have no drugs. Don't take drugs." Spencer's mother's interview is even more revealing about Spencer's negative emotional reactions to his parents' difficulties:

> It's, it's like he can't believe in me anymore ... he won't believe me if, like, I'm telling him I'm going to stop and I'm going to do better, and then I fall right back into the same pattern ... I don't know, like he's going to have some problems because he don't talk about nothing. He holds everything in and that's going to mess with him as he

grow up. Because he just needs to talk about things that bother him. If you hold things in that bother that, that causes something ... to go wrong with you ... [Lynda]

MAKING THE EMOTIONS-DELINQUENCY CONNECTION

It is not uncommon for youths themselves to make the connections between the anger and other negative emotions they experienced regarding their family circumstances and their own acting-out behaviors:

> Oh yeah, something that you didn't know is that when I was 15 years, well 14 years old, I was the baddest kid at Elmhurst middle school ... I used to get suspended almost every time I went to school ... Because I really didn't care ... I used to beat up kids. My father wasn't there ... I was just mad, man, I didn't really care.

Recall that we had initially interviewed the core respondents as young adults in 1995 (average age 29), when most of their children were still quite young. At that time, a number of respondents expressed concerns about their children's well-being, but many narratives also reflected optimism about their child's engaging personality or academic prospects (e.g., he could be president ...). Because many of their problem activities continued and children inevitably became more aware of them, it is also more difficult for parents to continue to assert that their actions have not or will not in the future have negative effects:

> She has seen a lot of stuff [for] her age as far as she being 12. She, she done seen a lot. What she has seen is part of my fault, too, because I could've put her in a better atmosphere or whatever, better position and stuff, but I didn't. I tried to but it didn't do no good. [Anita]

> I have belittled Tianna ... Just by using around her, using around her friends, being high. I embarrassed her ... Probably at home, in front of her friends, at school. I've did so much, you know, to that poor child. And I think the anger inside of her from me using and preaching, you know ... it's hard for your mom to be sitting here preaching education, no drugs, and stuff when your mom's completely the opposite. I was a drug addict; I didn't have no education. And I felt like Tianna ... sometimes she saw how ... "What right do

you have to say anything Mom? What right do you have to say anything to me?"

She (Lauren) wrote me a letter. She said, "Mom, you're a liar. You
told me and my brother you were never going back to prison. You be
lying," and just letters like that … she had got in trouble in school
and I was on the telephone … my daughter's school. She gets in
trouble all the time … She's a fighter. [Q: Get suspended a lot?]
Yeah … Detention, oh bad grades … Bad grades. It's like she's really
angry. She's taking it out on other people. [Stephanie]

As prior research has shown, the parents who have participated in the
OLS vary significantly in their own efforts to effect substantial change
(Giordano, Cernkovich, & Rudolph, 2002). However, as the following
quote demonstrates, even where parents have stopped abusing drugs/
alcohol or other types of illegal involvement, children may experience
stress from assuming at least some of the responsibility of attempting
to ensure that their parents do not return to their former lifestyles:

I could not stand my mom when she was drinking. She just …
'cause when she drinks she gets mean and she's disgusting when she
drinks. Just the way she acts. She acts immature. She's embarrassing. Her quitting drinking was good for everybody. I mean we talk
about everything now, and I'm really proud of her for sticking with
it. If she is stressed I try to calm her down so she doesn't want to go
out and buy a case of beer or something. [Carla]

The above quotes document a number of stressors that are unique to
having criminal parents: an increased likelihood that their children
will learn criminal definitions but also experience ambiguity/regret
about the process through which this learning has occurred, and
feeling that they must protect, police, and otherwise "parent" their
own parents. An angry reaction to these circumstances increases the
likelihood of expressing oneself through violence or other forms of
acting out. Drug and alcohol use and violence have been amply demonstrated as coping mechanisms within the family context, making
such adaptations to these family stressors significantly more likely.

IDENTITY FORMATION AS A "LOADED" PROCESS

A related set of dynamics specific to families characterized by parental deviance involves the concerns of children, other family members

and parents about their children's future prospects. As previously noted, undoubtedly all family interactions eventually include the observation that specific children are like or unlike their parents. However, based on the extensive references to these issues in the OLS narratives, our view is that identity issues are more dominant preoccupations for young people who are trying to avoid a replay of their parents' problem lifestyles. These concerns, too, carry a strong emotional valence, and are a specific-to-this-population source of stress.

> I heard that I'm just like her when she was younger because I do a lot of the same things, well that's a long story. [Janine]

> 'Cause we're so much alike. I don't know. 'Cause I'm exactly how she was when she was my age. Partying and … Neither one of us liked to go to school. I don't know. We're just exactly the same. Just the way we act. [LaVonda]

The concerns parents and other family members voice may further reinforce and amplify the children's feelings of stress and uncertainty:

> [I'm afraid] She's going to end up like me. I don't want her to live that life. I don't want her to be out there making money or using drugs or running in and out of jail. [Her dad says], "This little girl is just like you." She looks like me and everything. [Julie]

> Like, I'm never around, and it's kind of scary because Nathan has been caught with a gun, too … everybody says "He's just like you, he looks just like you."… Like I said before, I just stress to him that this is not what he wants to do. [Neal]

> It bothers me 'cause I know she doesn't listen to me, and I'm afraid she's gonna end up like her dad because he has a lot of the same traits that she carries. And I'm just afraid that she'll end up like him. … just the desire to have things and want it quick. Like that's why he sold crack, to get money quick and uh … he didn't have to work for it. And, uh … I'm just afraid that since she carries a lot of his traits like his attitude and his, uh … she's just like him inside and out, that she'll end up in prison. [Kristine]

WIDENING THE NET OF DELINQUENT ASSOCIATIONS

Although our emphasis is upon the influence of the biological parents, as previously noted, the child necessarily has social experiences

that extend beyond the parent-child bond. While this has the potential to provide alternative models and prosocial influences, as we discuss in Chapter Seven, often the parent's criminal lifestyle increases
the likelihood of contact with other antisocial individuals. Thus, the
parent's romantic partners, friends, and associates represent additional sources of criminal learning and opportunity, heightening the
risk for traditional forms of victimization. For example, Allie told the
interviewer that she had served time for petty theft:

> My dad's wife went into a store and started stealing stuff. And then
> they seen her, and when we was with her we got charged with acces-
> sory to petty theft because we was there and we were with her.

Brittani discusses her relationship with her father's girlfriend and
conveys the girlfriend's negative influence on her behavior. Note also
Brittani's apparent emotional reaction to this kind of influence:

> [Q: Who turned you on to crack?] My dad's girlfriend. No, I wanted
> to try it and see what it looked like, see how it made people feel. And
> I done it and then it's like I couldn't stop doing it. 'Cause she should
> have been there ... 'cause that was more like my stepmom, but they
> weren't married. She should have told me, "No, you're gonna end up
> like this." She never told me anything like that. She just put it in the
> pipe and said, "Here you go." That's all she did. [Brittani]

Whether told with a lot of emotion or in a more straightforward
manner, then, the children's narratives reflect that these events are
commonplace, everyday occurrences, but ones that they understand
on a different level are not appropriate or "right." Outside observers
might well focus on the child's young age and vulnerability, but it is
interesting that these young narrators are aware that adults should
be sources of support and modeling (*she should have told me no ...*),
not people who will supply them with crack or provide marijuana for
their parties.

PARENTAL CRIMINALITY AS AN INFLUENCE ON THE ADOLESCENTS' FRIENDS AND ROMANTIC PARTNERS

The parent has an impact on the associations that connect directly
to the parent's lifestyle, but as much of the prior research has shown,

extrafamilial relationships also become increasingly important during the adolescent period (Call & Mortimer, 2001). Since our focus here is on the dynamics of intergenerational transmission, a complete exploration of these relationships is beyond the scope of this analysis. However, we wish to highlight that the choices these young people make about their romantic and peer relations are also likely to be deeply influenced by the parent's life circumstances and behaviors. As discussed in earlier chapters, the parent's disadvantaged socioeconomic position clearly influences the neighborhood and school context the child inhabits, making it more likely that youths will come into contact with other young people at risk for problem behavior.

Aside from neighborhood propinquity as a source of friendship, however, there is also the "birds of a feather hypothesis," popularized by Hirschi (1969), which holds that delinquent youths are attracted to other delinquent youths because they share a similar behavioral profile. The selection of friends is thus seen as deriving from the delinquent youth's affinity for hell-raising, violence, and other delinquent activities. However, it is also useful to view these affiliation processes through a "family-of-origin" lens. Some youths within the sample described relationships that were meaningful to them, not because their friends were committed to delinquent activities, but because their friends had experienced family problems that were similar or analogous to theirs. Debi, for example, told the interviewer that she and her close friend shared problems and supported one another: "I'll call her and be like 'I talked to my mama today and she was acting like she didn't care' or something, uh ... she'll get to telling me how her mama didn't care and be like 'well just don't pay no attention to her. You got to let that go.'" Rob also has a very close friend whose mother's difficulties were a source of bonding and mutual solace:

> My friend Patrick, his mom had a drug problem. That's why he lives with his uncle and aunt ... We understand each other. Like, I've met his mom before and then like ... my mom and her friend dropped me off at Patrick's house before. And I felt weird 'cause she was all messed up on drugs ... And she like, she like about fell out of the door. He was like ... he was like, "don't feel bad 'cause my mom does it too sometimes"... like I feel bad for him, but I know he feels bad for me too.

ROMANTIC RELATIONSHIP EXPERIENCES

Most of the research on social-network influences during adolescence and emerging adulthood has focused on same-gender peers, but recent research has also documented that dating and romantic relationships can also be influential as a source of positive or negative influence. For example, using data from the national Longitudinal Survey of Adolescent Health and relying on direct measures of friends' and romantic partners' delinquency (self-reports elicited from the friends and partners themselves), Haynie et al. (2005) documented that the delinquency of the romantic partner was a significant predictor of the adolescent's self-reported involvement, even after controlling for the delinquent behavior of friends and other traditional correlates. More recently, Lonardo et al. (2009) found a similar association, relying on the TARS data set and including parental deviance as an additional control. Taylor et al. (2008) also found a longitudinal association between a partner's alcohol use and subsequent levels of drinking, controlling for respondents' initial level of drinking behavior. The OLS narratives also suggest that romantic partners can increase the child's problem-behavior involvement, but illustrate ways in which their family circumstances influence these partner choices and dynamics.

First, like friends, romantic partners are likely to be drawn from one's immediate "web" of affiliations, a reality that for these families heightens risk for affiliating with antisocial individuals. In more affluent neighborhoods, youths frequently socialize with same-aged others who attend their school, potentially further reinforcing prosocial lines of action, including academic achievement. In contrast, the school is less likely to be the social center for OLS youths, who on average, are involved in few extracurricular activities, are frequently absent, and are not typically high achievers, as we detailed in Chapter Five. The pattern of dating that often results is dramatically illustrated by Corrin, who is currently romantically involved with a man who is an acquaintance of her father and twenty years her senior. Both her father and Stanley are currently incarcerated, but Corrin has hopes that Stanley will cease his involvement in the drug scene when he is released from prison. Stanley's progress in desisting is a critical consideration because Corrin herself recently decided to pursue a life that did not include substance use and threw away her drug paraphernalia (crack pipes).

The narratives of parents and children are replete with references not only to the intergenerational transmission of crime, but also to involvement with unfortunate (from a crime standpoint) romantic partners. This form of social reproduction, then, adds to the child's overall level of risk. Dawn describes her daughter's tendency to develop relationships with undesirable boyfriends:

> I knew that she had self-image problems, and I knew that she would be, uh … fair game for … for idiots that came along with a story.

Danielle provides another example of unfortunate intergenerational continuities in partner choices. Danielle became pregnant by a boy named Rudy who had wanted her to get pregnant. Danielle did not want to get pregnant, but she did not use birth control. Danielle's mother does not mince words when she gives the interviewer her opinion of this boyfriend Rudy: "He's just a no good drug dealing, useless piece of shit."

Danika, quoted below, provides another example of the complexities of these influence processes. Earlier in her narrative she indicated that she was initially introduced to drugs by her mother and her friends. Her father is also currently in prison, suggesting multiple antisocial parental influences. Nevertheless, her boyfriend, Andy, clearly was not was not a prosocial addition to her network of intimate associations, making her eventual attempt to move away from drugs potentially a much more difficult process:

> … When I met Andy, yeah. And he was still doing coke, and me and him did coke maybe three times together in the first week that I met him and then, uh … I told him, I said, listen I said, "we can't do this no more." I said, "if you want to be with me you've got to stop." … "It's because." I said "it would be a start of a relationship … not that you would end up hitting me but the fact that we would end up having problems. Drugs destroy relationships and everything bad. And it's destroying me and it's destroying you and we need to grow up and fucking quit doing it."

In addition to the obvious risk that is presented by associating with a partner who uses drugs or engages in other illegal acts, in many cases, as Danika hints, the intergenerational transmission of relationship dynamics potentially contributes further to the child's risk portfolio. Just as marital violence was a common theme in the narratives of the adult respondents, children's narratives also frequently referenced violent behavior within the confines of their dating relationships. Prior research has shown that witnessing family and other intimate violence increases the child's own risk, and studies have shown further that the adolescent's own delinquency/violence is an important intervening factor. Thus, many of these young people have developed a more general violent repertoire that plays out within the heterosexual realm as well as on the school yard. Affiliation with antisocial partners then compounds the level of risk:

> ... it ended up with us in my living room and I was beating him in the face with my fist. And he didn't hit me, he just held me down and tried to stop it but I was upset. [Sarah]

> Yeah, we've been in physical fights before but nothing too serious. [Stacy]

> He's (Nick, ex-boyfriend), like, "where have you been?" I said, "it's none of your business." I said, "you're sleeping here on the floor because you can't stay at your dad's house. Yeah, we're not together but we are, you know what I'm saying? We're ... we're working on it. That doesn't mean, you know, that I can't go and do what I want." And he started pulling out the knife and he threw the dresser drawer at me and I ran out the door finally. and I had cuts all over me up and down. He punched me in my face. He was strangling me. Like, straight in my forehead punching me, and all my neighbors heard it. All of them heard it, but nobody came to my door. This was the second time in one month for sure that they have heard me screaming and yelling and him beating the shit out of me, and nobody did anything. And I ran down the door and ran to Ben's house, and Ben already had his door open. And he slammed the door shut and then Nick was pounding on the door. "Let her out. Let her out." And Ben went out there and was like, "you need to leave." Ben's gay, you know, he's more like, you know, just a sweetheart. And Nick beat the shit out of him. Left him laying on the deck, and Lindsay, the lady downstairs, she's a manly man, you know what I'm saying? She was ... but she's very feminine in her ways. She's got her own little thing going on. She's really cool. She, uh ... pulled Nick down the stairs and beat the shit out of him and when the cops showed up she was still beating the shit out of him, and he started running and, uh ...

she knocked out one of his teeth. She broke her fingers punching him because she knew what he did to me. She knew. [Kaley]

Kaley's account of her relationship with her former boyfriend Nick indicates the experience of a serious level of intimate-partner violence. Social learning theories have often focused on the relatively straightforward dynamic encompassed by the idea of "modeling," which hypothesizes that direct observation of a behavior heightens the individual's own likelihood of enacting a similar behavior when placed in an analogous situation. A symbolic interactionist approach to these intergenerational transmission processes adds to our understanding of the mechanisms involved, however, in that this perspective emphasizes the importance of interaction and communication in the process of constructing meanings. Meanings, in turn, serve as guides to action. Thus, the parent may engage the child in discussions (or the child may overhear discussions with others) that impart negative views about the opposite sex or emphasize the importance of defending oneself if attacked by others, including romantic partners. Such attitudes and life "lessons," then, contribute to the child's developing relationship "views" (see Furman & Wehner, 1994) and associated actions, increasing the likelihood of a violent confrontation. Indeed, the child may be more routinely exposed to these types of influences than to violent outbursts within the home.

As we discussed in Chapter Two, it is a challenge to capture this type of content within families, which is one of the reasons researchers typically study more straightforward variables, such as family structure or parental supervision. Thus, it is quite informative to consider the direct responses of OLS and TARS parents to a simple question about their child's dating life (How do you feel about your child dating?). This question was asked during the structured interview protocol and was one of only a few questions that allowed an open-ended response in connection with the laptop method of administration. While some universal themes and concerns are shared by TARS and OLS parents, there nevertheless remain stark contrasts in the content of their responses. It is also interesting to note that the OLS parents in particular often took the occasion to answer as if speaking directly to the child. This provides us with a relatively rare opportunity to in effect "eavesdrop" on such parent-child conversations (albeit hypothetical ones) and to highlight potentially consequential variations in the content of what is communicated to children about dating and romantic relationships more generally.

A SAMPLE OF THE RESPONSES OF TARS PARENTS

I think at 17 dating is okay and a part of the teen experience. Group dating is better for teens at that age. [Maureen]

I think that interest in the opposite sex is developmentally normal. Dating with some parental supervision (time to come home, activities) is good. [Kelly]

I feel he will make the right decisions or as a trusted adult. Family member for advice. [Libbey]

It's good for her to date. [Holly]

I feel it is ok as long as it is not the only thing she does. [Julie]

It's fine as long as grades and responsibility are taken serious. [Toby]

I am fine with it. [Abby]

I would discourage dating in high school. I would let her go out as a part of a group activity. [Amy]

I feel that dating is fine after 16. I just hope they have good common sense. [Cindy]

I feel it is okay, but just don't get too serious. [Kate]

I think it can be a healthy part of a teen's life. [Sandra]

A SAMPLE OF RESPONSES OF OLS PARENTS

If you got to have sex, use protection – but wait as long as possible, because boys will use you then leave you. If you're going to have sex, let it be your decision, no one else's. Treat people the way that you want to be treated. Be respectful. If a man put his hands on you, I'll kill him, and go to jail. No 2nd chance, if he hits, he'll do it again. We can always talk. [Ava]

Watch out for the hood rats, the bad girls that don't want to succeed, that don't want anything out of life and will hold you down! Watch out for those girls that want your money. Always wear a condom, get a career 1st, don't put your hands on a lady. If she is not good for you, just walk away. Wait 4 marriage. [Tammy]

You're not going over to no boy's house until you are 17. You can have phone calls or they can come here, but I have to meet them and you'll be supervised. Remember no means no. Let me know if anything touches you in the wrong way, I'll deal with it – I'll beat them up and then press charges. Protect yourself from sex. Use condoms so u don't catch disease. [Jolie]

Men can either love you and be there for you, or use you and leave. I want you to know that there are good men out there. Don't have sex, don't make the mistakes i did – i had a kid at 16 – be with a man who will respect you – don't let a man hit you ever – don't have sex until you're 18 or older, go to school – don't be what i have been – don't ruin your life like me. [Mary]

You should rule. Don't let a boy have control over you. He should treat you with respect. Don't have kids, you don't act old enough to have kids. Use protection especially with the boys you date. Your boyfriend is ugly – and you should watch how he treats you. If a man puts his hands on you, pick something up and knock him out. Take nothing from him. [April]

You can't believe a word that a man say – be careful. You can't depend on them, you have to depend on yourself. Wrap it up! Wear a condom – don't believe that a man is going to be faithful. You're too young to have kids right now. Be careful. Respect yourself, watch how you dress, watch what kind of guy you attract, dress trashy, they'll treat u badly. [Karen]

Don't get pregnant b4 eighteen yrs old – like I did, finish school – don't mess life up like I did. If a man puts his hands on you, especially a grown man, knock the shit out of him. Go slow … I didn't go slow. You can get AIDS and pregnant. When you do it, use protection, there is all kinds of stuff out there. [Tanya]

Get your education now. You have your whole life for girls, get your school down now. You better not get a girl pregnant right now because you'll have to be responsible, and that's what happened to me. If a girl hits you, hit her back, hit her hard enough to let them know, u don't hit me, but you better respect women. Never hit 1st. Use condoms, illbhere4ualways. [Elaine]

Go dutch – so a man won't think you owe him sex – keep your legs closed – if a man hits you, knock his ass out – beat the shit out of him – take him out and leave him alone – slow down, you got time – don't rush in – be more lady like – don't be more demanding – be safe. [Jeannie]

Hold out! Don't have sex so early. Don't date older men. Follow your heart, but remember that you're still young, no hurry to grow fast.

It's great that you ask my opinion, but hold out. You can handle your own – knock out a man who puts his hands on you. You're too young to have a baby. I had you 2 when i was 16/18 – I was still a baby. Don't do it. [Angela]

The above excerpts are all quotes from OLS mothers. It is interesting that the OLS fathers' admonitions are similar in tone and content:

Don't get pregnant at a young age, don't do the things that I did. Don't smoke weed. You're pregnant, don't let a boy beat you up. If he touches you, come to me, I'll take care of it. I told you I'd even give you fucking rubbers, but that dumbass didn't use them with you, and now you're knocked up, you should have have worn a rubber. Don't bed down with every boy. [Scott]

Slow down – way down, quit sleeping with so many guys, you're going to catch a disease and get pregnant and I am scared. Get on the shot. U have too much unsafe sex. I am afraid for u. Don't be like me. I've got kids splattered everywhere. I regret the things I've done, I've lost 4. How will you raise kids? Stop sleeping around, you'll get hurt. [Andy]

Don't trust a boy, until you know him for a long time. Most boys are only out for one thing (sex)! Date boys that are your age, (get rid of 27 yr old boyfriend). Date someone of your own race only – it makes you look bad to date mixed guys like you're doing. Your mother should have raised you better than that – I am mad at your mom for u dating black guys. [Darrell]

Watch what boys do! – watch what boys try to force on you i.e., drugs. Don't be around them if they do drugs. Watch how a boy treats you. A boy should treat you right, should present himself right. Get away from a boy who does drugs or tries to hit you – and let me know! I'll handle it! Use protection – don't date someone like me – please. [Steven]

I am going to be three rows back, watching you two at the movies on your first date! Always think about your future, don't let nobody take advantage of you. Don't mess with drugs, alcohol. Be a lady, be yourself. I trust you. You shouldn't be thinking about sex right now, think about your future. Tell me if he doesn't treat you right, I'll handle it. [Alex]

The above quotes effectively capture our perspective on the mechanisms underlying intergenerational transmission. Even though the topic is dating, the parents' comments impart advice, warnings, attitudes, and emotions that differ significantly across the two samples of parental responses. While many TARS parents reflected on the appropriate dating age and considered this next step for their child "a healthy part of a teen's life," the OLS respondents depicted dating as a world rife with "hood rats," men who will "use you," disease, drugs, early pregnancy, and violence. And even though these parents attempt to offer some hopeful alternatives ("I know that there are good men out there"), as we described in connection with many of their discussions of parenting, such messages communicate that potential disasters associated with dating are nevertheless always looming on the horizon. Further, even though on one level the message content appears to be prosocial (slow down, treat people the way you want to be treated), these excerpts also directly communicate that violent retaliations are sometimes an appropriate response. For example, some parents indicate that they will "handle it," if anyone hurts their child and even explicitly describe a violent action they will take ("I'll kill him and go to jail"; "I'll beat them up and press charges"), and others tell the child to "knock the shit out of him," "hit her back hard enough to let her know," "beat the shit out of him," "take him out," [or] "pick up something and take him out."

These comments are thus potentially useful in that they illustrate how everyday communications from the parent, along with the strong emotional valence that connects to this advice, increases the ratio of definitions favorable rather than unfavorable to the violations of law.

CHAPTER SEVEN

"Success Stories": It's All Relative

I'm going to do this. Like, my dad literally fell off his chair when I told him. When I stood in front of him like this and said "Dad I'm going to school to be a nurse," he fell. I mean, he never even expected me to graduate high school, because he expected me to be just like my mom.

[Kaley]

In this book, we have focused primarily on continuities in behavior problems and family dynamics that are linked to the difficulties experienced by the next generation. Yet numerous studies of children exposed to risky environments – from poverty to natural disasters – have documented that, like Kaley, some children are "managing to make it" in spite of this exposure (Furstenberg et al., 1999). Children who beat the odds have been labeled "invulnerable" or "resilient" (Anthony & Cohler, 1987; Haggerty et al., 1996; Luthar, 2003). We prefer the word "resilient" since the concept of invulnerability implies that the child has not been affected by or is impervious to the difficulties they have faced in those milieus. On the other hand, resilience connotes adaptability and an ability to "bounce back" that seems more consistent with the life-course approach and the dynamics we have explored in this investigation (Rutter, 1987).

Prior research in the area of youth resilience has highlighted the remarkable finding that a large number of youth, despite the presence of significant stressors, do appear to avoid serious difficulties and even to thrive. The presence of multiple risk factors is known to increase the likelihood that a child will experience developmental difficulties, but even where overlapping risks are present, many children do not evidence problem outcomes (Masten, 1994).

Werner and Smith's (1992) landmark longitudinal study of children growing up on the Hawaiian island of Kauai followed the development of a sample consisting of low- and high-risk infants. In the study, risk was defined in terms of poverty, a difficult pregnancy, or problem family environments. The follow-ups documented that despite being labeled at risk early, many of the respondents in the sample did not go on to experience developmental difficulties either in childhood/ adolescence or their adult lives. This study and others in this tradition have identified an array of individual and social factors – from even temperament to high IQ to the presence of at least one caring adult – that tend to be associated with positive adaptations. While a focus on such strengths or positives is important from the standpoint of theory building, this line of research also has potential implications for prevention and intervention efforts: observing how and why some children succeed in navigating risky environments can guide structured efforts to nurture those naturally occurring processes.

In this chapter we further explore the phenomenon of resilience and positive adaptation from the vantage point of a sample of children such as those who participated in the OLS. While we acknowledge the key role of factors often highlighted in prior research on resilience, our primary focus here is on the specific challenges faced by children who must cope with criminal or drug-using parents. Thus, although some protective factors (e.g., high IQ) may be universal as assets, other adaptations depend on the specific nature of the stressors to which the child is exposed. Our symbolic interactionist theoretical perspective, which emphasizes the degree to which meanings are necessarily "situated" within a particular context, supports this idea. Nevertheless, we hope that some aspects of our argument may also have utility for thinking about resilience within the context of other risky or problem circumstances.

ON THE LIMITS OF RESILIENCE AS A "KINDS OF PEOPLE" PHENOMENON

Prior to conducting the OLS child study, we eagerly anticipated the success stories we would inevitably encounter within the data and analyses that would clearly distinguish this subgroup from their not-so-successful counterparts. But while delinquency rates and other problem outcome measures certainly vary within the sample, the life histories of a majority of respondents resist clear-cut categorization. We can point to youths, such as Kaley, who plan to or are currently attending college, but an analysis of their life histories often uncovers that they encountered significant problems on the way to these current positive developments. For example, Kaley has already experienced an unplanned pregnancy that resulted in an abortion, experimented with alcohol and a variety of drugs (see Kaley's quotes in Chapter Six about tripping on mushrooms with her mother), and experienced intimate-partner violence at the hands of her ex-boyfriend. Finally, Kaley is currently involved with Kenny, who took his bong outside to smoke while the interview was taking place. Conversely, some of those who would be classified as delinquent based on their self-report scores or histories of recent arrests had taken positive steps to turn their lives around or expressed great pride in the care and protection they have offered their younger siblings. In this sample, then, resilience emerges as a precarious, dynamic process, rather than as a reliable characteristic or trait of specific individuals.

It is thus a challenge to isolate individual and social factors that are clearly associated with more positive trajectories for this population of children, when the number of resounding success stories is so low. This result likely traces directly back to the number and *severity* of risk factors in the children's lives, which are, in contrast, extraordinarily high. For example, while the children of Kauai were labeled high risk because of poverty or the mother's high-risk pregnancy, they nevertheless may have resided in families that functioned quite well, offering strong protection or a buffer against early environmental adversities. And while traditional protective factors such as high IQ appear to be of benefit even within the context of the OLS sample, there are limits to the reach of native intelligence when parents make numerous residential moves or when routine violence negatively affects the child's ability to concentrate on homework assignments.

These observations lead to our conclusion that for very high-risk youths such as those we have followed up here, not only is resilience a process rather than a fait accompli, but success itself must be conceptualized in relative, multidimensional terms. For example, Dave is not an academic high achiever, but he is proud that he has a good work history at Wal-Mart and has proved to his mother that he can make it on his own. On the other hand, Dana, who received a full scholarship to and currently attends a prestigious private university, is undoubtedly the highest academic achiever in the entire study (whether we consider the parents, children, or any of the caregivers who have participated in OLS since its inception). But Dana has recently taken on the care of her crack-addicted sister's children, is enmeshed in a tempestuous relationship with her unemployed boyfriend, and has mental health issues that threaten to derail her considerable academic achievements.

POSITIVE ADAPTATION AS EVIDENCED WITHIN THE LIFE-HISTORY NARRATIVES

Although each narrative is thus complex, many OLS children do show evidence of positive adaptation, or what is commonly viewed as resilience. Our decision to interview multiple siblings within many of the families (e.g., the Wilsons in Chapter Five) illustrates this variability. We observe even more variation within other OLS families: one youth is constantly in trouble at school, while a sibling earns A's and B's and is extremely active in his church youth group. The young people themselves undoubtedly have an imperfect understanding of the precise mix of social and personal assets that distinguish their more favorable trajectories. Nevertheless, the life-history narratives provide one window on the children's attempts to move forward or "bounce back" in the face of high levels of parental dysfunction and family difficulty.

Prior research on resilience provides a useful starting point for our discussion. The protective factors that have been identified typically include external features of the child's environment (e.g., the presence of at least one caring adult); internal or individual level assets (e.g., high IQ, positive attitude, even temperament); or positive developments that reflect some combination of the two (developing a commitment to and success in pursuing prosocial goals such as academic achievement; see e.g., Condly, 2006). These previously identified and relatively universal "positives" are in evidence within the OLS sample, and are important to an understanding of the situations of the more favorably positioned OLS youth. However, our objectives here are to focus attention on factors that have a special "fit" or resonance with the circumstances these youths have encountered. In particular, the symbolic interactionist perspective we highlighted in Chapter Six suggests the need to focus on (i) issues of identity, (ii) emotional and cognitive processes, and (iii) the phenomenon of human agency. This perspective also focuses attention on social network influences, which have direct potential as positive forces and indirect potential as influences on these social psychological processes. Thus, cognitions, emotions, identity-formation processes and the social experiences that foster them, although associated with intergenerational continuities, may also be tied to the child's ability to break from those family traditions. And unlike factors such as basic intelligence, these dynamics are also potentially malleable, a phenomenon that is useful for thinking about the content of prevention and intervention efforts. The potential for change and malleability emerges as a "double-edged sword," however, because even positive developments are often accomplished with little in the way of economic and social capital to cement youths' more hopeful, prosocial inclinations.

DEVELOPING AN IDENTITY-IN-CONTRAST

Identity formation is generally understood as one of the key tasks of childhood, and is an especially critical dimension of the adolescent period. The child's attitudes, emotions, and social experiences gradually crystallize as a constellation of self-views that are important as guides to action. Parents have a key role in the transmission of specific attitudes and emotional responses and as influences on the character of the child's social experiences, which are themselves a source of further definitions. In addition, the parent's own identity serves as one outsized template that children may drawn upon as they begin the process of crafting their own. It is important to underscore that this identity is multidimensional and often carries (on some level) positive meanings. For example, parents may not be particularly proud of the identity "convicted felon," and do not care to see this identity hook applied to their children, but have found it useful to be known in the neighborhood as the sort of person "you don't want to mess with." The multitude of learning opportunities involved and the more general tendency to identify with the parent may foster intergenerational continuity. Yet this result is not inevitable.

As we suggested in Chapter Six, the child draws much from parents as all-important "reference others," but necessarily comes of age in a different time and place. The specific nexus of attitudes, emotions, and social experiences that unfolds is not an exact replica of that of parents or siblings but instead is the child's alone. Children also possess the uniquely human capacity to reflect on the parents' and their own experiences to date and are thus not simply "passive recipients" of the information to which they have been exposed. Thus, some youths, based on the totality of their experiences, and their own social psychological reactions to them, move forcefully to develop an identity in sharp contrast to the one the parents have modeled:

I guess I kind of have a fear of having children because I guess there is kind of, you know, "like mother like daughter." But I'm gonna try my best to make it so it's not that way. I think when you're on drugs, you try to bring people down with you. And plus other people in my family have told me that I'm not gonna amount to anything and that "You think you're so much better than us. You're gonna end up just like us." I guess that's kind of why I dream so high. I want to prove to them that I will be better than them. [Jessica]

When my mom was ten years old … she was smoking marijuana and drinking alcohol. And, like, everybody expects me to be like just like my mom and everybody knows I just ain't like my mom. [Jason]

I like want to grow up and be nothing like her. Like, be better. And do something in my life and stuff. Like go to college and graduate and stuff. [Carly]

Things that my dad don't know about me, I want to know about my son so we can both know about each other, so I can know what he's doing in everyday life. And if he's having fun, or if he's ever sad or depressed, you know what I'm saying? My dad don't do that. He doesn't know nothing about me … I don't want to be like my dad; when I say I don't want to be like my dad, that's what I'm talking about. I want to be there for my kids, and I want to support my kids. I want to be at my kid's graduation or be at my kid's award assembly and stuff like that. Like, a father is someone who takes care of their kids. And I got a dad, you know what I'm saying, he's a donator to me. He just donated and left, and I don't want nothing like that. I want somebody to be a father. Something I never had. To me, you should have wore a condom if you didn't want me to be in the world. If you don't want to take care of me, you should have wrapped it up. They didn't do that. [Michael]

The data we discussed in Chapters Five and Six make clear that the press toward intergenerational continuity is strong. Thus, developing an identity-in-contrast is often not a singular decision followed by a smooth, problem-free march in the direction of achieving an alternative lifestyle. Kaley, the student we quoted at the beginning of this chapter, is adamant about her desire to be different from her mother. Nevertheless, she was not able to avoid significant potential derailments (including dropping out of high school and being involved with alcohol and drugs) prior to making the move to become a nurse:

I get scared that you know, me not going to school, like dropping out, that shit, you know, I'm ... like the day I dropped out I was like "shit," you know, I think I'm going to be like her. I just think that I might slip and fall ... but I think about it everyday. Like, I don't want to be like her. And the worse thing that somebody ever says to me and when they know it, if they know me, they know the meanest thing to say is "you're going to be just like your mom." Like, if I got out ... I went out and got all drunk or something, just had a fun time and somebody yelled at me like you know "you're going to be just like your mom." Like, if I ever heard that from dad, which I have heard before, the night that he was really mad at me for getting drunk, you know, that kind of thing I can't stand. That's why I really don't ... Because I don't ever want to be like her. I mean, yeah, I still do some things that I shouldn't do that she did that could lead me down her path, but I won't because I'm not that stupid.

Not only does Kaley "think about it [her general desire to be different from her mother] everyday," but specific difficulties or potential derailments become "loaded"; that is additionally stressful as they are filtered through this desire to move in a completely different direction from the path her mother has taken.

A central conundrum is that many of these youthful respondents expressed this general desire to carve out a lifestyle that contrasts sharply with that of their parents. Yet, as different aspects of their lives continue to unfold, many are less than successful in making this a concrete reality. One factor that appears to distinguish more successful youths from the less successful ones is simply the strength and depth of their commitment to this self-improvement project. This difference is reminiscent of observations we made in prior analyses of parents' own efforts to turn their lives around, that is to "desist" from criminal behavior and involvement in drug-oriented lifestyles (Giordano Cernkovich, & Rudolph, 2002; Giordano Schroeder, & Cernkovich, 2007). At the time of the first adult follow-up interview, when these original respondents averaged 29 years of age, a majority expressed a general desire to lead more productive lives, even if they were not currently doing so (I'm tired of being tired ….); yet the narratives of more successful desisters moved past vague pronouncements, reflecting specific cognitive, emotional, and social network developments that fostered these changes, making concrete their transformation efforts.

Similarly, the more successful young people we interviewed not only expressed negative attitudes towards their parents' problem lifestyles but also referenced current preoccupations and future goals that were potentially associated with satisfying and more prosocial "replacement selves." Thus, for these young people, forging an identity as "not like mom or dad" may be a necessary but insufficient step in the process of avoiding intergenerational continuity. Below we consider current and future roles that reflected more concrete identities-in-contrast and that tended to be associated with more favorable behavioral trajectories.

THE CARETAKERS

Children within all families take on somewhat distinct roles. But while some OLS youth appeared to be consumed with anger about their family situations and had become the problem children their parents could not handle, others had adapted a protective "caregiver" stance toward siblings or even the parents themselves. This is obviously not an ideal situation, but it can act as an identity template that points these children in a prosocial direction:

> I'm not saying that I had a bad life or a hard life, but it was sort of hard because my brother and stepdad never got along and I always

seen them fighting, and I would always have to act like the parent. I have been like that since I was like fourteen years old. So I'm used to being grown up. You know, I had to grow up earlier. But it's not as bad as it seems. [Pam]

This narrative segment is useful not only because it illustrates a respondent's view that she has taken on aspects of the parental role, but also because the quote highlights an accompanying perspective that may be beneficial or protective. Thus, Pam expresses a certain amount of pride, rather than anger/resentment about her situation, and hedges several times when she considers the difficulties she has faced ("I'm not saying that I had a bad life …. it's not as bad as it seems"). Christina recognized the role-reversal aspects and difficulties of her childhood, but she nevertheless also expressed pride in her maturity and concern for her siblings:

Most of my life I took care of me and my little sisters and my brother, so I was more like an adult when I'm supposed to be playing the child role. I was playing the adult's role because, I mean, she wasn't near, like, even when we were living with her, she wasn't, I'm not going to stay she wasn't stable. I mean, I was the one doing it, like cooking and stuff. I learned this stuff at a younger age. Like, I never really had the chance to be a child, so now that I have a chance to be a child, it's hard for me to be a child because I'm so used to being in an adult situation. I mean I can take things a lot better, like most sixteen-year-olds couldn't handle what I had to handle. Like for instance, my mama goes to jail, I mean, most sixteen-year-olds, they probably wouldn't know what to do mostly if their mama had to get up and go. I think that made me a strong person, yeah, I believe that. Yeah, I feel like I'm a role model in the way of, like when it comes to the boys, they [siblings] always come to me and ask me like "Christina should I do this?" and I just tell stuff I know. Because I have been here longer than them, a lot more experience than them, so I feel good about that.

Another respondent, Barbara, has adapted a protective stance toward her younger sister Jesse: "If she hangs out with like a bad person … I mean, I don't have any right to be much in her social life or anything, but I just don't want her hanging with people that, like, do drugs or anything." Barbara realizes that it is not typical and perhaps not even appropriate for her to be the one who adopts this protective stance. Yet, the more often she takes this position with regard to her sister's life, the more this may strengthen her own commitment to a prosocial identity and associated conventional lines of action. Dana, quoted below, also discusses her desire to be a good role model for her brother. In this instance, however, she references a shift in her role within the family, as she has successfully distanced herself from an earlier period of involvement in problem behaviors. Note that other changes are integral to this shift toward the prosocial:

> Because when I was using weed, like, my grades started slipping and now I ain't want to be like that. I want to be a good example for my little brother ... [used marijuana because] I felt that it was a source of me getting my stress out, but now I realize it wasn't ... it wasn't the weed that was getting my stress out; it was just talking that helped. Being able just to go to somebody and talk to them about the problem. That's what really helped me. Weed didn't really help me do that.

This quote suggests that wanting to be a good example for her brother can provide general motivation for Dana's renewed emphasis on school and decision to avoid drugs. However, it is also important to note that Dana's cognitive, social, and emotional changes appear to be in alignment with and buttress this new direction. These new attitudes (cognitions) are focused on the emotional realm, as Dana comes to recognize that accessing her network of social supports is a more effective strategy than marijuana use for coping with stress.

It is also important to note that these positive developments have apparently taken place without changes in the factors considered as key determinants (mediators) of intergenerational continuity, such as parental attachment and supervision. Control theory emphasizes a constant motivation to deviate that is essentially held in check by external sources of formal and informal social control. In contrast, a symbolic interactionist lens accommodates and indeed emphasizes situations in which social psychological changes influence motivational processes and, in turn, behavior change (Mead, 1934). Identity shifts represent a crystallization of these changes in attitude, and are themselves heavily implicated in behavioral choices.

It is also consistent with the symbolic interactionist perspective, however, that social experiences are considered central to an understanding of how definitions or meanings are initially constructed, as well as to how these definitions change. In this way, agentic moves of the sort Deb describes are accomplished at the individual level but are theorized as fundamentally social in origin. We do not have access to the full range of social experiences that may have fostered Barbara's worldview or Deb's change in perspective (whether deriving from their intimate contacts or their interactions across a wider circle of affiliations, including teachers, mentors, counselors). However, the resulting cognitive and emotional positions of these respondents are both distinct from the levels of control that characterizes their family situations and implicated in their positive trajectories.

Aside from the stresses associated with assuming the caregiver or protector role within the family, a limitation of this adaptation is that it may insulate or isolate youths from other positive activities and prosocial influences. Thus, Darlene has benefited greatly from an other-directed activity, volunteer work, which provides these outward-looking, beneficial linkages:

> I just like, you know, getting out there and meeting new people and becoming very active with the community. That's the main part that I like about it. And, you know, knowing that you're actually helping somebody that needs the need for the stuff that you're doing. So, that's the main thing that I like about volunteering.

Researchers have frequently highlighted the ways in which female socialization patterns foster what has been called an "ethic of care" (Gilligan, 1982). And, certainly, when viewed through the perspective of youths' own narratives, female children were more likely than their male counterparts to reference these other-directed or caregiving roles. However, this response is far from universal on the part of female respondents in the sample. Conversely, some males do focus heavily on other-directed themes within their narratives. We also considered other characteristics of youths who appeared to adapt and benefit from this type of family role, but the variations we encountered defy easy categorization. For example, it might be expected that the oldest children would be the most likely to develop a caretaker orientation, given their position within the family. And indeed, some narratives did reference this dynamic. For example, Lyniece, quoted in Chapter Five, noted, "my aunt always said I was the oldest so I have to take care of the rest of my sisters and brothers." Yet, the oldest children may have been exposed to more difficulties because they were born when the parents were teens and therefore particularly ill equipped to handle parenting responsibilities. Further, the oldest children may identify strongly with and have spent the most time with the parent during the parents' most active criminal years, thus increasing their exposure to a range of risks. It is interesting to note that in several instances, the younger children within these families, while lacking maturity and many of the tools needed to engage in parent-like activities (e.g., they cannot drive) have nevertheless moved into these protector roles. For example, Damien, aged 12 at the time of the interview, was doing well in school (earning mixed A's and B's) and reported no delinquent involvement or substance use. In his life-history narrative, Damien talks about how he often walked to neighborhood crack houses, in order to remove his mother from these environments:

R: I just, the places that she's going, I do, I figure it out.
Q: Do you think she's going to a house where she can do drugs?
R: Yeah.
Q: You just open the door and walk in?
R: Yep … they ask me that and I say, coming to get my mom
Q: And then does your mom come out?
R: Yeah. I say come on, you know you're not supposed to be here at this house. She's just, she just acts like she's mad, and then she'll be cool with me.

Eleven-year-old Danika is another success story, as reflected by good grades, answers to the structured problem-behavior scales, and comparisons to her siblings' difficulties. Her brother Jim dropped out of school in the tenth grade ("'cause I went to jail … I never went back"); he and his older sister were quoted in Chapter Five as getting in trouble with the police because of a domestic violence incident ("they said I pulled a knife on her – she pulled a knife on me …"). In contrast, Danika writes poetry (she wrote a poem for the interviewer) and indicated that she helps her mother remain sober by attending Alcoholics Anonymous (AA) meetings with her:

R: I sit by her, but sometimes I go with the kids.
Q: What do you think about AA when you go?
R: It's good. It helps people keep … It helps people not start back drinking.

Obviously, it is far from ideal that these young children have felt compelled to assume such adult-like positions and/or that they are preoccupied with and take responsibility for their parents' drug-abuse problems. Nevertheless, young people so positioned within the family often fare better (from an intergenerational transmission of crime standpoint) than their more angry siblings, who may in effect "wash their hands" of these family difficulties, even as they act out in similar ways. A significant complication is that while this adaptation appears generally beneficial in the short run, we cannot state definitively that the very young children we interviewed will be successful in avoiding problems as they begin to navigate the more risky terrain of adolescence. And even older adolescents may eventually succumb to the continued stress associated with the family's difficulties, the presence of antisocial models, and their own lack of success in navigating various adult transitions (e.g., lack of economic independence, affiliation with an antisocial romantic partner). Recall that Michelle, an adult respondent from Chapter Four, had routinely retrieved her own mother from crack houses; yet she described an incident that took place when she was twenty-one and her mother offered her the crack pipe as a way to distract her – subsequently Michelle herself became addicted to crack cocaine, and both women continued to use for many years.

Finally, these observations about the caregiver role appear to be at odds with results of Anthony and Cohler's (1987) research on "the invulnerable child." In a study of the children of parents with mental illness, they observed that the children who were able to distance themselves psychologically from that parent were more likely to avoid negative effects of the illness. This is an important and intuitive observation. It may be that there is an ideal position for such youths – a protective "middle ground" between the extremes of enmeshment and walking away completely from the parents' problems and siblings' needs.

CHILDREN OF GOD

A focus on spirituality and religious involvement is another positive adaptation made by a subset of these OLS respondents. In conducting the original follow-up interviews with the adults in 1995, we were surprised at the degree to which religion and spirituality permeated the life-history narratives of a significant number of the respondents. Guided by the prior research on factors associated with criminal desistance and persistence, we included many open-ended questions about spouses, employment, and the criminality of other network influences but no questions about religion. Nevertheless, many of the respondents spontaneously discussed – at length – the importance of their religious faith. This contrasted sharply with Laub and Sampson's finding that few of the Glueck men they studied appeared to benefit either from religion or spiritually oriented self-help groups. Indeed, Laub and Sampson (2003: 246) quoted one respondent, Mickey, as typifying the views of the Glueck men on religion ("It's a crock ...."). It appears that cohort shifts, and perhaps the rise of spiritually oriented self-help groups, are implicated in these distinct results. Nevertheless, the idea of religion influencing individual conduct is quite compatible with a control theory perspective. The conception of the individual as controlled by external forces is predominant not only in general treatments of religion (e.g., Durkheim, 1915), but also in studies focused on the connections between religion and crime. These notions also fit well with Hirschi's (1969) views of individuals as inherently prone to deviance; thus, whether or not individuals engage in crime depends on whether there are in place sufficient bonds to society to control individuals' natural impulses. The logic is that as an individual obtains bonds to religion and religious institutions, these bonds will deter the individual from realizing his or her natural proclivities to criminal activity.

Although religion's prosocial potential can usefully be viewed through the lens of social control, acquiring a spiritual foundation is also compatible with the principles of differential association theory, particularly the symbolic interactionist version we outline in this book (e.g., Giordano et al., 2002; Matsueda & Heimer, 1997; O'Connor, 2004). Thus, religion can be seen, not only as a source of external control over individual conduct, but also as a source for new definitions of the situation: for parents, it is a path that is distinct from their earlier criminal one; for the children, it offers alternatives to the antisocial definitions the parents have provided;

achieve in school, and routinely come into contact with
ating partners who do not prove to be a source of positive

of their social placement, then, religion provides one of
rces of "prosocial capital" that appears to be readily avail-
to the parent or the child generation of OLS respondents.
(1989) pointed out that in disadvantaged neighborhoods,
nvolvement provides one means for clearly distinguishing
nd individuals as "decent" rather than "street." But while
he OLS families would undoubtedly be viewed by others
itome of "street," the narratives nevertheless reveal much
to social networks and settings that have fostered the devel-
f their interest in spirituality.

rprisingly, many adult respondents often noted that they
me closer to God as a result of their involvement with AA
tics Anonymous, or from ministers who visited with them in
ttings. However, many also described contacts within their
te networks of relatives and friends as sources of influence/
on. For example, Rhonda, a core respondent, indicated that
er became a minister after he had gotten off drugs. Jessica,
adult respondent, had many discussions of religion with her
d a number of respondents included religious participation
discussions of earlier childhood experiences:

rgarten to eighth grade I was an alter boy. [Dean]

I was 12 years old we went morning, noon, and night. I mean,
lay and Tuesday, Wednesday, Thursday, Friday, Saturday, every
ay. [Shelly]

f the original OLS respondents did describe more personal
ate religious experiences as key to their transformations ("I
His voice, just lights all in my room …"), but the frequent refer-
o childhood and to adult social exposure provide additional
t for understanding the parents' general receptivity to the idea
ligious turn.

he quotes that follow illustrate, the adult respondents are gen-
not casual or blasé about the role of religion in their lives. We
a number of different OLS parents in order to highlight the

and for both, a relatively speci
"prosocial" individual. In the p
ence, whether through formal a
or church or based on personal
opment of a positive identity tha
sents a clear improvement over
crack addict, ex-felon) (see Maru
prise, we found that a subset of Ol
religion and their spiritual selves.

Relying primarily on the conte
dren's life-history narratives, we n
youths and their parents may hav
(ii) underlying mechanisms associa
finally, (iii) difficulties and compli
significant potential of this genera
lives of the OLS families we studied

WHY RELIGION?

Religion is one of the few positive
be objectively and subjectively availa
OLS parents and their children. As w
Four, the elements of what we have
ability package" (namely, a good job
a prosocial spouse/partner) have prov
sible, goals for many of the responder
most instances, not yet in the job mark
have experienced the consequences of
necting to traditional prosocial identiti
neighborhoods and schools, experience
or the stresses associated with their pa
Further, these youths do face difficulti
counterparts of a traditional respectabili
with stigma related to their parents' re

[1] Portions of this analysis are drawn from a more
ity and crime in the life course experiences of
Schroeder, & Cernkovich, 2007).

attempts t
potential
influence.

In light
the few so
able either
Anderson
religious
families a
many of
as the ep
exposure
opment

Not su
had bec
or Narco
prison s
immedia
inspirati
her fath
another
aunt, a
in their

Kind
Whe
Mon
Sun

Many
or pri
heard
ences
conte
of a r
As
erally
quote

apparent depth of interest in and commitment to religion felt by a
significant number of these respondents. In turn, these parents and
the others they reference as initial influences (i.e., the mother in the
adult's story is grandmother to one or more of the OLS children) are
potentially important sources of social influence on the children's
emerging interests in spirituality. This represents a different type
of intergenerational transmission, one that is more prosocial in its
potential:

> I know if I put Him first, I can never go wrong ... I pray to God. I
> pray, I pray. That's what keeps me going. I get on my knees no mat-
> ter where I'm at, and ask God to give me the strength. [Delia]

> I asked God to help me change, help me talk, to respect people, for
> them to respect me ... [Eileen]

> God blesses me. He does. They say He blesses all fools and babies.
> So I must be a fool. He sure looks after me. [Becky]

> Even when I went to Florida and picked up a catfish, and its skeleton
> was of Jesus Christ. There are so many things that you can find that
> are beautiful. [Steve]

> I'm doing good by the grace of God. Because God keeps me doing
> the right things ... it's really helpful. It keeps me feeling like I can
> keep going on ... like I can make it. The things that the preacher say
> from out of the Bible. I love that. He's just teaching you the ways to
> live. To live like the way God wants you to live right. [Karen]

> I have learned to trust God's word over my feelings and I've come to
> have a closer walk and a more joyful walk and more love in the Lord
> ... John 3:16: God so loved the world and that means everybody.
> [Karla]

> Well I didn't think like that until Buddhism. Now I go in to a stage
> of, you know, nirvana. It was like a cloud that just comes over me,
> you know. Any pain that I felt just goes away. [Mike]

> If you could have told me ten years or go or, say, the last time I seen
> you, seven years ago, that I would be singing in a choir regularly,
> going to church regularly, I probably would have thought you were
> crazy ... [Paul]

> Believe it or not I, actually, I got saved. [Dave]

Based on the content of the life-history narratives and answers to questions on the structured interview, we were thus well aware of the strong
interest of many of the adult OLS respondents in spirituality and their

religious faith. For example, 58 percent indicated that they felt close to God at the time of both follow-up interviews, and an additional 26 percent answered affirmatively at the time of one of the interviews. Given the typical concerns and interests of adolescents, however (e.g., their friends, current romantic interests), we were nevertheless somewhat surprised at the frequent references to God and spirituality within the context of the narratives of a number of the OLS children.

Darlene, aged 16, is currently living with a friend of her mother's, Delia, because Beth, Darlene's mother, is incarcerated (she had prior convictions for drug-related offenses; the current committing offense is forgery). Delia met Beth when the two were in rehab. Although Delia is making a good-faith effort to care for Darlene and her brothers and sisters, she expresses some trepidation, pointing out that she had lost custody of her own biological children, and indicating that she finds taking care of Beth's children to be a major challenge. The interviewer noted also that, although the children were physically with Delia, their lives nevertheless appeared somewhat unsettled. For example, some of their belongings were still at the apartment they had lived in with Beth, and some remained in bags at Delia's house. Darlene discusses her belief in God in connection with concerns about safety in the neighborhood in which Delia lives:

> .... like the other night the bus had almost stopped when me and my sister was on the bus. I was praying to God like "Please just let us get home safely," like, stuff like that. I mean I'm not going to say, I'm like "God this, God that, God that ..." I just believe in Him .... I just believe that He's in my life and He's the reason for me living and breathing.

Another respondent Francine also described how important spirituality was to her overall well-being:

> Well, God is ... like I said, he's the center of my life. As long as you've got God in your life you can, you know, I know I can do anything that I want. And as long as I pray to God, he'll give it to me as long as I do something good for him. And the reason why he's the best thing in my life ... that happened to me in my life is because before I found God, before I, you know, started going to church and stuff my life was just, you know, focused on boys, focused on really nothing at all. Once I found God my life just got lifted back up.

Although national studies indicate that females are more likely than their male counterparts to attend church and focus on issues of spirituality, some of the male children we interviewed also professed a strong belief in God and active involvement in a church community. As Adam put it, "We go to church constantly. If I miss it there would be chaos."

What does religion do? That is, in what ways is spirituality protective for youths who have carved out a spiritual identity?

(1) *Most religious teachings specifically reinforce prosocial actions.* Some activities or social contexts have the potential to be positive influences but are not fundamentally prosocial. For example, stable employment has potential as a catalyst for desistance from crime, but having a job, even if it is satisfying and provides a good income, does not specifically preclude involvement in crime, drug use, or getting into a fight. During the period of adolescence, involvement in extracurricular activities can reduce risks, but prior research has shown that adding recreation centers to low-income neighborhoods does not reliably reduce teens' involvement in delinquent behavior. In short, there is often sufficient time in the day to play basketball as well as to use alcohol and other drugs. Thus, in addition to its relative accessibility, religion appears to have much potential because many core concerns within religious communities and in the Bible relate directly to problem areas for these adults, as well as for their children. Importantly, religious teachings can provide a clear blueprint for how to proceed when the goal is to veer away from crime (in the case of the parents) or to avoid altogether the kind of problems the parents have faced (in the case of the children). Jane and Melissa, two adult OLS respondents quoted below, have managed to successfully desist from earlier criminal involvement:

> Reading the Bible. Getting instruction from the Bible. It clearly says in the Bible how we're suppose to act, how we're suppose to treat people. How we are suppose to deny ourselves and follow him. How we're suppose to leave self and ... and it's through that consciousness that I have stayed in constant contact with God that makes it not okay to let these people hanging on .... [Jane]
>
> It's about starting to obey the commandments. All of them. You know, that's how you start. You give up sin, you know what I mean?

You fight that. That's how you begin to hear. It took time. I was, you know, set in my ways, and you know I ... I like to go out on the weekends and, you know, drink or whatever ... but all that kind of stuff closes you down. [Melissa]

Narratives of children who consider themselves religious often reflect in similar ways on the knowledge they have gained from their exposure to a more spiritual way of life. Joe, for example, declares, "I love studying the Bible ... As long as I have Jesus, I'll be alright." Or consider David's more extended philosophical discussion:

Because I know right from wrong, and evidently that was something that he [his father] didn't know. I got, you know, evidently somewhere in his life, he got, you know, sidetracked to think that was all there was to life and he couldn't better himself. I don't know, I mean, my grandmother is a religious woman; my mom prayed for me and it worked out. I mean, like I told you on the computer, we all choose our own fate, we choose our own life. If you go into a gun fight with a gun, then there's a good chance you're going to shoot somebody or get shot at, the same thing. You know what you're going to do. And you should find something better for yourself.

As these narrative excerpts highlight, the adults and even the younger respondents not only adapt a religious language, but they indicate a very active reliance on spirituality as providing them with a useful cultural toolkit (Swidler, 1986). This "blueprint" thus includes general guidelines for behavior (as in references to the Ten Commandments and the scriptures), but is also viewed as a source for more specific advice and direction (as another adult respondent, Trisha, put it, "there is nothing that I do that I don't consult God first about it"). This is an important consideration as the individual moves forward and inevitably encounters novel situations, stresses, life events and negative social influences. Consistent with our symbolic interactionist viewpoint, David adopts an agentic stance regarding the differences between his path and that of his father ("we all choose our own fate"); also consistent with the social emphasis of this theoretical perspective, it appears that David has been influenced by the social definitions his grandmother and mother have provided. Thus, agentic moves and a different orientation are often necessary to interrupt the strong press in the direction of intergenerational continuities, but these necessarily occur within social settings that affect the nature of the child's opportunities, constraints, and specific emphases.

(2) *Spirituality is associated with positive emotions and is a key resource for emotion-coping.* The above discussion of religion as providing a blueprint for behavior and the construction of a prosocial identity is very consistent with differential association theory (religion provides an excess of definitions unfavorable to the violation of law), and with the focus on cognitive processes in our previous examination of the desistance process (Giordano et al., 2002; Sutherland, 1947). However, as we argued in Chapter Six, a significant limitation of most learning theories, including our own earlier version, is the exclusive focus on cognitive processes.[2] Thus, as emotions are a critical part of the fabric of human life, it is reasonable to expect that emotional processes connect not only to criminal involvement (behaviors such as violence and drug abuse are two categories that are especially intuitive in their connections to emotional processes), but also to the dynamics underlying a spirituality benefit (Agnew, 1997). Rambo (1993), who has focused specifically on the experience of religious conversion, argues that these experiences not only derive from and result in cognitive changes but also involve a strong emotional component as well. Corresponding to this, scholars interested in the sociology of emotions have emphasized that emotional processes can be seen as providing energy or motivation for new lines of action (Collins, 2004). Thus, respondents who describe spiritual feelings do not simply focus on the specific content of what has been learned (definitions unfavorable to the violation of law), but also convey strong positive affect concerning their spirituality and new lifestyle. For example, Tracy, a 30-year-old core respondent, described her situation as "just awesome"; Beth noted that "the calm and that peace within you – it's wonderful"; and Jessica, a complete desister, told the interviewer that she was "1000 percent happier because of Jesus." Spirituality, then, can be seen as a

---

[2] This critique also pertains to Sampson and Laub's theory of desistance, which does not focus heavily on emotional processes.

source of positive emotions in lives that have been characterized by
an array of negative ones, and also as a resource one draws on when
problem situations arise:

> I don't worry like I used to before. I know all things are in the Lord's
> hands, and I know he takes care of me. [Jennifer]

> I can if somebody says something to me that I don't like, you know, it
> doesn't bother me any more it's ... it meant (after being saved) that
> I could literally get ease with myself and not jump up and beat the
> crap out of somebody, or if somebody comes and gets something
> from me and didn't bring, you know, it back at a certain time I'd go
> and beat the crap out of them. [Karl]

These themes are also featured in children's narratives, as when
some of these youths indicate that their spirituality is a major means
for coping with stress and other negative emotions:

> ... just want to, like, let people know, not to like, to be stressed, well,
> not ... Well, you can be stressed out in life, but don't let stuff get to
> you. Just do what you've got to do in life and do what you've got to do
> to get done and not to let nothing bother you and everything else.
> Make sure that, you know, you believe in God and that as long as you
> believe in God stuff will be right for you. [Alexandra]

> With me going to church a lot and praying a lot, it's helped me get
> this far. 'Cause if I really wasn't in church or praying at all or didn't
> know any thing about God, basically, I probably wouldn't have been
> able to get this far. You know, I probably would have killed myself,
> you know, or ... [Katelyn]

> I just pray and tell God to make my life better, and that's all ...
> and help me get through, like, the struggle or whatever I was going
> through at the time. I just tell him that and everything just starts
> going good. [Kelci]

Hannah, 16, is another highly religious respondent, who earns mixed
A's and B's, and scores low on the delinquency and substance-abuse
scales. Although her depression score is high, she feels nevertheless
that her spiritual life is central to her ability to deal with stressful situations in her family life:

> I love learning about Jesus. I just want to learn why he died for
> us. And like, all the good thing he did, all the miracles. And like,

how earth started. I love learning stuff like that. I like when we do praises and worship. It makes me feel better. It makes all the stress go off of me.

For Hannah, learning about Jesus and focusing on these positive elements of her faith is beneficial, and the specific practices of praises and worship reduces her feelings of stress. Jesse discusses his religion in a way that suggests a motivational component, as we discussed in our treatment of mechanisms above: "Just, I mean, if you're stuck in a position and you don't think that you can get out, just keep praying and keep praying, until eventually it happens and you get the strength to do it or get out of it."

(3) *Another benefit of religiosity is that it may provide entrée to or solidify one's position with prosocial others.* The young people who have adapted a strong spiritual identity not only benefit from what we have labeled cognitive and emotional changes, but also from prosocial alignments both within their immediate families and those that result from their involvement in a church or other religious activities (e.g., youth groups). As we noted in our analyses of the adults' narratives, the beneficial effects of spirituality are likely to be significantly enhanced when they connect to more positive network affiliations. These may play a direct role in strengthening the move away from negative lifestyles as well as bolster the parents' and/or youths' developing spiritual orientations. Kim, a 17-year-old OLS child respondent, describes a boyfriend who became a positive influence in her life:

[Q: You met him at church like through youth group or something?] My sister ... My sister's friend invited us to go to church with her 'cause they were going to be there and she wanted me to meet him. [Q: Did you think that church was a cool place to meet a guy?] Yeah ... Um, I don't know. He ... He was real nice. [Q: Better than like at the mall or better than like at some Wal-Mart or something?] Yeah ... It's a lot different. It's not like that. He was like, he wasn't the kind of guy that, you know, [how] guys are ... usually guys are.

Similarly, Brittany's narrative focuses on the volunteer work that she began in connection with her church involvement, which led her to take advantage of and benefit from other volunteer experiences and, in turn, from the social contacts that connect to them:

> Right now, I'm volunteering like at school. I'm volunteering for tutoring and um … like doing clinicals, you know, volunteering at the hospitals and stuff. I'm doing that and right now at the church, I'm volunteering for food drives and blanket drives and stuff. And I've been doing that ever since ninth grade. [Q: What do you like about volunteering?] I just like, you know, getting out there and meeting new people and becoming very active with the community. That's the main part that I like about it. And, you know, knowing that you're actually helping somebody that needs … the stuff that you're doing. So, that's the main thing that I like about volunteering. And plus volunteer hours, you know, that will add up. And God will always look upon you for that. So, that's a lot … It has a lot to do with, you know, God and everything. If you do something good, you know, God will do something good for you.

Although Brittany focuses attention on various good works that she enjoys doing and the direct spiritual benefits, she does note that another benefit is "getting out there and meeting new people" and becoming very active in the community. Rebecca, quoted below, also focused on the role of her religion as a key source of life's meaning and a mechanism for coping with stressful events. Yet the narrative highlights that the process of developing this new orientation was intimately linked to her social contacts:

> Well, the thing that inspired me to start going to church was my [foster] sister Kristen. She was really involved in some church or whatever and I was going through a lot in my life when I was living with my cousin. And that was my only outlet to actually let go of everything that was holding me and making me so depressed and whatnot … and then it became like my thing for living, you know what I mean, it was like the things that sustain me, that gave me hope, when there was none. So … I got involved and I love what I was doing and I love the feeling I got from it, and I love the freedom that it gave me. And the happiness I felt after praising God, you know, and it just became me. And I don't know how not to do it, you know what I mean …

Rebecca's quote nicely illustrates her shift in perspective, as religion gradually assumed a more central role in her life and became a core aspect of her identity ("it just became me"). Jarrell, quoted below, highlights the role of his own changing attitudes and increased maturity, as he attempts to make positive life changes. Nevertheless, his agentic moves were apparently aided by his access to a prior relationship with a youth pastor who offered tangible as well as moral support:

> About a year ... Maybe a year and a couple months ago we were moving. We were getting evicted out of our house and stuff and she called my youth pastor and was like, "Um ... can he stay here until we get situated and get a place and everything?" And um, so, I moved in here and she finally found a place and stuff and ... And I just really ... you know, I found God really lead me to stay here, you know, for now 'cause it's just the thing that I need to do in my life, you know, the things that ... you know, I'm growing to be a man now and I've got to make a lot of different choices in my life. And so, I thought that it would be easier to make them here and so I decided to stay here for now anyways.

LIMITATIONS OF SPIRITUALITY AS A PROSOCIAL ANCHOR FOR THE OLS RESPONDENTS

Our analysis thus far has described benefits of religious involvement and specific mechanisms through which spirituality emerges as a key positive force in the lives of the both the adult respondents and their children. The discussion highlighted that religion provides a blueprint for how to proceed as a positive-thinking, prosocial individual; emotional benefits; and access to more prosocial others. These others reinforce the positive behavior patterns as well as spiritual involvement, and often serve as a counterpoint to some of the negative influences and events that may continue to occur within the family. Yet, results of quantitative analyses and even some aspects of the narratives themselves require us to add some caveats to this generally positive portrait of a spirituality benefit.

In analyses that specifically assessed the links between spirituality (the perceived importance of God) and religious involvement (church participation) of the parents and their self-reported criminal behavior (relying on the structured interview data), we found that only cross-sectional results were significant; that is, we observed the expected negative correlations between religiosity and crime, but these indices were not predictive of later levels of crime or drug use (e.g., 1995 spirituality as a predictor of 2003 crime). Other analyses examined the adult respondents' total pattern of criminal involvement across the two waves of adult interviews (whether the respondents were classified as desisters, persisters, or showed an episodic pattern across the two waves of data). These results again revealed that neither reports of spirituality nor church attendance were significant predictors of membership in these behavioral categories when we considered the longer window of time (Giordano et al., 2008).

Our analyses of responses of teens to similar items on the structured interview also failed to document a strong overall or aggregate relationship between religiosity and delinquent behavior. Neither the question about the importance of religion nor the measure of church attendance (child report) was significantly related to the child's level of self-reported delinquency or the likelihood of having delinquent friends. In another analysis, we did find a significant negative correlation between church attendance and religious importance and problem drug/alcohol use, but the association was not significant in a complete model that included standard controls such as parental attachment.

Clearly, a subset of the respondents appeared to have benefited greatly from their faith and involvement in the church. Why, then, is the relationship not stronger when we consider effects across these adult and child samples as a whole? Some reasons may be statistical or due to inadequate measurement. For example, since a high percentage of the respondents believed that God was important to them, this item may not have served well to discriminate between respondents. Related to this, these single-item indicators undoubtedly do not capture the apparent depth of interest in/commitment to spirituality that some of the narratives revealed. Nevertheless, it is also important to consider the more substantive limitations of relying on spirituality as a stand-alone anchor for change (in the case of the parents) or positive youth development (in the case of the OLS children).

(1) The immediacy of disadvantaged neighborhoods and social networks may swamp the positive effects of spirituality.

When we interviewed one parent, Angela, in 1995, she was living in a shelter for battered women. While Angela had several times been the victim of abusive relationships, at that time she was living in the shelter to avoid being homeless (all of the traditional shelters were full). Prior to this, she had lived in her car, along with her mother. At the time of the first adult interview, Angela admitted to the interviewer that she was addicted to crack (as was her mother), frequently engaged in prostitution, and had open warrants for her arrest. In the period between the two waves of interviews, however, Angela had become significantly more religious and focused on this as a key catalyst for changing her lifestyle:

> I've tried to turn it around. I've tried to live on the other side. I've tried to walk with God and be a good Christian mom and take care of my kids through the Bible. Bible studies day and night, from the morning we woke up reading the Bible and went to sleep reading the Bible, everyday for eight months straight, okay. [But] when I got kicked out of [another shelter] and put back in the same surroundings that I walked away from and stopped smoking drugs cold turkey, do you understand me? I stopped smoking drugs, all for God. That was God, that wasn't me. And then I got thrown back in the midst of that. I got my own place and I was trying to walk with God but I had a neighbor downstairs that used crack, used to phone me all the time, and I used to lay up here and cry and pray, ask [God] to restrict these urges but it didn't work. How can I change if I can't even get out of there? I have to be able to get out of there and I can't get out of it [crying].

Obviously, the children are influenced by all of these events, including Angela's significant efforts to be a "good Christian mom," and to teach them about the Bible. However, this mother's spirituality provides one of the only positive forces that she has been able to marshal in her attempt to offset a lifetime of addiction to crack, homelessness and housing insecurities, and other difficult circumstances. Thus, the longer personal history and structural disadvantages appear to overwhelm or swamp the positive potential of her newfound spirituality and her attempts to become a more effective parent.

Another respondent Jeanette, when interviewed in 1995, indicated that she had earlier experienced a problem with alcohol (and at least one DUI), but had turned her life over to Christ. Indeed, all of the life-history narratives were assigned shorthand titles, and while Angela's above was labeled "Rock-Bottom Homeless," Jeannette was given the label "Gone Clean, Spiritual." Further, responses to the 1995 self-reported crime index backed up the desister story line. At the time of the 2003 interview, however, Jeanette's self-report index documented drug use and other criminal activity within the year, and the life-history narrative was even more revealing:

> ... Wrong place at the wrong time. Wrong people, wrong crowd. Boyfriends. I fell into a problem with drugs. I did this for three years and me and the kids were separated. From '99 to 2001. I was bouncing around from house to house, place to place. Uh ... being out you know on the street. No sleep, no food, no nothing. All you could worry about was where's my next high going to come from. The next day what ... like, what can I steal today? Who's checks can I take today? You know. And, you know, at that time all I could do was worry about where I was going to get high at and how I was going to feed that habit. I was never caught boosting. I was picked up for forging and I was picked up for drug paraphernalia, and one time I was picked up for criminal trespassing and had a warrant on me, but they let me go.

Jeanette expressed great remorse about that period of her life, again had custody of her children, and appeared firmly committed to the idea of staying away from drugs. Spirituality remains an important part of her life. Yet her narrative also reflected a willingness to reunite with the children's father when he is released from prison:

> I'm open. I'm open, yes. If and when the time arrives if he can prove to me that he wants to maintain sobriety. That's right. You got to prove it to me. I had to prove it to my ... my kids, my family, my mother, my dad. Prove it to me. Oh they ... they're waiting for the day he comes home. They want him ... they want him back. They know I mean it. The only way Dad's coming home is if he's able to maintain sobriety. They know that. And they accept that. Because the kids need it. The kids want it. They all miss him, yep.

These excerpts illustrate that respondents do not necessarily choose companions to coordinate with their own drug use or criminal involvement, as the pure selection argument implies. In Angela's case, limited resources have circumscribed her housing options to the most marginal, high-crime area of the city, and Jeanette has been influenced by her children's reasonable wish to be reunited with their father. In short, the goal of completely transforming network ties may be an unrealizable task for many respondents, even when their spirituality has opened up the potential for moving in a more favorable life direction.

We also emphasized that while spirituality has a strong individual component, social ties often foster and strengthen the individual's religious commitment and involvement. The countervailing dynamic, then, is that if these spiritual others are not available to provide this reinforcement, the individual's own levels of participation may be difficult to sustain over the longer period of time. Obviously, when Angela was teaching her children about the Bible "day and night," this was a major preoccupation within the household. Her return to the use of crack cocaine, however, interrupted this religious emphasis, and created a host of potentially overwhelming problems for all members of the family. Blake found a religious mentor outside his family but did not sustain his own involvement over the long haul:

> … I used to be in the church and stuff a lot … I met this guy named Art, he's a counselor at JYC [Junior Youth Camp] and these [other] bible camps I use to go to. And I got real close to this guy; I was really into the Lord and stuff and then, uh … then three years ago I went to camp and everything was fine; I leave and he had his birthday two weeks later and the day after his birthday he died of cardiac arrest …. he was huge but he wouldn't hurt a fly. And he had such a big impact on my life. I believe he's one of my guardian angels now. Because you don't forget somebody that makes a big impact on your life like that. Granted, I'm not really into church and all that stuff now, but I feel he's still my guardian angel. I'll never be able to forget somebody like that. And see that? I've got it right there on my right arm [a tattoo].

Jarod's narrative, quoted below, is of interest, because it includes a religious emphasis but also highlights the importance of his relationship with a caring adult family member, who has apparently provided advice and direction on multiple domains of this teen's life, and a stability that coalesces effectively with his religious faith:

> My uncle plays a big role in my life and I'm glad, you know what I'm saying? I'm a strong believer in God, it's like God makes stuff happen for a reason, you know what I'm saying? He's got a goal for us all, you know what I'm saying? He put my uncle in my life and not my father in my life probably for a good reason because my father ain't shit, he ain't never going to be nothing, you know what I'm saying? But my uncle, he's doing big things, he tells me everything about women, about money, about cars, you know, how to buy a house and how they raise interest rates and stuff like that. He tells me everything.

(2) New problems that continue to arise may be associated with depression and angry emotions, heightening risk for violence or using drugs and other negative coping strategies.

Although many respondents indicated that religion had provided them with desirable feelings of peace and serenity and was a valuable coping resource, the lives of these adults and children inevitably move forward, and because of their early difficulties and negative social contacts, new problems often appear on the horizon. Violence and drug/alcohol use are two coping strategies that have (i) qualities of immediacy, (ii) connections to negative emotions, and (iii) familiarity to these respondents. In stressful situations, these methods for handling problems may compete successfully with more productive spiritual coping strategies (the parents have a long personal history and the children the social learning opportunities we described in Chapter Six). In the excerpt below we can see that Bob's former partner's drug use connects to an array of negative events and emotions and eventually to Bob's reliance on violence to solve a family problem:

> To be honest with you, I didn't want their mother to know where her kids were at, for the simple fact of what she was doing with them. She was on crack real bad, she was, um, doing all kinds of drugs. I found, the house was a wreck when I got out of jail. I mean I did six or seven months for felonious assault for stabbing one of the guys

that, you know, had my daughter buck naked, dancing in front of a couch full of dirty men.

The children, too, may realize that praying and church involvement represents a positive development in their lives, but they have also learned negative coping strategies that have long permeated their family environments. For example, Jarrell, who had recently moved in with a youth pastor, had been abused by a close relative, and while he did not discuss this in his own interview, his mother indicated that she recently learned that he had molested his younger, developmentally delayed sister, Marsha. Indeed, this appeared to be a major reason for his decision to move in with the youth pastor.

In the above discussion, we have assumed that religion is generally beneficial, but that other factors may serve to derail the progress respondents associated with their spirituality. However, it is also possible that in some respects, religious experiences/emphasis may prove limiting to the parents' and children's efforts to manage their lives. For example, many of the more spiritually oriented respondents appreciate the personal nature of their relationship with God. While people and even structured religion may disappoint, they know that God is always "there for them." But, to the degree that spirituality connects only to a private set of beliefs and experiences, others are not available to challenge the nature of those beliefs, provide tangible support, or reinforce the idea of adapting a prosocial way of life. Wendy, for example, described a close relationship with God that coexisted well with a particularly wild phase of her life: "But, honey, me and God then had a close relationship. I might do stupid things and he knew that, but he's like, 'I feel you.' I've gotta let Wendy live her life 'cause I know either way she's gonna do it. 'Cause see, I'm one of them type of person, I have to live it." Josh, a 17-year-old teen professes a strong belief in God, but indicates that he is currently not interested in making the type of behavior changes that he believes are associated with a complete commitment to his religious faith: "Because, like, if I get baptized then I got to stop doing, like, stuff that I like, the things that I do. Like, sometimes I might slip up and everything and cuss and all that. Like have sex and all that. You're not suppose to do that. I mean, I still ain't ready to stop doing that stuff."

Another belief of many of the OLS respondents and their children is that God takes care of all things, and directly intervenes in positive ways. As an example, Lindsey notes:

> **Q:** And how … how would God help you?
> **R:** Because he would … he was always basically there for us. He would always, you know …
> **Q:** How has God been there?
> **R:** He'd like send money down to us and help us.

Matthew also believes that God is directly available to help with all aspects of his life: "I just pray just to pray. It helps me out and like … Like I don't, like, got to worry about something when it happens or nothing. Because you don't have to handle the situation. God will."

This is a great source of comfort to these spiritually oriented respondents, but may be associated with difficulties in two respects. First, to the degree that these family members do not take efficacious actions to improve specific aspects of their lives, they will not have in place concrete supports to sustain the generally beneficial impact of their religious involvement. For example, some prisons that have adapted spiritually oriented programs for inmates have also given attention to job training and placement, recognizing that economic viability is a necessary component of inmates' success in avoiding future problems (Johnson & Larson, 2006).

A second potentially problematic aspect of this set of beliefs is that it may be associated with religious struggles or disillusionment when prayer or devotion does not produce an obvious "result." Recent research has documented that while spirituality generally is associated with more favorable health outcomes and even lower mortality, this is not the case for those who indicate that they have experienced religious doubts/struggles (Manning-Walsh, 2005; Pargament, 1997; Pargament et al., 2001). Thus, while it is common, even in general population surveys, for a crisis event such as death of a child, divorce, and the like, to precipitate a turn toward greater religiosity, in many instances such respondents' lives may return to relative stability after an illness, loss, or other crisis. In contrast, the lives of these respondents often continue to be difficult, a daily reality that may increase questioning, doubt, and associated stress that brings disillusionment, and for some, antisocial behavior involvement. Janie is only nine years old, but notes that her prayers are not always answered in the direct way that she would like: "I just think about it every night and pray before I go to sleep that our family be alright but in the next morning my, uh, cousin died. You .... you suppose to like count on God to sort of like protect your family and stuff." It is also interesting to note that Janie's mother's 2003 narrative is labeled "Struggling to maintain religious path in face of temptation." If Darla's own life begins to unravel again, this may interrupt her religious practices, and have a cascading negative effect on Janie's religiosity, her family life, and obviously, her own well-being.

This sense of disillusionment is even more palpable in the narratives of some of the adult respondents:

> I've always felt from a child all the way up that I've ... my life has been nothing but a ... a catastrophe, you might say. That I was put here just not for to have any happiness in my life. Not to have any love. Anybody that cares. And ... when He took my mother-in-law away. And they say God controls everything, well I've sit and I've looked at my life and it's like my life has been wrong since the day I was born. There's not ... there hasn't really been anything in my life that has went right. Well, it states in the Bible God controls everything. God controls all, well, it's like I ... I feel that God has put me here for nothing other than pain, to go through pain and to suffer because that's all I do. Is everyday I get up and ... and from the time I get up to the time I go to bed I ... its causes pain, hurt. [Christine]

A final, related set of beliefs that may prove limiting to a spirituality benefit is a strong focus on the devil or Satan as a source of negative events. Thus, even if individuals maintain a strong belief in God's beneficence, respondents sometimes spoke of evil forces that directly intervene in uncontrollable and negative ways:

> You know, I got to stay spiritually strong because if Satan is after me that bad, then it ain't going to stop. Well, put it this way, you know Satan is more stronger than what people think he is. Every bad thing on this earth has got to do with Satan. [Doug]

And, consistent with our symbolic interactionist perspective, narrative excerpts further highlight that while such beliefs are individually held, these appear, like all cognitions, to have been developed (Mead,

1934) through interaction and communication with others: "The devil don't work on people that he's already got. He wants the people that he don't got. That what a lot of the priests and stuff that I've talked to, you know, have told me, some of the case workers, and that does sound, you know, logical." A potential problem with assigning a strong active role for the devil is that this is readily available as an explanation for giving into temptation or to other difficulties that arise. This could also limit motivation or a perceived need to focus on concrete issues and goals (the idea of self-efficacy).

Despite the limitations that are associated with relying solely on spirituality as a primary identity hook and source of guidance, the references to God and religion remain among the most positive aspects of many of the OLS child and adult narratives. Sometimes the narratives of adult respondents focused in very positive ways on their roles as parents, and a subset described a strong relationship with a prosocial partner that was extremely important and helpful to them. Yet, as we discussed in prior chapters, many OLS parents have faced difficulties with the parenting role, and finding an appropriate spouse/romantic partner has also proven to be an elusive prospect for these respondents. And importantly, the OLS children have not yet reached an age when they are able to craft an identity around the role of spouse or parent. Thus, it appears that developing an identity as a "child of God" remains one of the few hopeful options available to these respondents.

STRONG FUTURE ORIENTATION: THE IMPORTANCE OF LONG-TERM GOALS

The two relatively prosocial, adaptive orientations or identities we described above are situated in the present, as some youths focused on "taking care of business" within the family and others gained strength from their strong religious faith. While we recognize that these are ideal types (i.e., a given youth's narrative could conceivably emphasize all of these adaptations), a strong focus on future goals was another orientation that appeared to be associated with positive emotional and behavioral well-being. Commitment to school is a traditional protective factor in studies of resilience, but the focus on even more distant long-term goals provided some OLS youths with the motivation required to stay away from the difficulties their parents and some of their siblings have faced:

> I just been saying that, like, my whole life. I just always want to be a lawyer and everybody say, because I like to argue and I don't stop arguing until I'm able to prove my point. that I would be good at it, so I just chose to be a lawyer. [Rachel]

> That makes me very proud of myself to be able to do that because my brother didn't even graduate. He dropped out when he was sixteen because he was just, he had trouble in school so bad. And I had trouble but I was not forcing myself to drop out because I was having trouble. I was going to do it whether I liked it or not. Didn't like it very well but now I do because I'm going to make it. [Alex]

> Well, in medical assistance, you know, I like to help people. I like to be there for somebody. So, I want to help people out in their life with the medical assistant part. But as far as, like, premed and forensics go in college, the reason I want to do forensics is because my aunt died … well, she was murdered. [Erin]

Our intent in this book has been to describe family circumstances and dynamics that are specific to this type of population of children. For example, the child's adoption of a caring, protective stance within the family (the caregiver role) may be beneficial, but taking on the caregiver role is not even a possibility within families where parents are functioning more effectively. Similarly, general population youth surveys often document that religiosity is negatively related to delinquency and drug use, but in these samples, religiosity often coalesces with traditional protective factors (e.g., a two-parent home, a prosocial orientation of parents) that provide a more reliable spirituality benefit. The OLS children, in contrast, often face everyday difficulties that challenge their faith/beliefs, or overwhelm the positive effects of religion on their lives. Similarly, the child's focus on long-term goals, while also generally positive, acquires a distinct meaning and potential impact within a sample such as the one we have focused upon in this investigation.

First, it appears that many of the goals the OLS youth focus upon are unrealistic. Their specific plans and dreams are in many instances not connected to educational attainment in the present that would set them on the success path that they desire. In addition, most have not received the kind of adult mentoring that would allow them to participate in higher education and, later on, in their chosen occupational careers. Of course, many young people aspire to occupations that are not the ones they eventually take up (Reynolds et al., 2006). Yet the adolescent whose father is a lawyer understands the basics of the legal profession and can provide tangible assistance in navigating the steps required to pursue a career in law (e.g., be able to answer such questions as, when should I take my LSAT test?). Similarly, if the child decides to take up medicine, the parent's cultural and social capital will tend to set in motion conditions favorable to achieving this goal. By contrast, Danika indicated that she planned to major in both modeling and law as an undergraduate. She had searched the Internet in order to find the perfect school that offered both majors. In Danika's social circle, no one was available to tell her that modeling does not require a college degree, that law requires advanced studies, and that focusing on two such disparate paths might not be the best strategy for achieving either goal. Finally, the university she had chosen was located in a distant state and featured on its Web site pictures of students and faculty holding classes on the beach. These realities further reducing the general feasibility of her plan and cast doubt on the quality of the educational experience she might receive if she were somehow able to secure a scholarship.

Some students (e.g., Jessica, who talked about becoming a medical assistant) described future goals that would appear to be associated with more realistic chances for success, but this was not a common pattern. And even Jessica combined this with another choice (forensics) that was highly unrealistic, apparently motivated more by her aunt's murder than a basic interest in a scientific career. But while these harsh realities suggest limitations to the respondents' focus on long-term goals, a tentative hypothesis is that this future orientation nevertheless has protective, beneficial effects. The adolescents recognize that the type of long-term achievements they discuss are less likely if they continue to get into trouble at school, affiliate with "bad companions," take drugs, or experience an early pregnancy. Thus, these aspirations can serve as a bridge that allows them to traverse the various risks associated with the adolescent period, particularly within the high-risk contexts they inhabit. Later on, disappointments may occur, but these respondents will nevertheless have avoided an early-starting pattern of deviance and nonconformity that makes even modest positive adult transitions unattainable.

Jake believes that he is destined for a lucrative football career. While this may also prove to be an unattainable goal in the long run, his focus appears to have immediate positive benefits and may have long-term benefits as well. Like many of the OLS youths, Jake does not wish to turn out like his father, but his goal orientation adds specifics to his goal of developing a contrasting identity and lifestyle:

> It makes you think how, how you want to grow up? Do you want to grow up and be like that or do you want to be better than that? That's all my mom would talk about. Is do you want to grow up to be like him or be better than my dad? And I always say, better than my dad. That's why I want to go to Texas. My dad never been to college. My dad didn't even, my real dad never even, I don't think he finished high school. And I'm gonna finish my years of high school, I'm gonna have fun at the same time. That's why I keep my, that's why I try to keep my GPA high, so I can play football. That's basically what I want to do, I love football. Football is just, man, that's, now that's something I can say I love. Football, man, just to play a sport, and if I was ever mad at my dad, I could just go on the football field and just take out all of my anger. And I could just have fun at the same time.

Jake's love of football thus not only serves as an anchor for a positive future identity, but is one that links directly to prosocial activities and affiliations during the adolescent period (involvement with coaches and teammates, keeping up his GPA, anger management). Nevertheless, his mother is also very supportive of Jake and is continually available to reinforce his prosocial plans. Because our study of the children is cross-sectional, we are unable to determine whether the focus on goals that are not entirely realistic is associated with later disillusionment, emotional difficulties, or problem behaviors that begin to unfold when these goals are no longer viewed as attainable aspirations. For example, Macleod (1995), in his classic study, *Ain't No Makin' It: Aspirations and Attainments in a Low-Income Neighborhood*, noted that the young men he observed and interviewed held positive hopes for their futures during the adolescent period but became increasingly demoralized by their lack of conventional opportunities when interviewed later in their twenties. Nevertheless, across the sample of very disadvantaged OLS youth as a whole, these future-oriented youths appear better positioned than their live-for-today counterparts, who were often fully enmeshed in problem lifestyles and behaviors.

ADULTS WHO CARE AND REPRESENT A STRONG CONTRAST

A few of the young respondents we interviewed were in the process of achieving along traditional lines (e.g., they had been accepted at a college or were attending one) and these individuals appear to be in many respects similar to those who have been described in prior research on resilient youth. An analysis of their narratives generally reveals the active, intense involvement of one or more adults (biological parents or other relatives) who in many instances were not the core respondents in the OLS study. For example, we began this chapter with a quote from Kaley, who was excited to tell her stepfather about her acceptance to a nursing school. She credits her relationship with her stepfather and his girlfriend with her ability to move beyond the difficulties she encountered when she lived (off and on for many years) with her mother. Kaley had not only developed a close relationship with her stepfather, but her stepfather and his partner represented a lifestyle that contrasted sharply with that of her mother's. Kaley's relationships with them were a source of attachment and monitoring, but they also provided economic and social stability and definitions unfavorable to the violation of law. Recall Kaley's references in prior quotes to frequent school and residential moves, and periods when she and her mother took mushrooms and other drugs together. Here she notes a strong contrast since she has lived with her stepfather:

> We ... plus we had Jenny. She was our stepmom, you know. I mean, if it wasn't for her I wouldn't know how to shave my legs. I wouldn't know make-up. I wouldn't know anything. She is my mother ... And eventually she moved in with us, and she would drive an hour and a half to work everyday and yet she would still wake us up and get

us ready for school. Make us, you know, our lunches. Be home in time, you know what I'm saying, to make dinner and to have, you know what I'm saying, family time. She tried so hard and I was so difficult because, you know what I'm saying? I had my mom. I had her. I didn't know. I was a royal bitch to her growing up but she still taught me you know; there were those times every Saturday we would go shopping together. She would constantly take me to get my hair cut. We would, you know, she would give me something out of her closet all the time or her diamond earrings. And she taught me ... She taught me, you know, to be polite. Not to be like my mom. So if it wasn't for her I wouldn't, you know, act this way. And just ... Jenny raised me; she's my mom and ... When I'm around them I ... I'm not me. I'm more worried about being proper, you know, nothing low cut, nothing too tight, nothing, you know what I'm saying ... Like everything ... my shoes have to be scrubbed. I mean I'm a ... I freak about that stuff. When I'm around them I watch every word I say. I'm ... I'm not me.

He's [stepdad] a very safe man, you know. You don't run around town. You don't disrespect people. You don't talk bad. You don't do potty mouth because it isn't lady like, you know. Jenny always taught me you shower twice a day. You know, you put lotion on. You can shave your legs really quick in the shower. You know, you don't ... you don't have ... see, I would always like, "well I'll shave my legs in a couple weeks." No, you do it real quick in the shower, you know what I'm saying. Everyday. And you don't have to worry about it, you know, getting all funky. And put on lotion everyday and shop at Victoria's Secret and buy their sprays and their lotions, and that's what I was raised on. Her taking me out every Saturday and going shopping. That's how we bonded and that's how we ended up becoming so close. I can tell her ... I could tell her [anything], you know what I'm saying? But the thing about her is, she tells my dad.

OTHER POSITIVES WITHIN THE NARRATIVES

In this chapter, we have focused on young people who on some level are doing well in "managing to make it," despite their early family difficulties. It is important to highlight that the number of classic success stories is small indeed. Nevertheless, the youths whose situations we have described appear to exhibit fewer problem outcomes, and they are in general characterized by greater emotional well-being than many of the young respondents in the OLS sample. In addition, these youths can be seen as improving upon their parents' early trajectories and, in many cases, the lifestyles of their siblings.

Although we have focused most of our attention on particular respondents or "cases," it is also useful to consider some additional positive dynamics that the narratives reveal, even though they may not result in stand-alone identities or anchors associated with resilient adaptations. For example, while the presence of caring, prosocial adults represents an ideal network situation, it is one that is not within the grasp of a large number of these young respondents. Thus, affiliation with caring, generally prosocial peers may also be a source of social support and positive direction.

> Oh, a couple of them [her friends] I can talk to about that. I tell them where my mom is – [jail]. They say they feel sorry for me and stuff. If I just keep all this stuff to myself it would really, my attitude would be really different I think. I'd be angry at the world. When I tell somebody it feels much better. [Lindsey]

Previously, we discussed the dynamics associated with friendship choices, including the tendency to select friends who may have experienced family problems that are similar to their own. This is a potentially useful observation because it highlights that a strong interest in pursuing delinquent activities may not always be the primary motivation for these affiliations. And while this may in some instances amplify the child's risk (since both friends have been socialized within risk contexts), this is not inevitable. For example, the interviewer noted that "Jon has a close friend, Alex, who is in a similar situation. They support and encourage each other to keep their eyes on the future and their lofty goals":

> My best friend Alex, my best friend, man, since school, we used to run together, everything, we did it all, me, him, and Chris. Chris, we branched off but he's still doing his thing, but that's still my boy, you know what I'm saying? I grew up with him, too, his mom and dad, he's got the sob story with me. Same way with Alex, no daddy ... [Q: So Alex feels the same way that you do, he wants to make it?] Yeah, oh yeah, I promised him no matter what that I'm going to look out for him.

Another potentially important observation is that even though many parents continued a pattern of drug abuse or crime during their children's formative years, the relationship between the child and parent was not inevitably strained or without positive features and effects. For example, Tiffany found her mother to be an extremely supportive parent, even though she was unable to live with her. She talked on the phone with her most days after school:

> Like, I would talk about things that are going on at school. About the girls that argue or relationships or anything. And she'll sit there and talk and understand. But other girls, they like can't talk to their mama or their mom won't listen or get mad at them or something.

The above quote highlights the social psychological reaction to the parent's circumstances as a key consideration, since Tiffany was able to benefit from her mother's support rather than focusing on her anger and disappointment about not being able to live with her. The quote below provides another example of the importance of perspective and shows that this need not reflect that certain "kinds of people" are simply more capable of accessing the support they need. Sarah's more positive social circumstances were a direct reflection of her own gradual change in viewpoint:

> And it was really, like, because I wasn't talking to nobody I felt like wasn't nobody really there for me. Nobody really for me to talk to but now I realize that there is. They [her sisters] ... they always there and they always open and willing to talk to me ... I wasn't talking to anybody. I keep my feelings bottled up inside. I feel like I didn't want to put my stress on they shoulders. When they all realized it's a mutual thing. We do it together, we just don't do it alone. We go through this together.

Similarly, Aaron, quoted below, experienced a "cognitive transformation" about the importance of distancing himself from negative influences and the fast lifestyle. This shift in viewpoint was not linked to traditional external prosocial influences or to being held in check by external forces (the control notion). This, too complicates the idea that resilient versus nonresilient youth is a straightforward dichotomy:

> We stayed on Belleview Avenue, straight hood, for real. You know what I'm saying? I'm not that type of dude; I never was but you get involved, you start selling drugs, you start doing this. It was not the

life I would have chose. Everybody know "fast money is don't-last money"; that's just how you grow up in the hood. Everybody knows that. You can buy tennis shoes, you can buy that, but I want bigger things, [but] you have to work. Every dope man and druggie eventually gets caught.

Katie is another respondent who has not completely isolated herself from negative influences but maintains a strong, generally prosocial attitude that allows her to distance herself from their negative actions:

Yeah, that's all, that's what half of my friends do is drink and I'm, oh yeah that's nice. Like my friend she had her nineteenth birthday and she's like "Do you want to come over we're getting drunk?" and I'm like "Yeah sure I'll come over" but I never showed up.

Consistent with this, later on in the interview she tells the interviewer about how she plans to deal with such friends at her graduation party:

Q: Tell me, um, so your concern is that there will be alcohol at the party or the graduation?
R: Yeah.
Q: Okay. Do you think that you'll get much control over that?
R: Yeah I will. All I have to say to them if they bring it, they're leaving. I don't care if there is only two people left at my graduation party, they're leaving.

These examples are useful because they illustrate that youths often strive to maintain a positive lifestyle, or redirect an initial rocky start without the traditional elements (presence of a caring adult, success in academics) that we tend to associate with the resilience process. These valiant efforts have a counterpart in the adult respondents' own life stories, where we have described, for example, some respondents' attempts to isolate themselves in apartments so that they are able to resist the pull of negative peer influences, while others become immersed in Bible study and the life of a church. A continuing problem is that when these "agentic moves" are not accompanied by structural, cultural, and social supports, the positive momentum is, for some, difficult, if not impossible, to sustain.

CHAPTER EIGHT

Theoretical and Policy Implications
of the OLS Study

This longitudinal study presented a unique opportunity to follow up the children of young people who as adolescents had engaged in serious, sometimes repeated, acts of law violation. After these respondents were released from the juvenile institution in which they had initially been interviewed in 1982, many of them continued a pattern of crime and drug abuse well into their adult years. When we interviewed them in 1995, in addition to self-reported crime and adult arrests, the women and men who participated in the OLS frequently also reported numerous other disadvantages and life problems, including depression, a lack of employment, housing instability, and continued association with antisocial family members, friends, and romantic partners. And while male self-reported crime scores were higher and prison stays for males on average longer, we did not find that women in the sample quit crime abruptly with the birth of their first child, an outcome that some prior research has indicated. The women were, however, more likely than their male counterparts to either live with their children or have contact with them, which is consistent with women's central childrearing role in our society. At the same time, the OLS women were significantly more likely than is typical for women in the general population (according to U.S. census figures) to indicate that at least one and sometimes all of their children were not currently living with them or had not lived with them at some earlier point.

The second follow-up interviews we conducted in 2003, with these respondents, and at least one of their biological children, were primarily focused on issues of parenting and child-well-being. Relative

to the steep, downward age-crime curve that is typically documented
in traditional surveys, as we discussed in Chapter Four, this cohort of
graduates from the state institution for juvenile offenders often continued to be involved in drug-oriented lifestyles and to report many
other legal problems. Indeed, many follow-up interviews with respondents were conducted in prison or jail, underscoring this pattern of
persistent difficulties. Perhaps it should not be surprising, then, that
the OLS children's levels of delinquency, violence, and serious drug
use were significantly higher than those observed in a sample of similarly aged youths who participated in the TARS, answering identical
questions.

As our analyses showed, some youths clearly fared better than others. But the key finding of this follow-up is that so few children could
be neatly classified as success stories, at least as success is traditionally
defined in studies of resilient youth (e.g., high academic achievement,
emotional health, no evidence of involvement in problem behavior).
The life-history approach makes this clear relative to the distribution
of scores on typical self-reported delinquency instruments, for several
reasons. First, even where children scored low on delinquency, their
narratives, along with those of parents and caregivers, often highlight
other problems such as disruptiveness at school, truancy, or mental
health problems that make it difficult to classify these children as clear
successes. Similarly, many self-reported delinquency scales, including
the version used in this study, reference the 12-month period immediately prior to the interview. Again, the narrative detail we elicited
from the respondents often referenced previous phases, or "eras," of
the children's short lives that included serious involvement in delinquent acts, aggression, drug use, and contact with the justice system.
A related problem is that the youngest of the children we interviewed
had not yet passed through the critical teen years, when peer contact and freedom of movement increases along with the potential for
involvement in risky behaviors. Thus, it is difficult to conclude that
either Jeena, who had recently given up smoking crack but continued
to associate with a crack-addicted boyfriend, or 11-year-old Ashley,
whose narrative was titled "Fifth-Grade Bully," will be able to successfully avoid future difficulties. The straightforward comparison
of the OLS parents' delinquency scores as adolescents and the OLS

children's own scores (see Table 4) does depict significantly lower levels reported by the latter. However, the content of the life-history narratives continually reminds us that these data did not begin to provide a comprehensive portrait of the difficulties this cohort of children had faced, nor of the specific effects their parents' problems had on their development and well-being.

THEORETICAL IMPLICATIONS OF
THE OLS FOLLOW-UP

As outlined in Chapter Two, control theory and to a lesser degree social learning theory are two frameworks that are often marshalled to explore the family dynamics associated with continuity in anti-social outcomes across generations. These two theoretical perspectives highlight important but distinct processes that in most respects are compatible. In our view, the symbolic interactionist framework described in Chapter Six adds to our understanding of mechanisms involved in intergenerational transmission, beyond the factors emphasized in these two theoretical traditions.

Control theory highlights the importance of parental attachment and effective supervision as key processes that serve to inhibit delinquency involvement. These dynamics have been examined in connection with more general studies of delinquency, and are also seen as important to an understanding of intergenerational transmission. Recall the hypothesis developed by Thornberry et al. (2003) that the effect of adolescent delinquency on the later behavior of children is largely indirect, resulting in a greater likelihood of exhibiting lax or otherwise ineffective parenting. The authors also conclude that, although there are multiple pathways linking parent and child behaviors across generations, the direct path is "in many ways, the least informative path because it sheds little, if any, light on the causal processes involved." Thus, Thornberry et al. do not fully explore the notion that the direct path (i.e., associations between parent and child outcomes that are significant even when other factors, such as parenting practices or family poverty, are introduced as controls) provides evidence of more direct transmission processes, as elaborated in Sutherland's theory of differential association. This is the case even though Thornberry et al.'s prior work emphasizes the importance of social interaction processes and the ways in which embeddedness in deviant networks, "serve[s] to foreclose conventional lifestyles and entrap the individual in deviant lifestyles" (Thornberry & Krohn, 2001: 296). Instead the authors conclude that the primary outcome of this criminal embeddedness is to "reduce the chances that the person will become an effective parent when he or she has children" (Thornberry & Krohn, 2003: 174). Hirschi takes a harder line against the idea of direct transmission in suggesting that parents, even if deviant, rarely reveal this to their children. Thus, it is argued that social learning is not a significant dynamic underlying delinquency in general and intergenerational transmission in particular.

The interviews we conducted provide substantial evidence of lax or ineffective parenting practices, consistent with Hirschi's theoretical emphases and the findings of Thornberry and other researchers. However, our results highlight numerous ways in which direct transmission occurs within many of the OLS families. Some examples are striking, such as Susan's mother angrily striking the teacher after she found out the teacher had disciplined Susan at school; Kaley's statement that she had used mushrooms with her mother; or Viv's description of how her husband had taught their son to clean marijuana for future sale. However, mundane "everyday" lessons appear to be transmitted on a routine basis as well. Our analyses suggested the following general observations about the process of providing what may accumulate as "definitions favorable to the violation of law" and, in turn, as the unfolding of problem behaviors on the part of this younger generation.

(1) *Parents do not want their children to become delinquent.* It is important to distinguish the parent's general long-term hopes for the child, which are almost always prosocial, from situated messages that nevertheless translate to higher risk that the child will become involved in antisocial behavior. Thus, for example, parents may not want their children to grow up to be arrested on assault charges but often believe that it is imperative to teach them to defend themselves at a very young age.

(2) *Definitions are delivered across a range of "transmission" methods.* The parent conveys attitudes and demonstrates behaviors through

modeling (the child's observations), as well as through interaction and direct communication with the child, other family members, and the parents' larger network of affiliations. In addition, this wider circle of parental contacts, including the spouse or romantic partner and parents' friends, may contribute further to an excess of definitions favorable to the violation of law.

(3) *Behaviors defined as delinquent acts make up only a small part of the content of what is transmitted across generations.* In addition to providing antisocial definitions, parents continually convey attitudes and values concerning the noncrime world (education, conduct within romantic relationships, economic matters) that may nevertheless add significantly to the child's overall risk. Thus, not only does smoking marijuana in front of or with the child have an impact, the parent who allows a child to stay at home from school to care for siblings communicates much about the value the parent puts on education; over time the child's disengagement from school and academic failure increase the likelihood of a delinquent outcome. Similarly, an intense focus within the family on romantic entanglements (their own and those of the children and other relatives) may overshadow interest in and follow-up about the child's homework assignments, and cue the child that the romantic realm offers more drama and excitement. We have referred to this informally as "the soap opera effect." The parent's highly conflictual relationship style may also contribute to the likelihood of aggression within the child's later romantic relationships, which decreases the conventionalizing potential of these heterosexual liaisons.

(4) *Opportunities abound for parents to provide definitions favorable to delinquent acts, aggression, or drug use, as well as to engage in lax, or otherwise ineffective parenting practices.* The results of this study suggest the need to temper Hirschi's general assertions that learning and control theories are incompatible, and that parents shield their children from their own antisocial behavior. Lack of attachment and proper supervision are reliable predictors of delinquency, but it is limiting to conceptualize the dynamics of intergenerational transmission entirely in light of what is missing or lacking within the family. Attention to the basic tenets of differential association/social learning theories requires that we also consider the content of life within

families, including the nature of communications and emphases that may contribute to continuity across generations. The neo-Meadian perspective we developed highlights the centrality of subjective processes, including the role of emotions.

Both the findings of the OLS study and the examples drawn from the life-history narratives we elicited from the parent and child respondents provide a portrait of multiple, overlapping risks that require a theoretical treatment of the intergenerational transmission process, which is itself multifaceted. By focusing on the importance of "definitions," differential association theory adds to control theory's emphasis on external constraints on the individual. Similarly, the symbolic interactionist perspective that we developed incorporates those dynamics but adds an emphasis on *subjective processes* and the reciprocal relationship between the child and the social environment. Thus, the child is not an entirely passive observer of what takes place within the family but is always acting and reacting. This point has often been made with respect to parental control efforts, for example, the idea that rebellious or difficult children may in effect set in motion particular parenting practices by which they are in turn influenced (Crouter & Booth, 2003). Even more fundamentally, the child reacts cognitively and emotionally to control attempts, and even to a lack of control (e.g., understanding that other children have parents who are more vigilant in monitoring their whereabouts or feeling afraid and angry about being left alone with an inappropriate guardian). Similarly, social learning mechanisms have most often been conceptualized as "exterior" as well as behavioral or cognitive processes, as children absorb and later mimic the behavioral profiles of others in their social networks. Thus, a key point, elaborated in Chapter Six, is that even the process of transmitting definitions is not likely to be an affectively neutral affair – emotions are also critical to consider.

The child faces heightened risk for using drugs by virtue of exposure to parents' use but also recognizes the normal-but-not-normal qualities of life within the family, and makes comparisons to other children, times, and places (*Other moms wouldn't give their children alcohol and drugs for their party; I remember what life was like when mom was sober*). The subjective element, then, includes emotional reactions to what is taking place that potentially amplify what is already a formidable complement of risks. The nature of these emotional reactions is variable, however. Thus, given equally difficult family circumstances some children may react angrily to their parents' difficulties, while others assume a protective, caring stance. These reactions and varying interpretations affect the child's behavior patterns as surely as individual traits such as intelligence, which has long been associated with more resilient adaptations, do.

The symbolic interactionist perspective also contributes to our understanding of intergenerational processes by focusing on the child's developing identity. Identity can be a source for intergenerational transmission or, potentially, for altering the strong cultural press favoring continuity within the family. Individuals are more than receivers of control attempts or an accumulation of parental attitudes. As they mature, children increasingly desire a sense of coherence about the world and about themselves, even as they become more adept at handling seemingly contradictory elements. Further, all children reflect on how they are similar to or different from their parents; yet this becomes a more central preoccupation/anchor for identity development within the context of families such as those who participated in the OLS. Levels of disadvantage characterizing families vary, but identity departures and the play of agency are evident as children struggle to carve out a different path. Children may take concrete steps, for example, to align with whatever prosocial network members are available in their social environments, while distancing themselves, emotionally, physically (or both) from negative sources of influence. They may also develop associations outside the family that have a beneficial effect (e.g., the spiritually oriented youth), or fix on a future goal that serves as a useful identity hook and offers protective motivation for navigating the risky terrain of the adolescent years.

The role of social psychological processes and a more situated, malleable, and agentic perspective on intergenerational transmission is suggested by the variability evident within as well as across children's narrative accounts. Thus, while the number of youths who reported ever being involved in delinquent acts, violence, or drug use is high, the number of those who narrate such behaviors as a phase or as not being part of their core identities is even more impressive.

Further, the children's stories of shifts and changes do not always trace back neatly to dramatic life events or external circumstances such as a change in caregivers. This observation contributes to our more general critique of some aspects of the life-course perspective as traditionally outlined, with its heavy focus on key transitions and events. The subjectively experienced worlds of children need additional research attention, as these can figure heavily into the unfolding of problem outcomes, as well as to the process of making positive moves and changes. We analyzed the role of such subjective elements in prior examinations of the parents' patterns of persistence in or desistance from crime. By extension and based on the current analysis of these narrative data, it appears that children's attitudes and emotions are also critical mediators; that is, they are central elements of the dynamic processes that link or present elements of contrast between the two generations.

The above observations about the role of subjective processes add to an understanding of mechanisms underlying intergenerational transmission. This emphasis is potentially useful because it fills in needed detail about how and why it occurs and also about negative cases, that is, about the situations of those who have managed to avoid a replay of their parents' difficulties. However, a fully comprehensive approach requires attention to both control and differential theory emphases and to these social psychological processes and reactions. Indeed, the child's objective circumstances (e.g., lack of appropriate supervision, parents' deviant behavior taking place within the home) are a key part of the family content to which the child responds/ reacts.

Undoubtedly, our emphasis on the subjective realms of experience links directly to the lack of variation in observed concrete familial assets across the sample as a whole. For example, traditional "pluses" such as a two-parent family structure, stable employment, and the presence of prosocial partners are in very short supply, making it difficult to observe the play of these more objective sources of variation in the character of the OLS respondents' family lives. This has a parallel in our focus on subjective processes in prior research on adult (the OLS parents') patterns of behavior. In contrast to a number of other studies, notably those conducted by Sampson and Laub, neither marital status nor job stability was systematically related to the odds that these women and men had desisted from crime. This is not because marriage is unimportant as an influence with good conventionalizing potential, but because the highly disadvantaged positions of these respondents (due to prior criminal lifestyles, economic marginality, and social isolation), makes it difficult for them to forge and sustain the type of marriage likely to have a prosocial impact. For example, only 22 percent reported being married at both adult follow-ups, and most often not to the same individual.

These central tendencies within the OLS sample may also be implicated in the lack of significant relationship found between many specific parental characteristics and various child outcomes. Since a majority of parents are economically disadvantaged, for example, it is difficult to observe ways in which variations in economic wherewithal influence child well-being; yet this is surely a critical backdrop for understanding the central tendencies we observe in the generation of children born to this cohort of respondents.

Similarly, based on 12-month self-reported data, the children were significantly less delinquent than their parents at a similar age; however, the positive developments in the lives of many children and adults have a frail, tenuous quality in contrast to more tangible structural and cultural advantages. While spirituality has clearly been an important part of the lives of many respondents, for example, the long-term effects appear uncertain given that this strong spiritual orientation is often a stand-alone development, not backed up by other structural and cultural supports. This contrasts with the more typical scenario observed in random sample surveys. In these, religiosity often dovetails with a host of other traditional protective factors (two-parent family, prosocial parental attitudes and behaviors) that together provide a solid anchor for the child's healthy behavioral and emotional development.

The findings of the OLS study have implications not only for the development of more comprehensive theoretical treatments of the phenomenon of intergenerational transmission, but also for intervention efforts focused on highly vulnerable youth like those who participated in the OLS study. Such applied implications are not divorced from the theoretical issues we have discussed but connect directly to them. Below we describe several elements of our theoretical perspective and study findings that have implications for the current emphases of family and youth serving organizations, recognizing that more research is needed to support the conclusions we base largely on this single investigation.

(1) The need to move beyond the exclusive focus on effects of parental incarceration.

Denise Johnston, director of the Center for the Children of Incarcerated Parents, recently noted that while the increased interest in the children of prisoners has been an important development that has energized research and advocacy efforts, this emphasis is nevertheless not without its costs/limitations:

> After more than five decades of study, there is almost no information about the experiences of these children that are unrelated to incarceration, the content and quality of their lives before and after their parents are incarcerated or about those children whose parents commit crimes, get arrested, and get jailed but do not go to prison. Perhaps those of us who are researchers, policy makers, and/or practitioners in this field should be asking ourselves: Have we gone down the wrong road? (Johnston, 2006: 703)

The perspective we adopted in connection with the OLS study is consistent with Johnston's critique and her call for a broader approach, and also with our goal of offering a life-course view of the children's experiences. Efforts to improve the lives of children of incarcerated parents have proceeded on the assumption that the most devastating events in their lives stem from the parent's incarceration. Accordingly, efforts to improve children's lives often focus on maintaining or enhancing parent-child attachment during this time, a view that links effectively to control theories. Arditti (2005), for example, recognized the need for a multifaceted perspective on the problem (or what she terms an "ecological" approach), but she hypothesized that the parent's contact with the criminal-justice system is the key circumstance that negatively influences family and child well-being in these other respects. For example, Arditti suggests that the concept of "disenfranchised grief" captures the emotional reactions of children and other family members, arguing that they experience a type of loss that is "not openly recognized and not defined as socially significant" (2005: 253). Feelings of stigma and shame about the parent's incarceration are related processes that have also been discussed repeatedly in both theoretical and advocacy-oriented treatments of this topic (Hairston, 2007). Applied efforts organized around these problems have sought to provide youths with counseling or other supportive forums in which to discuss their feelings of loss and shame and have also focused on increasing the child's contact with parents during the incarceration period through methods designed to facilitate visitation and improve the experience itself (see Hairston, 1998; Sturges, 1999). Girl Scouts Beyond Bars (Moses, 1995) and programs designed to keep infants in prisons with their mothers (Zaitzow & Thomas, 2003) are examples of structured programs that seek to develop or enhance parent-child contact and bonding.

Practitioners and researchers interested in incarceration effects recognize that these families and children face numerous other challenges, but they often trace many of these other difficulties to incarceration's effects, rather than to the parent's antisocial lifestyle or disadvantaged status (e.g., very low educational attainment). For example, Arditti suggested that economic strain and family instability (e.g., as reflected in a high percentage single-parent households) and the presence of alternative caregivers were processes that, if not set in motion by, then were clearly exacerbated by the incarceration experience. Johnston, in a critique of this position, noted that a majority of men and a substantial minority of women interviewed in connection with a large-scale prison survey indicated that they did not live with children *prior* to the incarceration experience; thus, children in these households may have garnered significant experience with economic marginality, alternative caregivers and single-parent households prior to the parent's prison stay.

The life-course perspective we outlined and the data we presented in Chapters Three through Seven of this book accord well with Johnston's perspective. It is "going down the wrong road" to focus on the negative effects of parental incarceration only to the degree that we ignore the children's lives prior to and after such periods of involvement with the criminal-justice system. As we have argued throughout, these incarceration periods may be integral to the problem circumstances with which these children must cope, but they have not set all of these circumstances in motion. Further, as Johnston noted, some offenders spend much, if not all, of their time outside the radar of the official system. Based on the results presented here, if we conclude that it is useful to describe children of incarcerated parents as falling through the cracks (i.e., they are well served by neither the criminal-justice system nor child protection/welfare agencies), then this description may even more accurately characterize the children of offenders whose parents are *not* under criminal-justice jurisdiction. It is a greater challenge to provide services to this type of population, but the findings of our study highlight the urgent needs of such children. One reason that children of prisoners have been a target of intervention/services is that they become a concrete, identifiable subgroup by virtue of the parent's prison involvement. The prison may also serve as a location for the delivery of such services. However, by the time adult men and women receive a sentence that includes incarceration at the state level, their lives have often been characterized by arrests, local jail time, and even more importantly, heavy involvement in deviant lifestyles. In short, it is often late in the day for many of their children.

Prevention and intervention efforts aimed at vulnerable youth have long been concerned with the issue of how to identify and then serve children who are likely to be at greatest risk (Farrington & Welsh, 2007). Criteria ranging from low scores on peer status nominations (i.e., measuring how well youths are liked by other grade-school children) to living in a disadvantaged neighborhood have been identified as risk factors. Yet longitudinal research indicates that the number of "false positives" using such criteria is high: many unpopular children do not go on to become delinquent, and some popular ones do; a majority of inner-city youth manage to avoid involvement in serious difficulties. It is intuitive to expect that the children born to serious juvenile offenders may well be a particularly vulnerable subgroup, but this long-term follow-up has allowed us a look into the future, as we described in detail the multiple, overlapping layers of risk that characterize the lives of 158 of such children. The original youths we followed into adulthood do have incarceration experience, as this was a criterion for their initial selection, but intervening in connection with this earlier system involvement (to improve the lives of both the core respondents and their children) would appear to be more timely and efficient than either prevention strategies that cut a wider swath (e.g., targeting children living in disadvantaged neighborhoods) or that focus only on the children of adult prisoners.

(2) Need to target family dynamics highlighted by social learning perspectives.

Whether programs are designed to serve the children of incarcerated parents or populations like the OLS families and their children, focusing on parenting practices constitutes an important, but on its own incomplete, strategy for interrupting the family processes that foster intergenerational continuity. Eddy and Reid (2002) recently outlined four promising approaches for addressing the problems of incarcerated adults and their children drawing principally on the emphases of general programs with a solid track record in the prevention/intervention field (visiting home-nurse programs, parent management training, multisystemic therapy, and multidimensional treatment foster care). Most of these programs focus heavily on parenting practices (e.g., teaching the parent how to provide consistent and supportive supervision), although other domains of the child's life (e.g., school performance) are also targeted.

Based on the results of the OLS study, our view is that without greatly increased attention and resources directed to the issue of the parents' underlying drug and alcohol problems (and sometimes violent behavior), these types of programs will likely turn out to be limited in their effectiveness. We have argued throughout that the parents' deviant behaviors have direct effects that transcend specific parenting practices, both in terms of transmitting antisocial attitudes/behavior patterns and increasing the child's exposure to a wider social network of deviant affiliations (other deviant family members, romantic partners, friends, associates and peers whose family situations are similar) that result in emotionally and behaviorally costly outcomes. These issues are not only theoretical; they influence choices about how best to intervene given the reality of limited resources.

To illustrate, we revisit a quote from an interview with a core respondent, Donna, in connection with the first adult follow-up interview completed in 1995. Donna, aged 30, forges the basic distinction we wish to highlight here, while articulating an opposite point of view:

> All my kids are on the honor rolls. My children have been through counseling, Family Focus. My kids will complete school. My kids will not be like I was. I am real strict. I might be a drug addict, and I may not get up but even if I'm not up, they will get up for school, dress proper for school, don't disrespect any teachers or anything like that. My children don't do that. Don't break the law. My girls don't even leave the backyard unless I take them.

Donna expressed high hopes for her children, emphasized her vigilance in monitoring them, and was proud that all have been involved in a family-counseling effort (the reference to Family Focus). Yet her long-term drug problem undoubtedly has made it more difficult for her to maintain a high level of consistency and effectiveness in carrying out the parenting practices she describes, undermines the authority she is attempting to display, and creates a host of other family dynamics/problems that transcend the concept of parenting style. At the time of the second adult follow-up, the shorthand title for Donna's narrative was "Female Fugitive from the Law Trying to Get Straight." At this follow-up, which took place eight years later than the initial adult interview, Donna no longer expressed the hope and confidence that characterized her earlier comments, and recognized that her drug problem was fundamentally incompatible with parenting in an effective manner. For example, she discussed her feelings about her 17-year-old daughter Brandi's own drug use:

> I said ... we got in a conversation about Brandi using one time. She used marijuana and cocaine and, uh ... I said, Do you want to end up like me? I was really upset, [but] it's hard for your mom to be sitting here preaching education, no drugs, and stuff when your mom's completely the opposite.

At the time of the second interview, Donna's 19-year-old son, Chad, was living with other relatives; Kristin and Cheri, now aged 15 and 12, had been adopted out, and Brandi had been emancipated and was living on her own. That the children needed such alternative living arrangements indicates in a shorthand way some of the many difficulties the children had faced in the time period between the two interviews. For example, Donna's ex-husband apparently sexually abused her daughters ("... and he eventually admitted it and said that he had made a mistake and that it will never happen again"), and Donna's narrative pointed to some of the problems the children had developed (e.g., "They've got Kristin on depression pills ..."). We were also able to locate and interview Brandi directly. The interview took place in the backyard of her apartment, as she was reluctant to show the interviewer the inside of her home. Brandi described her initial thoughts about trying drugs: "[I thought] Well, I'm not having that much fun not doing things that I'm not supposed to be or whatever. Maybe I'll just try the drug and see. It can't be that horrible. And I won't end up like my mom because I'll stop before I get addicted."

Brandi also corroborated Donna's account of the abuse she had experienced, and focused on the instability that characterized her childhood and adolescent years. In addition to being placed in a succession of foster homes after age 11, Brandi also described a period very early in her life when she had not lived with her mother (prior to the first adult interview when all children were living at home). "I didn't live with my mom for the first five years of my life. Nobody exactly explained it to me, but from what I do understand she wasn't taking care of me and my brother at all." This quote is of interest because it highlights that while children may not remember precisely what occurred when they were very young, these periods can nevertheless have a large impact, and become an important part of the personal narrative. In addition, from both Donna and Brandi's interviews, it became clear that the period immediately preceding Donna's first interview was one of the only phases in her adult life when she was not using drugs. Donna indicated at that time that she was in treatment but told the interviewer she had missed several sessions with her counselor ("I didn't have the seven dollars yesterday"). It is also noteworthy that, even during the first interview, she did not describe her drug involvement in a way that distanced her from this identity and behavior ("I may be an addict and I may not get up, but ..."). Consistent with the tentative nature of her "desistance," the second follow-up interview reveals a 38-year-old mother who continued to have trouble with the law and, after an additional eight years, is still "trying to get straight." In our view, learning about effective rule setting and follow-through during parenting classes is unlikely to prove a comprehensive approach to Donna's considerable difficulties and, in turn, those of her children.

The longer window provided by a life-course perspective also suggests that even those positive parenting practices Donna described at the time of the first interview were likely influenced by her (temporary) cessation of drug use and were not a separate dynamic, as she argued in the quote above. Being free of substance abuse would appear to be a basic condition that would allow parents the stability needed to learn and enact some of the positive parenting techniques to which they are exposed in parenting classes. Alternatively, the deficits in parenting that occur during periods of active use are so "outsized" (e.g., disappearing for weeks or months, exposing children to antisocial partners, sharing drug paraphernalia with their children) that it is very unlikely that attending parenting classes will be sufficient to ameliorate them.

Thus, our findings provide a caveat to conclusions such as the following from Murray and Farrington's (2006) discussion of evidenced-based programs for children of incarcerated parents: "If children of prisoners are at risk because of inadequate parenting, parenting programs could be used to reduce parenting risks for children ..." The authors go on to review Eddy and Reid's (2002) description of parenting programs that have demonstrated effectiveness in community-based settings. While we agree with these researchers that it is important to build prisoner-based parenting programs around well-tested models, our larger point is that, given the reality of limited programming resources, drug/alcohol treatment may be an even higher priority. Within the life course of individual respondents, marked differences in parenting and in children's feelings of comfort and safety are traceable to periods of abstinence and relapse. In addition, partner and other network choices are dramatically affected by the parent's substance use. Further, drug/alcohol use amplifies risks for marital conflicts, family violence, and other forms of victimization (e.g., sexual abuse) within the home. And finally, as our prior analyses of the OLS adult data and many other studies have shown, drug use is a significant predictor of involvement in a broader pattern of criminal activity, including violent behavior, or what Uggen and Thompson (2003) call "ill-gotten gains," and in the seriousness and length of these criminal careers.

Phillips et al. (2006) recently conducted an epidemiological study that examined the association between parental criminal-justice contact, other parental risk factors (including substance use and mental health problems), and family-related risks. Relying on data from respondents in rural counties in North Carolina, they concluded that while parental arrest explained some variance in these risks, parental substance use and mental health problems had more direct effects, particularly on family structure and on what they termed "quality of care" (this dimension of family risk included the presence of physical or sexual abuse as well as, for example, inadequate supervision). Although the study did not specifically forge the link to negative outcomes on the part of the next generation, their conclusions are similar to those we draw here based on a substantially different type of sample, design, and methodological approach. Their analyses clearly showed that the parents' difficulties and their effects on the family were not limited to negative consequences of official system contact (arrest). In addition, these researchers reached similar conclusions about programming needs and emphases, elegantly summarizing a view we share based on the OLS results:

> The most pervasive risks among children with histories of parental arrest in this study were parental substance abuse and mental health problems. Ironically, however, there has been a de-emphasis on offender rehabilitation programs over the past two decades (Petersilia, 1999), which might address these parent risks. Accordingly, the criminal justice system may not only be increasing the likelihood of children being subjected to economic strain and family instability through "acts of commission" (i.e., through parental arrest and incarceration), but also through "acts of omission" (i.e., not providing adequate and effective interventions to address parental substance abuse and mental health problems that this study shows are also linked to children's exposure to family risks).

> At the same time there has been a shift away from a rehabilitation orientation in corrections, there has been an increase in programs that address the parenting role of offenders, e.g., parent education,

visitation programs, and scouting. A National Institute of Corrections
publication heralds these programs as a way to reduce intergenerational incarceration. In light of the findings reported in this article,
it is difficult to imagine how one could expect these programs to
achieve such a lofty goal if, in fact, the criminal justice system is
simultaneously contributing to youths' experiencing family risks
that are linked to delinquency and, at the same time, not giving priority to addressing parent problems that can also contribute to children becoming involved with criminal authorities. The importance
of correctional programs that address parent issues (visitation,
scouting, parent education, etc.) for children seems to lie primarily
in their potential to mitigate the more immediate negative emotional consequences of parental arrest and incarceration. The value
of these programs should not be discounted. Nonetheless, it seems
unrealistic to expect them to have a substantial impact on preventing intergenerational incarceration if other aspects of the criminal
justice system are not aligned with that goal. (2006: 694–695).

(3) Need to take into account the children's points of view.
Interventions designed to serve children of offenders should take
into account the children's points of view, recognizing that their
attitudes and emotional responses may not always coincide with the
parent's perspective. The OLS follow-up adds to prior research on
intergenerational transmission, including studies that have documented an increased level of risk to children born to delinquent
youth or to adult prisoners, by providing a window on the children's
perspectives. We found that while treatments of parental incarceration effects often place heavy emphasis on feelings of loss and other
negative emotions that stem from absence due to incarceration,
youths themselves often focused on the parent's broader lifestyle and
behaviors, especially their substance use. The negative emotions the
children experience are important to understand not only because
they may serve to amplify the child's own risk for delinquent involvement or other problem outcomes, but because this information could
inform interventions designed to serve these families and children.
For example, a goal of many programs is to enhance opportunities
for children to visit their parents while they are in jail or prison; yet
for some youths this period may serve as a respite from the extremes
of negative emotions and family dramas that characterized life with

an actively using parent. Similarly, numerous discussions focus on the child's feelings of stigma about having a parent who is incarcerated, but the interviews we conducted indicate that the parent's behaviors when they are not incarcerated may also be viewed by the child as highly embarrassing and stigmatizing. It is important to recognize the full complement of attitudes and emotions children may experience, including heterogeneity in children's responses, and changes over time in a given child's reactions.

A comprehensive approach to reducing risk will target both the subjective realms of the child's experience and the objective circumstances that produce these negative reactions. A number of programmatic efforts provide training or other assistance in the area of anger management, but it is especially important for potential service providers to confront the logical and rational basis of many children's strong emotional reactions. This idea differs considerably from the notion that anger stems from "thinking errors," or a "hostile attributional bias" that causes the individual to erupt over trivial matters (Dodge & Somberg, 1987; Wilson Bouffard, & Mackenzie, 2005). The neo-Meadian perspective we outlined emphasized the degree to which emotion and cognition are coordinated rather than oppositional processes. This is a general theoretical point but one that has implications for the design of counseling or other intervention approaches. Such efforts would likely be more effective if they were to incorporate supportive counseling for the larger problems within the home, concrete steps to solve these problems (e.g., by assigning a high priority to substance-abuse treatment for the parent generation), as well as instruction in productive coping/anger management strategies.

(4) Need to develop a more nuanced approach to family reunification.

Most child welfare and criminal-justice agencies that are in contact with families such as those who participated in the OLS study focus on reunification as a top priority. Parents love and want to be with their children, and most often, children want to be with their biological parents. Nevertheless, it is critical to back up this laudable goal with intensive services and follow-up so that these families can have a realistic chance of success. And, based on the severe and continuing nature of risks within many of these families, in some instances residing with the parent is not the best option for the children involved. Alternatives need to represent an improvement, and not another source of risk.

Our conclusions in this sensitive area are quite tentative, since the limited programming available has not always provided offenders high-quality drug/alcohol treatment, other counseling and employment services, and appropriate follow-up, all of which would likely improve outcomes within reunified families. Nevertheless, our data show that some parents' difficulties are so pervasive and apparently intractable that it is unlikely that even the best efforts of social-service providers will be able to ameliorate them. The typical OLS non-parent caregiver is a family member of the core respondents we followed up here, and thus the alternative setting to which children are exposed may present at least some of the same risks. The children's living circumstances may improve slightly in these alternative settings, but in most instances there appears to be very little oversight of these alternative placements. This point has been made frequently with regard to the placement of children when a parent is sent to prison; while this represents a concrete crisis point, a larger percentage of children are left to such informal alternative arrangements when parents are heavily involved in drug-oriented lifestyles (see especially Dunlap et al., 2002; Johnson Dunlop, & Maher, 1998).

Unfortunately, the data we presented indicated that the children not living with the biological parent do not, on average, evidence lower rates of problem outcomes, and reports of abuse are also high in this group. These results likely reflect some combination of the child's early experiences within the family of origin, the nature of the alternative placements, instabilities associated with a back-and-forth pattern (where the parent regains and loses custody several times), and reactions to these difficult circumstances. The child who was removed early on and placed in a loving home for an extended period of time was the exception rather than the rule, making it difficult to ascertain how such children might fare over the long haul.

Holland (2005) conducted an analysis of those children who participated in the National Longitudinal Survey of Youth, distinguishing foster-care youth from other respondents. In analyses that examined their later life outcomes, she found that foster care youth as a sub-group, not unexpectedly, did not fare as well as those who lived with their biological parents; nevertheless, when she distinguished foster-care youth who "aged out" of the system from those who were reunified with parents, the former exhibited more favorable outcomes. This study was not designed specifically to explore such issues, but it suggests the importance of conducting additional research that can provide a solid knowledge base around which to evaluate the utility of several less-than-ideal strategies for intervening in the lives of at-risk youth. As stated earlier, children's own perspectives add an important dimension, recognizing that their feelings will vary based on their ages, and the specifics of their family situation. For example, Holland included a qualitative component in her study, interviewing a number of adults who had aged out of the foster-care system. Although this undoubtedly reflected their more mature perspectives as adults, a majority of those interviewed indicated that they wished that they had been removed from their homes sooner. Brandi, Donna's 17-year-old daughter, quoted earlier (the young woman who had recently been emancipated, that is, allowed by the court to live on her own), had apparently reached a similar conclusion: "I just was hoping she stayed out of my life. 'Cause every time we do get close she just ends up hurting me again."

(5) It is important to assign a high priority to the provision of services to women with early problem/delinquent backgrounds and to the well-being and safety of their children.

The literature focuses heavily on the societal and family effects of father absence due to incarceration, an emphasis that is intuitive given the sheer numbers of men relative to women who are incarcerated at any given point. We have been critical in this book of the singular emphasis on children of prisoners, but even if we limit our focus to incarcerated populations, adapting the longer life-course lens is useful: the figures are significantly higher for the number of women who have some prison or jail experience and, accordingly, for the number of children whose lives are affected by a mother's system involvement. The subgroup of women who struggle with substance-abuse is larger still and is likely implicated in recent observed increases in the number of women prisoners (Wellisch, Anglin, & Prendergast, 1993). Taken together, all of these problem circumstances contribute to the child's true level of exposure to family-related risks.

Aside from the sheer disparity in numbers of offenders, another factor that influences perceptions of the severity of the problem is the relative seriousness of male crimes compared with female crimes. When compared to boys or men, the delinquent acts of girls and the crimes of women are, on average, of a less serious nature – this is the case even if they have been officially labeled a delinquent by the court or sent to prison. The young women who participated in the OLS can be considered serious offenders when we compare their levels of delinquency to those reported by most girls who are participants in population-based surveys; yet on average, their levels of involvement are still not as serious as the self-reports/adjudicated crimes of the OLS men. But even if women's average prison stays are shorter and their crimes not typically of a spectacular sort, this does not automatically equate to a situation of low risk for the children involved. Why?

(a) The pervasiveness of deviance in many of the women's family histories. Since most girls manage to avoid any involvement in delinquency, those who have exhibited problems sufficient to warrant state-level intervention are likely to come from backgrounds characterized by a panoply of risks, including criminality and deviant behavior on the part of parents and other family members. The narrative data we elicited from the original OLS respondents highlighted this, and national statistics accord with this observation. For example, data from one study indicate that incarcerated women were even more likely than their male counterparts to have had at least one family member who had been incarcerated (Snell & Morton, 1994). These family dynamics are important to a comprehensive understanding of the etiology of serious female offending, but are also a part of the family context the child inherits. These other family members contribute to women's encapsulation in worlds characterized by drug use and other deviant behavior, the severity and length of their own drug-abuse/criminal careers and risk for incarceration, high levels of victimization, and in turn to their children's own risk environments.

Importantly, these family members frequently become the alternative caregivers during those periods when a parent is absent either due to incarceration or involvement in a drug-oriented lifestyle.

(b) Gendered dynamics associated with the assortative mating process. The focus in this study on family deviance as a background for understanding female offending presents an apparent contrast to theorizing that emphasizes the role of male partners in relation to offending patterns. Recall, for example, Richie's (1996) book detailing multiple ways in which women could be considered, in effect, "compelled to crime" by virtue of their contacts with men – from reacting violently to repeated acts of victimization to committing crimes at the urging of a spouse/romantic partner. The difference in theoretical emphasis undoubtedly relates at least in part to the different types of sample groups involved in these two studies. The early-starting delinquent girls we followed up in connection with the OLS had typically developed problem behavior profiles prior to their involvement with adult romantic partners; in our view it is important to recognize the extent of family-related disadvantages because these are implicated not only in their initial start along delinquent pathways, but also in the character of partner choices/dynamics later in the life course.

We thus find the "bad boyfriend" explanation of female crime somewhat limiting, (particularly when the focus is upon more serious offenders such as those we have followed up in this investigation); nevertheless, as we highlighted in Chapter Four, the OLS women often did go on to develop relationships with highly antisocial men. We suggested that the choice of a romantic partner involves more than passive selection (wherein both inhabit similar social space and thus are more likely to become a couple). Our symbolic interactionist perspective, a variant of social learning theory, emphasizes that the individual does exert some agency in moving toward individuals who represent a particular lifestyle and worldview. In contrast to the complete selection argument, however, the social learning perspective highlights that once involved in an intimate relationship, the individual is likely to be influenced significantly – for good or for ill – by the behavioral proclivities of this romantic partner. Where both partners are involved in drug-oriented lifestyles, for example, this concordance amplifies further the individual's own initial level of risk. In addition, negative relationship dynamics are likely to be increased in situations characterized by this double dose of deviance. The children are likely to be deeply affected by these negative consequences of "homophily" as well.

Why is this process gendered? The assortative mating process is not fundamentally or inherently gendered: there is a general trend favoring initial similarity on a number of characteristics, whether the focus in upon male or female partner selection. However, we can consider this process to be, for all practical purposes, gendered, given known base-rate disparities in male and female involvement in criminal activity. Since most women are not heavily involved in criminal activity or are less so than their male counterparts, even without knowing much about a particular female partner, we can surmise that the average male offender may gain a slightly more prosocial companion when he selects his female partner. Based on the results of the OLS study, and again, upon simple probabilities, the opposite is also true. In addition, as a number of scholars have previously pointed out, women with significant criminal or substance-abuse histories are often more heavily stigmatized/marginalized compared to males with similar backgrounds. This makes it difficult for such women to locate "respectable" marriage/relationship partners, even if they have a general inclination to do so. Thus, the children of female offenders may be negatively influenced not only by their mother's problem behaviors and the deviant environment that characterizes the latter's family of origin, but also by their exposure to the behaviors of their mother's partners, and the volatile combination of the two. This double layer of risk will not always have an exact parallel where the referent is the partnering experiences of male offenders, who, on average, are more likely to affiliate with at least a slightly more prosocial individual. In turn, this spouse, often the biological mother, will prove a source of some stability for children even where the father continues to be involved in criminal acts, or is absent due to a period of incarceration.[1] This relates to the final consideration

---

[1]   As suggested in earlier chapters, this is not always the case, as a number of male OLS offenders had forged relationships with women who were violent or heavily involved in drug-oriented lifestyles; conversely, some women developed loving relationships with prosocial men (see also Capaldi et al., 2008).

in our assessment of the needs of children such as those we have followed up in this study:

(c) *Mothers remain extremely important caregivers for a majority of children.* Although father involvement in child-rearing tasks has become increasingly normative, mothers remain primary caregivers within many families, and in relation to many aspects of their children's daily lives. Again, this highly gendered phenomenon is not inevitable, but it is nevertheless extremely common, even as gender roles have become more equitable within the context of contemporary families. For example, Milkie et al. (2002) found that mothers compared with fathers were more likely to be involved in discipline, play, monitoring, and the provision of emotional support to children. In addition, since it is less typical for mothers to become substance abusers or to be absent from their children's lives (whether due to drug involvement or to incarceration), this is often perceived by children as an even greater hardship or source of stigma and other negative emotions – adding to their own risk for problem behaviors and other negative outcomes, and to mothers' feelings of demoralization and associated emotional/behavioral risk.

We hope the above considerations and findings of the study as a whole serve to highlight the urgent need for services and support for young women who have evidenced a pattern of antisocial behavior. Yet these recommendations should not deter policy-makers and practitioners seeking to provide services to male offenders or to their children. The limited resources currently expended for intervention/rehabilitation services should be greatly expanded, so that it is not necessary to make choices between the needs of women and men or, for example, about whether to offer a parenting class or a drug-treatment program. The results of this study suggest that providing a range of services and intensive follow-up to seriously delinquent girls and boys should be a high priority, not only to help them redirect their own lives, but also to ensure a safer, more stable family environment for the next generation.

In addition, the focus on effects of OLS parents' life circumstances on children's well-being is meant as a modest corrective, or counterpoint, to literature that focuses almost exclusively on incarceration effects. However, we agree with prior research that these periods of incarceration are very costly to the adults, the children, and the larger society. Thus, our perspective and findings should not be read as a call for increased levels of incarceration, but rather for increased attention to the underlying problems that foster the array of family difficulties described in this investigation.

References

Agnew, Robert. (1992). Foundation for a general strain theory of crime and delinquency. *Criminology* 30(1):47–87.

(1997). Stability and change over the life course: A strain theory explanation. Pp. 101–132 in Terrence Thornberry (Ed.), *Developmental Theories of Crime and Delinquency*. New Brunswick, NJ: Transaction Publishers.

Agnew, Robert, Timothy Brezina, John P. White, and Francis T. Cullen. (2002). Strain, personality traits, and delinquency: Extending general strain theory. *Criminology* 40(1):43–72.

Akers, Ronald L. (1977). *Deviant Behavior: A Social Learning Approach*. Belmont, CA: Wadsworth.

(2002). A social learning theory of crime. Pp. 135–143 in Suzette Cote (Ed.), *Criminological Theories: Bridging the Past to the Future*. Thousand Oaks, CA: Sage.

Anderson, Elijah. (1989). Sex codes and family life among poor inner-city youths. *The Annals of the American Academy of Political Social Science*. 501:59–79.

(1990). *Streetwise: Race, Class, and Change in an Urban Community*. Chicago, IL: University of Chicago Press.

Anthony, James C., and Bertram J. Cohler (Eds.). (1987). *The Invulnerable Child*. New York: Guilford Press.

Arditti, Joyce A. (2005). Families and incarceration: An ecological approach. *Families in Society* 86(2):251–258.

Bachman, Jerald G., John M. Wallace Jr., Patrick M. O' Malley, Llyoyd D. Johnston, Candace L. Kurth, and Harold W. Neighbors. (1991). Racial/ethnic differences in smoking, drinking, and illicit drug use among American high school seniors, 1976–89. *American Journal of Public Health* 81(3):372–377.

Barnard, Marina A. (1993). Violence and vulnerability: Conditions of work for street working prostitutes. *Sociology of Health and Illness* 15(5):683–705.

Bloom, Barbara. (1995). Imprisoned mothers. Pp. 21–30 in Katherine Gabel and Denise Johnston (Eds.), *Children of Incarcerated Parents*. New York: Lexington Books.

Boney-McCoy, Sue and David, Finkelhor. (1995). Psychosocial sequelae of violent victimization in a national youth sample. *Journal of Consulting and Clinical Psychology* 63(5):726–736.

Bottcher, Jean. (2001). Social practices of gender: How gender relates to delinquency in the everyday lives of high-risk youths. *Criminology* 39(4):893–932.

Box, Steven. (1971). *Deviance, Reality and Society*. London: Holt, Reinhart, and Winston.

Bradley, Gifford W. (1978). Self-serving biases in the attribution process: A reexamination of the fact or fiction question. *Journal of Personality and Social Psychology* 36(1):56–71.

Braithwaite, John. (1989). *Crime, Shame, and Reintegration*. Cambridge, MA: Cambridge University Press.

Burt, Cyril L. (1925). *The Young Delinquent*. London: University of London Press.

Cairns, Robert B. (1979). *Social Development: The Origins and Plasticity of Interchanges*. San Francisco, CA: W. H. Freeman.

Cairns, Robert B., Beverly D. Cairns, Hongling Xie, Man-Chi Leung, and Sarah Hearne. (1998). Paths across generations: Academic competence and aggressive behaviors in young mothers and their children. *Developmental Psychology* 34(6):1162–1174.

Call, Kathleen T., and Jeylan L. Mortimer. (2001). *Arenas of Comfort in Adolescence: A Study of Adjustment in Context*. Mahwah, NJ: Lawrence Erlbaum Associates.

Capaldi, Deborah M., Hyoun K. Kim, and Joann W. Shortt. (2004). Women's involvement in aggression in young adult romantic relationships: A developmental systems model. Pp. 223–241 in Martha Putallaz and Karen L. Bierman (Eds.), *Aggression, Antisocial Behavior, and Violence among Girls: A Developmental Perspective*. New York: Guilford Press.

Capaldi, Deborah M., Hyoun K. Kim, and Lee D. Owen. (2008). Romantic partners' influence on men's likelihood of arrest in early adulthood. *Criminology* 46(2):267–299.

Capaldi, Deborah M., Rand D. Conger, Hyman Hops, and Terence P. Thornberry. (2003). Introduction to special section on three-generation studies. *Journal of Abnormal Child Psychology* 31(2):123–125.

Cernkovich, Stephen A., and Peggy C. Giordano. (2001). Stability and change in antisocial behavior: The transition from adolescence to early adulthood. *Criminology* 39:371–410.

Cernkovich, Stephen A., Peggy C. Giordano, and Meredith D. Pugh. (1985). Chronic offenders: The missing cases in self-report delinquency research. *The Journal of Criminal Law and Criminology* 76(3):705–32.

Chesney-Lind, Meda, and Randall G. Shelden. (1998). *Girls, Delinquency, and Juvenile Justice.* Belmont, CA: Wadsworth.

Collins, Randall. (2004). *Interaction Ritual Chains.* Princeton, NJ: Princeton University Press.

Condly, Steven J. (2006). Resilience in children: A review of literature with implications for education. *Urban Education* 41(3):211–236.

Conger, Rand D. (1976). Social control and social learning models of delinquent behavior: A synthesis. *Criminology* 14(1):17–40.

Conger, Rand D., Glen H. Elder Jr., Frederick O. Lorenz, Katherine J. Conger, Ronald L. Simons, Les B. Whitbeck, Shirley Huck, and Janet N. Melby. (1990). Linking economic hardship to marital quality and instability. *Journal of Marriage and the Family* 52:643–656.

Costello, E. Jane, Alaattin Erkanli, John A. Fairbank, and Adrian Angold. (2002). The prevalence of potentially traumatic events in childhood and adolescence. *Journal of Traumatic Stress* 15(2):99–112.

Crouter, Ann C., and Alan Booth. (2003). *Children's Influence on Family Dynamics: The Neglected Side of Family Relationships.* Mahwah, NJ: Lawrence Erlbaum Associates.

De Haan, Willem J. M., and Ian Loader. (2002). On the emotions of crime, punishment, and social control. *Journal of Theoretical Criminology* 6(3):243–253.

Dobash, Russell P., R. Emerson Dobash, Margo Wilson, and Martin Daly. (1992). The myth of sexual symmetry in marital violence. *Social Problems* 39(1):71–91.

Dodge, Kenneth A., and Daniel R. Somberg. (1987). Hostile attributional biases among aggressive boys are exacerbated under conditions of threats to the self. *Child Development* 58(1):213–224.

Doherty, Elaine E., Kerry M. Green, Heather S. Reisinger, and Margaret E. Ensminger. (2008). Long-term patterns of drug use among an urban African-American cohort: The role of gender and family. *Journal of Urban Health* 85(2):250–267.

Dugdale, Richard L. (1877). *The Jukes: A Study in Crime, Pauperism, Disease and Heredity, also Further Studies of Criminals.* New York: Putnam.

Dunlap, Eloise, Andrew Golub, Bruce D. Johnson, and Damaris Wesley. (2002). Intergenerational transmission of conduct norms for drugs, sexual exploitation and violence: A case study. *British Journal of Criminology* 42(1):1–20.

Durkheim, Emile. (1915). *The Elementary Forms of the Religious Life.* New York: Free Press.

Eddy, J. Mark, and John B. Reid. (2002). The antisocial behavior of the adolescent children of incarcerated parents: A developmental perspective. Paper presented at the National Policy Conference, From prison to home: The effect of incarceration and reentry on children, families, and communities, January, Washington, DC.

Edin, Kathryn, and Maria Kefalas. (2005). *Promises I Can Keep: Why Poor Women Put Motherhood Before Marriage*. Berkley, CA: University of California Press.

Elder, Glen H. Jr. (1996). Human lives in changing societies: Life course and developmental insights. Pp. 31–62 in Robert B. Cairns, Glen H. Elder Jr., and E. Jane Costello (Eds.), *Developmental Science*, New York: Cambridge University Press.

Emirbayer, Mustafa, and Jeff Goodwin. (1994). Network analysis, culture, and the problem of agency. *The American Journal of Sociology* 99(6):1411–1454.

Engdahl, Emma. (2004). A theory of the emotional self: From the standpoint of a neo-Meadian. Ph.D. dissertation, Department of Sociology, Örebro University, Örebro, Sweden.

Farrington, David P. (1993). Understanding and preventing bullying. Pp. 381–458 in Michael Tonry (Ed.), *Crime and Justice*, Vol. 17. Chicago, IL: University of Chicago Press.

(1995). The development of offending and antisocial behavior from childhood: Key findings from the Cambridge Study of Delinquent Development. *Journal of Child Psychology and Psychiatry* 36:929–964.

(2003). Key results from the first forty years of the Cambridge Study in Delinquent Development. Pp. 137–183 in Terence P. Thornberry and Marvin Krohn (Eds.), *Taking Stock of Delinquency: An Overview of Findings from Contemporary Longitudinal Studies*. New York: Kluwer Academic/Plenum Publishers.

Farrington, David P., and Brandon C. Welsh. (2007). *Saving Children from a Life of Crime: Early Risk Factors and Effective Interventions*. New York: Oxford University Press.

Federal Bureau of, Investigation. (2004). *Crime in the United States, 2003: Uniform Crime Reports*. Washington, DC: U.S. Department of Justice.

Furman, Wyndol, and Elizabeth A. Wehner. (1994). "Romantic views: Toward a theory of adolescent romantic relationships." Pp. 168–195 in Raymond Montemayor, Gerald R. Adams, and Thomas P. Gullota (Eds.), *Personal Relationships during Adolescence*. Thousand Oaks, CA: Sage Publications.

Furstenberg, Frank Jr., Thomas D. Cook, Jacquelynne Eccles, Glenn H. Elder Jr., and Arnold Sameroff. (1999). *Managing to Make It: Urban Families in High-Risk Neighborhoods*. Chicago, IL: University of Chicago Press.

Gaarder, Emily, and Joanne Belknap. (2002). Tenuous borders: Girls transferred to adult court. *Criminology* 40(3):481–517.

Gabel, Katherine, and Denise Johnston (Eds.). (1995). *Children of Incarcerated Parents.* New York: Lexington Books.

Giddens, Anthony. (1984). *The Constitution of Society: Outline of the Theory of Structuration.* Berkley, CA: University of California Press.

Gilligan, Carol. (1982). *In a Different Voice: Psychological Theory and Women's Development.* Cambridge, MA: Harvard University Press.

Giordano, Peggy C., Jill A. Deines, and Stephen A. Cernkovich. (2006). In and out of crime: A life course perspective on girls' delinquency. Pp. 17–40 in Karen Heimer and Candace Kruttschnitt (Eds.), *Gender and Crime: Patterns in Victimization and Offending.* New York: New York University Press.

Giordano, Peggy C., Monica A. Longmore, Ryan D. Schroeder, and Patrick M. Seffrin. (2008). A life course perspective on spirituality and desistance from crime. *Criminology* 46(1):99–131.

Giordano, Peggy C., Monica A. Longmore, and Wendy D. Manning. (2006). Gender and the meanings of adolescent romantic relationships: A focus on boys. *American Sociological Review* 71:260–287.

Giordano, Peggy C., Ryan D. Schroeder, and Stephen A. Cernkovich. (2007). Emotions and crime over the life course: A neo-Meadian perspective on criminal continuity and change. *American Journal of Sociology* 112(6):1603–1661.

Giordano, Peggy C., and Stephen A. Cernkovich. (1997). Gender and antisocial behavior. Pp. 496–510 in David M. Stoff James Breiling and Jack D. Maser (Eds.), *The Handbook of Antisocial Behavior.* New York: John Wiley and Sons.

Giordano, Peggy C., Stephen A. Cernkovich, and Allen Lowery. (2004). A long-term follow-up of serious adolescent female offenders. Pp. 186–202 in Martha Putallaz and Karen L. Bierman (Eds.), *Aggression, Antisocial Behavior, and Violence among Girls: A Developmental Perspective.* New York: Guilford Publication.

Giordano, Peggy C., Stephen A. Cernkovich, and Donna D. Holland. (2003). Changes in friendship relations over the life course: Implications for desistance from crime. *Criminology* 41(2):293–327.

Giordano, Peggy C., Stephen A. Cernkovich, and Jennifer L. Rudolph. (2002). Gender, crime, and desistance: Toward a theory of cognitive transformation. *American Journal of Sociology* 107:990–1064.

Giordano, Peggy C., Toni J. Milhollin, Stephen A. Cernkovich, M. D. Pugh, and Jennifer L. Rudolph. (1999). Delinquency, identity, and women's involvement in relationship violence. *Criminology* 37:17–39.

Glaser, Barney G., and Anselm L. Strauss. (1967). *The Discovery of Grounded Theory; Strategies for Qualitative Research*. Chicago, IL: Aldine Publishing Company.

Glaser, Daniel. (1956). Criminality theories and behavioral images. *American Journal of Sociology* 61:433–44.

Glaze, Lauren E., and Laura M. Maruschak. (2008). *Parents in Prison and Their Minor Children* (NCJ 222984). Washington, DC: U.S. Department of Justice, Bureau of Justice Statistics.

Glueck, Sheldon, and Eleanor Glueck. (1950). *Unraveling Juvenile Delinquency*. New York: Commonwealth Fund.

Gottfredson, Michael R., and Travis Hirschi. (1990). *A General Theory of Crime*. Stanford, CA: Stanford University Press.

Hagan, John, and Patricia Parker. (1999). Rebellion beyond the classroom: A life-course capitalization theory of the intergenerational causes of delinquency. *Theoretical Criminology* 3(3):259–285.

Hagan, John, and Ronit Dinovitzer. (1999). Collateral consequences of imprisonment for children, communities, and prisoners. *Crime and Justice* 26:121–162.

Haggerty, Robert J., Lonnie R. Sherrod, Norman Garmezy, and Michael Rutter (Eds.). (1996). *Stress, Risk, and Resilience in Children and Adolescents: Processes, Mechanisms, and Interventions*. New York: Cambridge University Press.

Hairston, Creasie F. (1998). The forgotten parent: Understanding the forces that influence incarcerated fathers' relationships with their children. *Child Welfare* 77(5):617–638.

  (2007). *Focus on Children with Incarcerated Parents: An Overview of the Research Literature*. Baltimore, MD: The Annie E. Casey Foundation.

Harper, Cynthia C., and Sara S. McLanahan . (2004). Father absence and youth incarceration. *Journal of Research on Adolescence* 14(3):369–397.

Haynie, Dana L. (2001). Delinquent peers revisited: Does network structure matter? *American Journal of Sociology* 106(4):1013–1057.

Haynie, Dana L., Peggy C. Giordano, Wendy D. Manning, and Monica A. Longmore. (2005). Gender, romance, and delinquency involvement. *Criminology* 43(1):177–210.

Healy, William, and Augusta F. Bronner. (1926). *Delinquents and Criminals, Their Making and Unmaking: Studies in Two American Cities*. New York: Macmillan.

Heimer, Karen, and Candace Kruttschnitt (Eds.). (2006). *Gender and Crime: Patterns in Victimization and Offending*. New York: New York University Press.

Hirschi, Travis. (1969). *Causes of Delinquency*. Berkeley, CA: University of California Press.

Hirschi, Travis, and Michael Gottfredson. (1987). Causes of white collar crime. *Criminology* 25(4):949–974.

Holland, Donna D. (2005). A life course perspective on foster care: An examination of the impact of variations in levels of involvement in the foster care system on adult criminality and other indicators of adult well-being. Ph.D. dissertation, Department of Sociology, Bowling Green State University, Bowling Green, OH.

Horney, Julie. (2006). An alternative psychology of criminal behavior: The American Society of Criminology 2005 Presidential address. *Criminology* 44(1):1–16.

Horney, Julie, D. Wayne Osgood, and Ineke Haen Marshall. (1995). Criminal careers in the short term: Intra-individual variability in crime and its relation to local life circumstances. *American Sociological Review* 60(5):655–673.

Huesmann, L. Rowell, Leonard D. Eron, Monroe M. Lefkowitz, and Leopold O. Walder. (1984). Stability of aggression over time and generations. *Developmental Psychology* 20(6):1120–1134.

Jessor, Richard, and Shirley L. Jessor. (1977). *Problem Behavior and Psychosocial Development: A Longitudinal Study of Youth.* New York: Academic Press.

Johnson, Byron R., and David B. Larson. (2006). The InnerChange Freedom Initiative: A preliminary evaluation of a faith-based prison program. *The InnerChange Freedom Initiative Newsroom.* Executive summary. New York: The Manhattan Institute.

Johnson, Bruce D., Eloise Dunlap, and Lisa Maher. (1998). Nurturing for careers in drug use and crime: Conduct norms for children and juveniles in crack-suing households. *Substance Use and Misuse* 33(7):1511–1546.

Johnston, Denise. (2006). The wrong road: Efforts to understand the effects of parental crime and incarceration. *Criminology and Public Policy* 5(4):703–719.

Katz, Jack. (1988). *Seductions of Crime: Moral and Sensual Attractions in Doing Evil.* New York: Basic Books.

(1999). *How Emotions Work.* Chicago, IL: University of Chicago Press.

Katz, Rebecca S. (2000). Explaining girls' and women's crime and desistance in the context of their victimization experiences: A developmental test of revised strain theory and the life course perspective. *Violence against Women* 6(6):633–660.

Kilpatrick, Dean G., Benjamin E. Saunders, and Heidi S. Resnick. (1998). Violence history and comorbidity among a national sample of adolescents. Paper presented at Lake George Research Conference on Posttraumatic Stress Disorder Program, March, Bolton Landing, NY.

Konopka, Gisela. (1966). *The Adolescent Girl in Conflict.* Englewood Cliffs, NJ: Prentice-Hall.

Kreider, Rose M. (2007). Arrangements of Children: 2004. *Current Population Reports*. Washington, DC: U. S. Census Bureau.

Krueger, Robert F., Terrie E. Moffitt, Avshalon Caspi, April Bleske, and Phil A. Silva. (1998). Assortative mating for antisocial behavior: Developmental and methodological implications. *Behavior Genetics* 28(3):173–186.

Kruttschnitt, Candace, and Kristin Carbone-Lopez. (2006). Moving beyond the stereotypes: Women's subjective accounts of their violent crime. *Criminology* 44(2):321–352.

Kruttschnitt, Candace, and Peggy C. Giordano. (2009). Family influences on girls' delinquency. Pp. 107–126 in Margaret Zahn (Ed.), *The Delinquent Girl*. Philadelphia, PA: Temple University Press.

Laub, John H., Daniel S. Nagin, and Robert J. Sampson. (1998). Trajectories of change in criminal offending: Good marriages and the desistance process. *American Sociological Review* 63:225–238.

Laub, John H., and Robert J. Sampson. (2003). *Shared Beginnings, Divergent Lives: Delinquent Boys to Age 70*. Cambridge, MA: Harvard University Press.

Leonard, Eileen B. (1982). *Women, Crime, and Society: A Critique of Theoretical Criminology*. New York: Longman.

Leverentz, Andrea M. (2006). The love of a good man? Romantic relationships as a source of support or hindrance for female ex-offenders. *Journal of Research in Crime and Delinquency* 43(4):459–488.

Liebow, Elliot. (1967). *Tally's Corner: A Study of Negro Street Cornerman*. Boston, MA: Little, Brown.

Loeber, Rolf, and Magda Stouthamer-Loeber. (1986). Family factors as correlates and predictors of juvenile conduct problems and delinquency. Pp. 29–149 in M. Tonry and N. Morris (Eds.), *Crime and Justice*, Vol. 7. Chicago, IL: University of Chicago Press.

Lombroso, Cesare. (1876). *Criminal Man*. Milan: Hoepli.

Lonardo, Robert A., Peggy C. Giordano, Monica A. Longmore, and Wendy D. Manning. (2009). Parents, friends, and romantic partners: Enmeshment in deviant networks and adolescent delinquency involvement. *Journal of Youth and Adolescence* 38(3):367–383.

Lowery, Allen R. (2001). A long-term follow-up of serious female offenders. Ph.D. dissertation, Department of Sociology, Bowling Green State University, Bowling Green, OH.

Luthar, Suniya S. (Ed.). (2003). *Resilience and Vulnerability: Adaptation in the Context of Childhood Adversities*. New York: Cambridge University Press.

Macleod, Jay. (1995). *Ain't No Makin' It: Aspirations and Attainment in a Low-Income Neighborhood*. Boulder, CO: Westview Press.

Manning-Walsh, Juanita. (2005). Spiritual struggle. *Journal of Holistic Nursing* 23:120–140.

Maruna, Shadd. (2001). *Making Good: How Ex-Convicts Reform and Rebuild Their Lives.* Washington, DC: American Psychological Association Books.

Massey, Douglas S. (2002). A brief history of human society: the origin and role of emotion in social life. *American Sociological Review* 67(1):1–29.

Masten, Ann S. (1994). Resilience in individual development: Successful adaptation despite risk and adversity. Pp. 3–25 in Margaret C. Wang and Edmund W. Gordon (Eds.), *Educational Resilience in Inner City America: Challenges and Prospects.* Hillsdale, NJ: Lawrence Erlbaum Associates.

Matsueda, Ross L. (1992). Reflected appraisals, parental labeling, and delinquency: Specifying a symbolic interactionist theory. *American Journal of Sociology* 97(6):1577–1611.

Matsueda, Ross L., and Karen Heimer. (1997). A symbolic interactionist theory of role-transitions, role-commitments, and delinquency. Pp. 162–213 in Terence P. Thornberry (Ed.), *Developmental Theories of Crime and Delinquency.* New Brunswick, NJ: Transaction publishers.

McCord, Joan. (1977). A comparative study of two generations of Native Americans. Pp. 83–92 in R. F. Meier (Ed.), *Theoretical Concerns in Criminology.* Beverly Hills, CA: Sage.

McMahon, Martha. (1995). *Engendering Motherhood: Identity and Self-Transformation in Women's Lives.* New York: Guilford Press.

Mead, George H. (1934). *Mind, Self, and Society from the Standpoint of a Social Behaviorist.* Chicago, IL: University of Chicago Press.

    (1964). *On Social Psychology: Selected Papers.* Chicago: University of Chicago Press.

Messerschmidt, James W. (1993). *Masculinities and Crime: Critique and Reconceptualization of Theory.* Lanham, MD: Rowman and Littlefield.

Milkie, Melissa A., Suzanne M. Bianchi, Marybeth J. Mattingly, and John P. Robinson. (2002). The gendered division of childrearing: Ideals, realities, and the relationship to parental well-being. *Sex Roles* 47(1/2):21–38.

Miller, Eleanor M. (1986). *Street Woman.* Philadelphia, PA: Temple University.

Miller, Jody, and Christopher W. Mullins. (2006). Stuck up, telling lies, and talking too much: The gendered context of young women's violence. Pp. 41–66 in Karen Heimer and Candace Kruttschnitt (Eds.), *Gender and Crime: Patterns in Victimization and Offending.* New York: New York University Press.

Mischkowitz, Robert. (1994). Desistance from a delinquent way of life? Pp. 303–330 in Elmar G. M. Weitekamp and Hans-Jürgen Kerner

(Eds.), *Cross-National Longitudinal Research on Human Development and Criminal Behavior.* Boston, MA: Kluwer Academic Publishers.

Moffitt, Terrie E., Avshalom Caspi, Michael Rutter, and Phil A. Silva. (2001). *Sex Differences in Antisocial Behavior: Conduct Disorder, Delinquency, and Violence in the Dunedin Longitudinal Study.* Cambridge, MA: Cambridge University Press.

Moses, Marilyn C. (1995). *Keeping Incarcerated Mothers and Their Daughters Together: Girl Scouts Beyond Bars* (NCJ 156217). Washington, DC: U. S. Department of Justice, National Institute of Justice.

Murray, Joseph, and David P. Farrington. (2005). Parental imprisonment: Effect on boys' antisocial behaviour and delinquency through the life-course. *Journal of Child Psychology and Psychiatry* 46(12):1269–1278.

(2006). Evidence-based programs for children of prisoners. *Criminology and Public Policy* 5(4):721–735.

(2008). The effects of parental imprisonment on children. Pp. 133–206 in Michael Tonry (Ed.), *Crime and Justice: A Review of the Research,* Vol. 37. Chicago, IL: University of Chicago Press.

O' Connor, Thomas P. (2004). What works, religion as a correctional intervention: Part I. *Journal of Community Corrections* 14(1):11–27.

Ogle, Robbin S., Daniel Maier-Katkin, and Thomas J. Bernard. (1995). A theory of homicidal behavior among women. *Criminology* 33:173–93.

Oppenheimer, Valerie Kincaid. (2003). Cohabiting and marriage during young men's career development process. *Demography* 45(1):127–149.

Pacherie, Elisabeth. (2002). The role of emotions in the explanation of action. *European Review of Philosophy* 5(1):53–91.

Pargament, Kenneth I. (1997). *The Psychology of Religion and Coping: Theory, Research, Practice.* New York: Guilford Press.

Pargament, Kenneth I., Harold G. Koenig, Nalini Tarakeshwar, and June Hahn. (2001). Religius struggles as a predictor of mortality among medically ill elderly patients: A two-year longitudinal study. *Archives of Internal Medicine* 161:1881–1885.

Petersilia, Joan. (1999). Parole and prisoner reentry in the United States. Pp. 479–529 in M. Tonry and Joan Petersilia (Eds.), *Prisons.* Chicago, IL: University of Chicago Press.

Phillips, Susan D., Alaattin Erkanli, Gordon P. Keeler, E. Jane Costello, and Adrian Angold. (2006). Disentangling the risks: Parent criminal justice involvement and children's exposure to family risks. *Criminology and Public Policy* 5(4):677–702.

Pogarsky, Greg, Alan J. Lizotte, and Terrence P. Thornberry. (2003). The delinquency of children born to young mothers: Results from the Rochester Youth Development Study. *Criminology* 41(4):1249–1286.

Powers, Jane Levine, John Eckenrode, and Barbara Jaklitsch. (1990). Maltreatment among runaway and homeless youth. *Child Abuse and Neglect* 14(1):87–98.

Rambo, Lewis R. (1993). *Understanding Religious Conversion*. New Haven, CT: Yale University Press.

Raphael, Steven, and Michael A. Stoll (Eds.). (2009). *Do Prisons Make Us Safer? The Benefits and Costs of the Prison Boom*. New York: Russell Sage.

Reynolds, John, Mike Stewart, Ryan MacDonald, and Lacey Sischo. (2006). Have adolescents become too ambitious? High school seniors' educational and occupational plans, 1976 to 2000. *Social Problems* 53(2):186–206.

Richie, Beth E. (1996). *Compelled to Crime: The Gender Entrapment of Battered Black Women*. New York: Routledge.

Riege, Mary G. (1972). Parental affection and juvenile delinquency in girls. *British Journal of Criminology* 72:55–73.

Rittenhouse, Ruth. (1963). A theory and comparison of male and female delinquency. Ph.D. dissertation, University of Michigan, Ann Arbor, MI.

Robbins, Cynthia. (1989). Sex differences in psychosocial consequences of alcohol and drug abuse. *Journal of Health and Social Behavior* 30(1):117–130.

Rosenberg, Morris. (1990). The self-concept: Social product and social force. Pp. 593–624 in Morris Rosenberg and Ralph H. Turner (Eds.), *Social Psychology: Sociological Perspectives*. New Brunswick, NJ: Transaction Publishers.

Rutter, Michael. (1987). Psychosocial resilience and protective mechanisms. *American Journal of Orthopsychiatry* 57(3):316–331.

Sampson, Robert J., and John H. Laub. (1993). *Crime in the Making: Pathways and Turning Points through Life*. Cambridge, MA: Harvard University Press.

 (1996). Socioeconomic achievement in the life course of disadvantaged men: Military service as a turning point, circa 1940–1965. *American Sociological Review* 61:347–367.

Schott, Susan. (1979). Emotion and social life: A symbolic interactionist analysis. *American Journal of Sociology* 84(6):1317–1334.

Schroeder, Ryan D., Peggy C. Giordano, and Stephen A. Cernkovich. (2007). Drug use and the desistance processes. *Criminology* 45(1):191–122.

Seeburger, Francis F. (1992). Blind sight and brute feeling: The divorce of cognition from emotion. Pp. 47–60 in Viktor Gecas and D. D. Frank (Eds.), *Social Perspectives on the Emotions*, Vol. 1. Greenwich, CT: JAI Press Inc.

Seffrin, Patrick M., Peggy C. Giordano, Wendy D. Manning, and Monica A. Longmore. (2009). The influence of dating relationships on friendships networks, identity development, and delinquency. *Justice Quarterly* 26(2):238–267.

Seymour, Cynthia B., and Creasie Finney Hairston (Eds.). (2001). *Children with Parents in Prison: Child Welfare Policy, Program, and Practice Issues.* Piscataway, NJ: Transaction Publishers.

Shaw, Clifford R. (1930). *The Jack-Roller.* Chicago, IL: University of Chicago Press.

Shaw, Daniel S. (2003). Advancing our understanding of intergenerational continuity in antisocial behavior. *Journal of Abnormal Child Psychology* 31(2):193–199.

Simon, Robin W., Donna Eder, and Cathy Evans. (1992). The development of feeling norms underlying romantic love among adolescent females. *Social Psychology Quarterly* 55(1):29–46.

Simons, Ronald L., Chyi-In Wu, Rand D. Conger, Frederick O. Lorenz. (1994). Two routes to delinquency: Differences between early and late starters in the impact of parenting and deviant peers. *Criminology* 32(2):247–276.

Smith, Carolyn A., and David P. Farrington. (2004). Continuities in antisocial behaviour and parenting across three generations. *Journal of Child Psychology and Psychiatry* 45(2):230–247.

Snarey, John. (1993). *How Fathers Care for the Next Generation: A Four Decade Study.* Cambridge, MA: Harvard University Press.

Snell, Tracy L., and Danielle C. Morton. (1994). *Women in prison: Survey of state prison inmates, 1991* (NCJ 145321). Washington, DC: U.S. Department of Justice, Bureau of Justice Statistics.

Stanton, Ann M. (1980). *When Mothers Go to Jail.* Lexington, MA: Lexington Books.

Sterk, Claire E. (1999). *Fast Lives: Women Who Use Crack Cocaine.* Philadelphia, PA: Temple University Press.

Straus, Murray A., Richard J. Gelles, and Suzanne K. Steinmetz. (1980). *Behind Closed Doors: Violence in the Family.* Garden City, NY: Anchor/Doubleday.

Stryker, Sheldon. (1980). *Symbolic Interactionism: A Social Structural Version.* Menlo Park, CA: Benjamin/Cummings.

Sturges, Judith E. (1999). Concerns of visitors and correctional officers at two county jails. *American Jails* 13(1):27–30.

Sutherland, Edwin H. (1947). *Principles of Criminology,* 4th ed. Chicago: J. B. Lippincott.

Swindler, Ann. (1986). Culture in action: Symbols and strategies. *American Sociological Review* 51(2):273–286.

Tarde, Gabrielle. ([1890] 1912). *Penal Philosophy.* Translated by Rapelje Howell. Boston, MA: Little, Brown, and Company.

Taylor, Heather L., Monica A. Longmore, Wendy D. Manning, and Peggy C. Giordano. (2008). Qualities of adolescent romantic relationships and alcohol and drug use: A person-centered approach. Poster presented at the biennial meetings for the Society for Research on Adolescence, March, Chicago.

Terry, Charles M. (2003). *The Fellas: Overcoming Prison and Addiction.* Belmont, CA: Wadsworth.

Thornberry, Terence P., Adrienne Freeman-Gallant, Alan J. Lizotte, Marvin D. Krohn, and Carolyn A. Smith. (2003). Linked lives: The intergenerational transmission of antisocial behavior. *Journal of Abnormal Child Psychology* 31(2):171–184.

Thornberry, Terence P., and Marvin D. Krohn. (2001). The development of delinquency: An interactional perspective. Pp. 289–305 in S. O. White (Ed.), *Handbook of Youth and Justice.* New York: Plenum.

(Eds.). (2003). *Taking Stock of Delinquency: An Overview of Findings from Contemporary Longitudinal Studies.* New York: Kluwer Academic/Plenum Publishers.

Travis, Jeremy, Elizabeth C. McBride, and Amy L. Solomon. (2005). *Families Left Behind: The Hidden Costs of Incarceration and Reentry.* Washington, DC: Urban Institute.

Turner, Jonathan H. (2000). *On the Origin of Human Emotion: A Sociological Inquiry into the Evolution of Human Affect.* Stanford, CA: Stanford University Press.

Uggen, Christopher. (2000). Work as a turning point in the life course of criminals: A duration model of age, employment, and recidivism. *American Sociological Review* 67(4):529–546.

Uggen, Christopher, and Melissa Thompson. (2003). The socioeconomic determinants of ill-gotten gains: Within-person changes in drug use and illegal earnings. *American Journal of Sociology* 109(1):146–185.

Warr, Mark. (1998). Life-course transitions and desistance from crime. *Criminology* 36(2):183–216.

(2002). *Companions in Crime: The Social Aspects of Criminal Conduct.* Cambridge, MA: Cambridge University Press.

Wellisch, Jean, M. Douglas Anglin, and Michael L. Prendergast. (1993). Numbers and characteristics of drug-using women in the criminal justice system: Implications for treatment. *Journal of Drug Issues* 23(1):7–30.

Werner, Emmy E., and Ruth S. Smith. (1992). *Overcoming the Odds: High Risk Children from Birth to Adulthood.* Ithaca, NY: Cornell University Press.

West, Donald J., and David P. Farrington. (1977). *The Delinquent Way of Life.* London: Heinemann.

Western, Bruce, and Christopher Wildeman. (2009). The Black family and mass incarceration. *The Annals of the American Academy of Political and Social Science* 621(1):221–242.

Western, Bruce, and Sara McLanahan. (2000). Fathers behind bars: The impact of incarceration on family formation. Pp. 309–324 in Greer Litton Fox and Michael L. Benson (Eds.), *Contemporary Perspectives in Family Research: Families, Crime and Criminal Justice,* Vol. 2. Stamford, CT: JAI Press.

Whitbeck, Les B., and Dan R. Hoyt. (1999). *Nowhere to Grow: Homeless and Runaway Adolescents and Their Families.* New York: Aldine de Gruyer.

Widom, Cathy Spatz. (1984). Sex roles, criminality and psychopathology. Pp. 187–213 in Cathy Spatz Widom (Ed.), *Sex Roles and Psychopathology.* New York: Plenum.

  (1989). Child abuse, neglect, and violent criminal behavior. *Criminology* 27:251–71.

Wilkinson, Deanna L. (2003). *Guns, Violence, and Identity Among African American and Latino Youth.* New York: LFB Scholarly Publishing.

Wilson, David B., Leana A. Bouffard, and Doris L. Mackenzie. (2005). A quantitative review of structured, group-oriented, cognitive behavioral programs for offenders. *Criminal Justice and Behavior* 32(2):172–204.

Zahn, Margaret A. (Ed.) (2009). *The Delinquent Girl.* Philadelphia, PA: Temple University Press.

Zaitzow, Barbara H., and Jim Thomas (Eds.). (2003). *Women in Prison: Gender and Social Control.* Boulder, CO: Lynne Rienner Publishers.

Index